★ ★ ★

THE LIBERAL REDNECK MANIFESTO

★ ★ ★

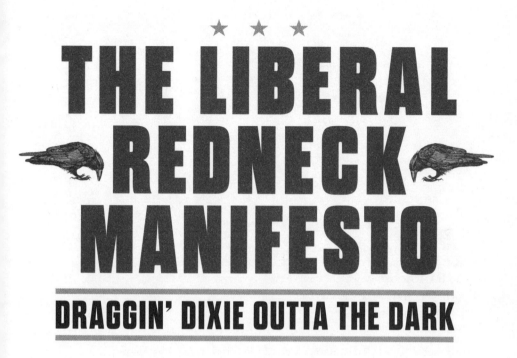

THE LIBERAL REDNECK MANIFESTO

DRAGGIN' DIXIE OUTTA THE DARK

★

TRAE CROWDER, COREY RYAN FORRESTER, AND DREW MORGAN

Illustrated by Eric Loy

ATRIA BOOKS

NEW YORK LONDON TORONTO SYDNEY NEW DELHI

ATRIA BOOKS

An Imprint of Simon & Schuster, Inc.
1230 Avenue of the Americas
New York, NY 10020

First Atria Books hardcover edition October 2016

ATRIA BOOKS and colophon are trademarks of Simon & Schuster, Inc.

For information about special discounts for bulk purchases, please contact Simon & Schuster Special Sales at 1-866-506-1949 or business@simonandschuster.com.

The Simon & Schuster Speakers Bureau can bring authors to your live event. For more information or to book an event, contact the Simon & Schuster Speakers Bureau at 1-866-248-3049 or visit our website at www.simonspeakers.com.

Interior design by Renato Stanisic
Illustrations by Eric Loy

Manufactured in the United States of America

10   9   8   7   6   5   4   3   2   1

Library of Congress Cataloging-in-Publication Data is available.

ISBN 978-1-5011-6038-7

ISBN 978-1-5011-6041-7 (ebook)

For Spook, Granny Bain, Flo, Clem, and Ruby Geraldine—
y'all are our roots.

Introduction

Holy shit, y'all! You're readin' a book by us. *Us.* That's wilder than hill people on mushrooms during a thunderstorm.

We ain't writers! I mean, we are, but as comedians, we just write jokes usually. You prolly knew that. Maybe not. Well, that's what we are: traveling joke salesmen. And we kinda figured we'd always be just that (with hopefully a movie or TV show role peppered in). We were happy to live a life of no to moderate fame, eating fried food at three in the morning in a town no one had heard of and fallin' asleep on floors and in terrible hotels with names like Tanya's Hideaway Bar and Inn. What's Tanya hidin' from? Lord knows.

Then Trae made a video and called himself the Liberal Redneck, and the world sort of changed. Life's weird.

"Wait. Like an actual book? Y'all tryin' to address Dixie with a damn book?! Like a readin' book?!"

Yes. We are. It's a book about the love/hate relationship you have with your homeland. It's a book about the South and all its problems, but also all its beauty. We thought it was time to talk about where we're from with both empathy and tough love—and have some damn laughs

Porch Talk with Trae
Y'ALL DON'T GET IT

Okay, first of all, a note: this book is written from our, the authors', shared perspective. However, throughout and when appropriate, we're going to individually sit down with y'all on a metaphorical back porch and get a little personal, a little intimate—a little *sexy*, if you will. A second note: these talks will not be particularly sexy. But they will be those other things. So with that said, here's our first Porch Talk, with the "Liberal Redneck" himself, Trae:

If there's one thing I've been asked more than anything else so far, it's, Why? Why did you make those videos? Well, that question is hard to answer because honestly—and *I know how this sounds*—I kind of feel like my whole life has been leading up to those videos. Jesus Christ, let a man write *one damn book* and he thinks he's James Franco, amirite? I know. I'm insufferable. You should talk to Corey and Drew about it sometime. But it's true. I made the videos because they represent who I am and how I've felt my whole life. For the record, here's one of the early ones: https://search.yahoo.com/yhs/search?p=liberal+redneck&ei=UTF -8&hspart=mozilla&hsimp=yhs-001.

Growing up in Celina, Tennessee, population Not A Lot (we have no traffic lights), I was hailed as a literal prodigy. I'm not that smart, trust me, but, comparatively speaking, they treated me like a fat redneck Good Will Hunting. Fat Will Hunting. Good Billy Bob Hunting. Goodwill Huntin': The Story of How I Got My Clothes. You get it. It was a whole thing. And I got made fun of and shit for it, too, being "the smart kid." I was always different.

Then I moved away and realized that, while I was "the smart kid" in my hometown, I was "that hick dude" everywhere else. I mean, even in places like Knoxville and

Nashville, but especially once I started leaving the South some. The way my accent made people react, the things people assumed about me—it always pissed me off.

But that bitterness, that resentment at being constantly underestimated and misjudged, well, it's kinda like a bad tattoo: it never goes away. Not really. Because, hell, it happened in comedy too. Audiences would hear my accent and immediately think, "Oh, well, the Cable Guy's here." I would have road comics tell me, "You're going to have to lose that accent, man." Shit like that. And so it kind of just became my mission to show people that an apparent redneck can be funny without talking about his farts or his dog or his dog's farts (and *no*, I'm not talking shit about Corey's act), and also that he can be well spoken and insightful about things besides stock car racing too, goddamn it!

So I made those videos to take a stand for people who don't get many words of support with a drawl drippin' from 'em. But as the support swelled, and the comments got, uh, colorful, I realized those videos *also* were a chance to defy the bigots who make those stereotypes seem true and to show as many people as I possibly could: You think you know us? You think you got us all figured out down here? Well y'all don't get it. But that's okay. I'll show ya. *We'll* show ya. Because that's another thing: I'm not some redneck unicorn. I'm not special. There are *plenty* of liberal-thinking, intelligent country folk out here, and we're tired of people either not knowing or not caring that we're down here, trying to fight against the ignorance and the hate and doing it from the front lines, by God. It's time we made our presence known.

That's why I made the videos, and that's why we're writing this book.

along the way. Feelin' conflicted because you support gay rights but can't help that you *still* crave Chick-fil-A? Buddy, we get it. Mad as hell about what the local college's football coach *and* the hypocritical local senator said at their recent press conferences? Love buffets but hate yourself after you go? Well, boy, do we have something to make you feel better!

"Is it pills?"

No, damn it, it's this book! We're talkin' about all that's right about life below the Mason-Dixon line and also all that's wrong—like the damn pills. Anyone who has grown up in the South in the last thirty years understands, whether they've ever thought about it or not, that there's a central dichotomy that permeates every aspect of Southern life. Even if you don't know what half them five-dollar words mean, if you're from here, you get what we're talkin' about. A divide underlies the actions and words of every native Southerner. And no, it ain't "Ford versus Chevy." The internal conflict that has defined what it means to be from the South is that of "Pride versus Shame." For example, jean shorts. We invented 'em. They hit. They also somehow don't hit. Proud. Also ashamed.

To those outside the South, the "shame" side of things is easy enough to understand. After all, there's plenty to be ashamed of down here (the Stars and Bars, Jim Crow, Florida Georgia Line, etc.). And we feel that way a lot. *Duck Dynasty?* Shame! Truck nuts? Shame! Institutional racism? Hell, *double shame!* We get it, is what we're saying. The shame is well founded. Spending all your extra money on a houseboat rental and a keg over Labor Day weekend hits. But for whatever reason, when your in-laws find out, you feel a little guilty—like you ort not done that. That's what being from here is like, kinda.

And many native Southerners live almost entirely on the shame side of the scale, leaving home the first chance they get, going out of their way to lose their accents and hide where they're from. It's a lot easier to resist ordering biscuits and gravy if you move to Connecticut and become gluten free, after all. These people who've left behind their Southern home, sympathetic though their stance may be, are not helping. If everyone who's worth a damn just leaves as soon as possible, then what's left? How will things ever get better? Sure, the demolition derbies and meat shoots (that's where you shoot guns to win hams) will kick more ass without those pussies around, but race relations probably won't improve too much.

Still, the people on the shame end of the scale are much easier to understand and deal with than those on the pride side of things. And these people are legion down here. After all, how could they not be, when everyone else just runs away? For those of you outside the South, when you think of "rednecks," "hillbillies," "hicks," or "Southern Baptists," these are the people you're picturing. They fly the Stars and Bars high from the back of their jacked-up trucks, the flagpole rising up between the bumper stickers on either side of the back glass with phrases like "Drankin' Beers and Shootin' Deers" and "Honk If I'm Payin' for Your Health Care" (because we all know the country's entitlement programs are propped up by the tree-trimming and pumping-gas-at-a-boat-dock industries). Well, we're ready to dive in on what exactly it is they're proud of. It can't be the 2.2 GPA they maintained at one of the worst public schools in a state ranked forty-ninth in education. Is it their ability to pound fourteen beers during the ball game and still drive home?

No. There actually is *a lot* to be proud of down here. And that's the part that's so hard for outsiders to understand. They easily grasp the shame, but the pride leaves them dumbfounded. But, hell, fact is, we do some things better. College football? Check the scoreboard. Whiskey and bourbon? Shit ain't close. We celebrate as good or better than anyone else in the whole country. Hell, that's half the reason why we get so patriotic—when lovin' America and supportin' the troops means gettin' hammered on a lake and shootin' fireworks at each other's faces, it's hard not to feel like you *are* in the best country on earth. We know how to party.

The southeastern United States is home to some of the best food, music, athletes, soldiers, whiskey, women, and weather this country has to offer. The home of Mark Twain and André 3000 is worth redeeming. And that's where this book comes in. We're going to tackle everything people think they know about the South, both the good and the bad, the glorious and the shameful. We're going to approach this herculean task as honestly as possible and in the process will hopefully present to outsiders a side of Dixie they never knew existed.

We may even come up with some ways of discussing "tolerance" and "decency" that both bigoted right-wing assholes and self-righteous prejudiced liberals from all over this country might be able to get on board with. (Don't choke on your juice cleanse, Tristan, you got some learnin' to do too.) And lastly, we're going to drag our homeland kicking and screaming into the present, whether the prideful mouth breathers or the naysaying outsiders like it or not.

Welcome to the New South.

The New South Bill of Wrongs

FIRST AMENDMENT

No one shall give a damn about your religion. Freedom of speech doesn't mean you can say whatever you want about prayer and God and rules and gays, and everyone else has to take it. It means you can say whatever you want about all that, but I can then say back to you, "Your church is a cult, and all the women in it are fat." So suck it up, Brother Daryl.

SECOND AMENDMENT

A "well-regulated militia" means regulated by the government. We need prudent regulation for guns. Let's all accept that. We don't need anyone to have machine guns. We can wait a little while on a background check (but if you're white with a bowl cut, then you have to go to the back of the line, Preston). Support prudent legislation designed to keep other guns away from the mentally ill and criminal elements. If you're paranoid that all these laws are designed to take away *your* gun, then we're going to assume you're mentally ill or criminal. But now let's be clear: guns rock. Hunting is awesome. Keep your guns. But, like, we gotta regulate 'em, y'all. We *have* to.

THIRD AMENDMENT

Soldiers ort be respected, but war won't be. I'll thank a vet, but that senator has to stop parading them (and especially their corpses) around like they're trophies. And take that damn sticker off your giant truck you don't work out of. Those soldiers paid for the gas that keeps it running with their lives—that sticker don't make up for that. Wearin' stickers while voting for war ain't support. If you supported your kids the same way you do the troops, they'd be dead in the back of a hot car.

FOURTH AMENDMENT

If you're gonna be antigovernment, be consistent. The police are the government. Stop pretending like government overreach is a problem everywhere but in the criminal-justice world. Also, Black Lives Matter.

FIFTH AMENDMENT

Repeat after me: "I want a lawyer."

SIXTH AMENDMENT

Take that shit to trial. It's *not* a coincidence that four of the ten amendments of the original Bill of Rights deal with curtailing government overreach in criminal prosecutions. We will say it again: hating the government but loving the justice system is hypocritical and shows your privilege. And seriously, take that shit to trial.

SEVENTH AMENDMENT

Women's bodies will not be used as political fodder or a weapon against them. Just treat everyone like you would want your momma to be treated in any given scenario. Would you say your momma "had it coming for dressin' like that"? Would you let strangers dictate where your momma got health care based upon their political views?

EIGHTH AMENDMENT

The government shall not "crack down" on drug crime while taking kickbacks from industries and companies perpetuating addiction and abuse. You can't fight wars on drugs—only on people. The drug war kills people, not drugs. Anytime you hear a politician talk about being tough on drugs but then say nothing about pharmaceutical companies, doctors, or insurance providers needing reform as well, you call them what they are: hacks. And hit them in the fa—we mean, vote against them.

NINTH AMENDMENT

Raise your kids. They're your responsibility, not your parents'. Also, ease up on Planned Parenthood. They help poor mothers. Yes, they also perform abortions. We get that many of you hate that, but you have to compromise in life. We hate your politics, Aunt Tammy, but your gravy hits, so we allow it.

TENTH AMENDMENT

It's time to catch up to the rest of the country. We seem to love states' rights in the South. Hating the federal government and telling them we don't need 'em is the great Southern pastime. Well, okay, let's tell the Feds to fuck off. But with great power comes great responsibility. Education, business, minority-class rights, etc.—we're behind in everything. No longer. If we're gonna stand on our own, we have to start taking better care of our own people. We have to do better and stand taller—but near the cooler, of course. Skew.

1

Redneck Revelry

So, what *is* a Liberal Redneck? Well, honestly, the "liberal" part is fairly self-explanatory. A "progressive," a "leftist," a "huge pussy"—you understand what we're saying. The "redneck" part, though, is a little more difficult. It means a lot of different things to a lot of different people—most of them bad. Now, for the record, we authors really didn't understand all this until it was far too late.[1]

Don't get us wrong: we knew it was a loaded (like our uncle's potato) term. Like many of our peers, we have something of a chip (probably ranch flavored) on our shoulder about people thinking we're dumbasses/racists/hicks/inbred just because we're from the South. So part of the mentality was, "Well? We *are* rednecks. Fuck if they like it or not." But see, we grew up in the 1990s/early 2000s, all three of us. We thought when people heard the word *redneck*, they thought of Jeff Foxworthy. Turns out, many think of Jefferson Davis. We weren't particularly crazy

---

I. In other words, until Trae had already gotten Internet-famous by that Liberal Redneck name, the stupid idiot.

about people looking down their noses at us for the former, but we're absolutely not okay with people looking through their rearview mirrors at us for the latter. So we need to set the record straight, off top.[2]

Being a "redneck" depends on who and where you are. Let's do a little background on the word itself and find out how we got here in the first place.

A SLUR IS BORN

The term *redneck* originated, by all accounts, down in the Mississippi Valley sometime in the nineteenth century. It first referred to the sunburn a poor white man would get on the back of his neck from working in the fields all day. So it was meant not only to slur a person based upon his class but also his color. *Technically*, rednecks may have been white, but the ruling class wanted to make it abundantly clear that poor whites were not their equals. For the record, blacks of the time also adopted the term. From its earliest uses, *redneck* was meant to describe poor white Southern people (especially men) who were considered low-class or inferior.

Now, being slurred for being poor or inferior often wins a man sympathy, but such is not the case with *redneck*. And that's because the word also carries with it other, more nefarious connotations that also can be traced back to its origin. You ever wonder how them dumbasses got sunburned so bad on the neck in the first place? I mean, they ain't have no Hawaiian Tropic yet, but still—they couldn'ta thrown some shade on that bitch?[3] Well, they *could*, they just chose not to. Or so the story goes,

---

2. "Off top" is rap for "before anything else." We like rap. Get on board.

3. "Throw Some Shade on That Bitch" is also the name of our favorite 2 Chainz song. Actually, that's not true. Our favorite is "I Luv Dem Strippers."

anyway. See, the recently freed slaves who they were forced to work the fields with wore wide-brimmed light hats that provided some measure of shade. Well, the redneck forefathers clearly couldn't be associated with anything so brash and uncouth as Common Fucking Sense, so they opted to not wear those hats in order to set themselves apart from their black counterparts. As being dumber and more stubborn, apparently.[4]

In the years following the inception of the term, *redneck* became more and more associated with bigoted and racist connotations and less and less with class and lifestyle. By the mid-twentieth century, to many people, a redneck was *any* closed-minded white bigot, regardless of his upbringing—which seems weird to us, because we would assume that literally every single rich white American woman in the 1950s was unapologetically racist, for example, and yet we can't imagine that "redneck" was being tossed in their direction very much. Still, the racism, the homophobia, the general shittiness—all those things became the primary characteristics of a redneck to people.

There wasn't much to be proud of about any of that, obviously. So for those who grew up in this period or who were raised with the same primary usage for the word, it would be unfathomable for any reasonable or free-thinking person to ever even *dream* of self-identifying as a redneck.

And yet this was a fact that was largely lost on us as authors.

Why? Well, because something happened during our childhood and coming-of-age years that skewed the way we viewed the word. See, in the latter part of the twentieth century, rednecks started doing what rednecks do best: being just proud as *hell* of some shit that most people agree is pretty damn stupid. In this case, the moniker itself.

---

4. A tradition that many of our brothers continue proudly to this day.

FUN WITH SLURS

★

It's a long-running joke that there's no well-established racial slur that's considered truly offensive to white people. And we agree—especially as it pertains to the truly white. The WASPy, half-caf latte crowd, for example, is *infinitely* more offended by other people's very existence than it could ever be by a word. Most poor white people, who are so far removed from WASPs that they might as well be a completely different race, don't mind being called "redneck." Hell, we plaster that shit on our trucks and tattoo it on our dicks, so obviously we ain't *too* put off by it. It's just hard to offend poor white people with a slur. Hell, it's hard to offend poor white people by doing anything other than talking shit about their truck. But that sure hasn't stopped people from trying.

Here are the best of the rest when it comes to Southern slurs:

Cracker. Ahh, the good old standby. Like a warm cup of cocoa, this one. Look, we don't mean to get all high-horsey on ya or nothin', but, frankly, it's hilarious how pathetic an attempt at a slur the word *cracker* is. We always just assumed it was from soda or saltine crackers (which wouldn't make sense nowadays, because those crackers come in sleeves . . . get it?). Ya know, like food. Because everybody just *hates* to be referred to as food. But apparently it's way worse: etymologists think it actually comes from *whip-cracker*, which was a term for a foreman on a plantation. Which, granted, is just terrible. But, hell, if 98 percent of people think you're talking about damn Toll Houses, then who gives a shit? No one is offended by the term *cracker*.

Peckerwood. We really like this one. Apparently it's just an inversion of the word *woodpecker*, which antebellum blacks used as a contrast to the blackbird they identified with. Or something. We just like the way it sounds. It really rolls off the tongue. "Peckerwood." Now, it would still be extremely hard to take someone seriously if right before a fight he hollered out, "All right, it's go time, you fuckin' *peckerwood*!" Tell us you wouldn't laugh. You'd laugh. Oh, but it also turns out it was adopted by the Aryan Brotherhood as a part of prison subculture beginning in the 1960s . . .

So, uh, yeah, we don't really like it anymore.

White Trash. See, now, this shit is just lazy. We mean, seriously, other races? "*White trash*"? It's just our color and then a bad thing. There's no pizzazz. There's no wit. Disappointing, really. Be that as it may, *white trash* has existed as a slur since the early 1800s, when it was adopted as a term for the whites who worked among the slaves on a plantation. Harriet Beecher Stowe included a chapter called "Poor White Trash" in *A Key to Uncle Tom's Cabin* (which is the only cabin white people have ever hated), and the rest is insult history.

Trailer Trash. Brought to you by the writers of *white trash* comes this unimaginative and derivative sequel, *trailer trash*. See, what they did here, guys, was they took the less-evocative "white," which referenced the person's *skin*, and they replaced it with "trailer," which referenced their *home*. Fuckin' got 'em.

Hick. Okay. Now, we can't be 100 percent sure about this—and give people some time after Obama leaves office and all—but we *believe* that *hick* is the only slur that can accurately be described as being presidential. The term originally referred to poor rural whites who were ardent supporters of Andrew Jackson, who was known as Old Hickory (and also as an absolutely raving lunatic boogity-boogity crazy son of a bitch—not to mention the seventh president of the United States). So there. Eat shit, people-who-came-up-with-*cracker*. But whatever it meant once, it quickly became synonymous with the rest: a poor white piece of shit, basically. In fact, in our anecdotal opinion, *hick* is probably the most commonly used slur for poor white Southerners, except, of course, for the subject of this chapter, *redneck*, and *redneck*'s little brother:

Hillbilly. Ah, yes. Hillbillies! Mountain folk! You know 'em: the ones what play the banjo and like a nice, purdy mouth. What they lack in teeth they make up for in not caring about having teeth. Just hardworking, salt-of-the-earth, *objectively terrifying* people. We're kidding, of course. We kid because in our experience, *hillbilly* is the only one of these slurs that can actually hang with *redneck* in terms of the volume of negative stereotypes related to it. Also, for what it's worth, Trae and Corey always self-identified more as *rednecks*, but Drew, being from a place that's a little more . . . Appalachian, has always thought himself more of a *hillbilly.* In all honesty, to most people outside the South, these are pretty much interchangeable. But in terms of sheer bite, *hillbilly*, like the rest of these also-rans, does not and cannot hold a candle to *redneck*.

THE REDNECKAISSANCE[5]

Beginning in earnest in the 1970s, poor white Southerners collectively decided, consciously or not, that if everybody *else* was gonna call 'em rednecks anyway, then, by God, they were gonna make the most of it. For the record, we generally think that "taking back a word" like that is a pretty noble exercise. Take the opposition's ammunition from him by using it on yourself before he can use it on you. The LGBTQ community hits on this front. This is known in academia as the "B-Rabbit

---

5. That's right. The Redneckaissance.

Approach."[6] But when the word you're adopting so proudly is known mostly for cross burnin', pig fuckin', and Jew hatin', well, you're gonna take some lumps. But that ain't never stopped a redneck before.

What really kicked off the "Redneck Revolution," if you will,[7] was Georgia boy Jimmy Carter being elected president in 1976. During his campaign, he (very lukewarmly) embraced being called a redneck by the opposition as a way to endear himself to working-class voters. And it worked. But let's be honest here: Jimmy Carter weren't much of a damn redneck. He was a wealthy-ass lifelong politician. He started out as a farmer—on a plot of land his daddy gave him. Don't get us wrong: we like Jimmy Carter. Hell, if we thought he *was* a redneck, then you'd have to admit he was a Liberal Redneck, so he's like a pseudo-forefather for us. Or something. But look: he was just too damn uppity, y'all. All there is to it. But he still had a *tremendous* impact on redefining the word *redneck*. Though maybe it's more accurate to say that his momma, Miss Lillian, had a tremendous impact. Because in addition to Jimmy, she *also* gave birth to his younger brother, Billy Carter. And that sumbitch? Hoo-wee, buddy! Now, *he* was a goddamn *redneck*.

BILLY BOY

Billy Carter was somethin' else. His brother was the goddamn president of the United States, and he had an easier time controlling fuckin' Congress than he did his baby brother. Billy Carter talked shit, got hammered, pumped gas, and whipped out his dick to take a piss in front of foreign dignitaries on an airport runway. Billy Carter blew

6. This is not true, but Eminem's *8 Mile* hits, so fuck it.

7. Or if you won't. Don't matter—our book.

out his last damn on his third birthday. He drank so much beer that a beer company gave him his own beer, called Billy Beer. (Don't let your dreams be dreams, kids.) And through it all, he was baldly, proudly *red as hell*. He openly self-identified as a redneck, and while doing so, he sortly damn won the hearts of the nation. Suddenly there was a whole 'nother side to being a "redneck." Billy Carter had a hell of a lot to do with that.

So with Billy Carter basically spearheading (beerheading?) the way, redneck culture swept the country. People wrote movies, people wrote books,[8] people dipped snuff and wore boots. It was a whole thing. The word *redneck* had been redefined, at least by its new adopters, as a way to describe being working class and proud rather than bigoted, hateful, shitty, etc. This new definition gave a term to the mind-set and lifestyle of simple, tough-as-nails people who didn't need any help from outsiders to get by. Bands like Molly Hatchet, the Allman Brothers, and, of course, the indomitable Lynyrd Skynyrd all wrote songs pointed straight down the barrel of the negative stereotypes that had been aimed at our people for so long. The Redneckaissance was in full swing.[9] And then, beginning in the 1990s, things took a turn for the silly.

YOU *MIGHT* BE A CARICATURE

We need to preface this section with something of a disclaimer: Jeff Foxworthy is a goddamn legend. He's a finalist for the Stand-up Comedy Mount Rushmore. As comedians, us talking shit about Jeff Foxworthy would be tantamount to us talking shit about Jerry Seinfeld. We're not

8. We're sure those books were just fine.

9. "Freebird" is our Sistine Chapel.

DARK FOXWORTHY

★

For years now, we the authors have had an ongoing bit between us internally called "Dark Foxworthy," and we'd like to share it with you now because we love you and because we love hittin'. And in our opinion, this hits. The concept is basically "What if Jeff Foxworthy had no filters?" Imagine that Jeff wasn't the mainstream comedy virtuoso that he was but instead was an angry fringe comic who had no qualms about illuminating the darkest reaches of redneck culture—*but* did so with the exact same joke structure. Let us demonstrate:

(Note: Please read these in your head in the cheesiest, most exaggerated Jeff Foxworthy impersonation you can muster. This is important to us.)

If yoooou've ever punched your daddy after you both punched your momma . . . *you might be a redneck!*

If yoooou've ever told your granny, "Your boyfriend owes me money from a bet we had our sophomore year" . . . *you might be a redneck!*

If yoooou've ever blown a guy because you thought he *might* have Percocets . . . *you might be a redneck!*

If yoooou've ever banged a girl in a stained tank top in the infield of a NASCAR race while your buddies cheer you on and assure you she's "for sure" seventeen . . . *you might be a redneck!*

If yoooou've ever stolen your momma's EBT card and given it to a man known as Lay-Low for weed . . . *you might be a redneck!*

If yoooou've ever voted against your own economic self-interests because you were hopelessly misguided by the empty promises of religious charlatans offering you false salvation at the hands of a clearly apathetic God . . . *you might be a redneck!*

You get it. Shit like that.

here to do that. We, all three of us, grew up with Foxworthy's comedy and absolutely *loved* it. As did much of the country.

Now, having said that, it's pretty hard to argue that the "genre" of comedy that he basically invented did our people or the word *redneck* many favors in terms of public perception. When his stuff exploded in the nineties (and, buddy, that shit exploded harder than Michael Bay's boners or a Vacation Bible School director's head after the HB2 law), immediately the zeitgeist was filled with images of "rednecks" as moronic hayseed ne'er-do-goods.[10] We live in trailers, we eat roadkill, we buy dumb shit with money we ain't got, we could stand to do better with hygiene, we use Marlboro points as currency, we drag our kids behind our trucks through a field in a garbage can (hits, though)—the list goes on and on. To his colossal audience, Foxworthy quite literally defined, albeit with an intended wink, what it meant to be a "redneck," and that definition was . . . less than flattering.

Despite the largely uncomplimentary picture this new wave of pop culture painted, redneck humor was also *hugely profitable*. And as we all know, that's all the lizard people really care about. Particularly the California lizard people.[11] Their forked tongues immediately registered the heat emanating from the cash machine that was Redneck Comedy, and they dived in scaly-head-first. Before long, we had the Blue Collar Comedy Tour, and with it came the natural end point of this particular brand of funny: Larry the Cable Guy.

Now, as comics, we have to admit that the man is gifted as hell. We're not saying he lacks talent. And by all accounts, he's nice as hell. But for anyone left out there who doesn't know: it's an act. He ain't

---

10. **We know what the damn phrase is. Y'all ever heard of nuance? Shit.**

11. **I.e., Hollywood.**

Southern. He doesn't talk that way; he doesn't act that way. His name is not Larry. His name is Dan. And Dan created the character of Larry the Cable Guy and used that character to very shrewdly and expertly exploit and capitalize on a culture that he himself doesn't belong to. And good for him. He made a hell of a lot of money and achieved things that most comics can only dream of. But his character and his catchphrases ("Git-R-Done!"[12]) to many embody the moment when redneck comedy jumped the shark.[13] Culturally speaking, we had become caricatures. Cartoon people. Jokes that were almost exclusively laughed *at*. This is what we are now.

That ain't Foxworthy's fault, by the way. He was an innovator and a comedic force of nature.[14] Where we have ended up culturally as "rednecks" was probably going to happen no matter what. It's kind of the natural progression for it, if you think about it. It starts out as a slur and an insult, we do our best to redefine the word, we take that shit *just a little too far*, and we wind up where are now. But all that being said, Foxworthy and Blue Collar and the Cable Guy, whether they intended to or not, they started us down this road. Not Ron White, though. Ron White is the fuckin' shit, and we'll fight anyone who says otherwise.[15]

Side note: our music has unfortunately followed a very similar progression, and we don't think that's a coincidence. Country music (or at least what is popularly known as country music) started out as a source

---

12. **The fucking Voldemort of comedy catchphrases.**

13. **Or in this case, the largemouth bass.**

14. **Seriously, guys, we love Foxworthy.**

15. **The Blue Collar Comedy Tour was Foxworthy, Larry the Cable Guy, and Ron White. Foxworthy also very graciously allowed a sentient hemorrhoid of his that he'd named Bill Engvall to tell jokes because Jeff is a prince.**

of pride and has now become a gushing, stinking sulphur geyser of white-hot fucking shame. Which sucks. See chapter 6, "Pickin' and Spinnin'," for more on this.

So here we are. The word *redneck* has been on quite the Roller Coaster of Meaning.[16] From slur to silly shit and everywhere in between. But what does it mean to people *now?* Well, to answer that question, we need to quote every politician who ever lived and say: *It depends.*

WE KNOW WHAT YOU THINK

What the word *redneck* means to you obviously depends on who *you* is. Is you a Yankee? Is you black? Is you gay? Is you foreign? If so, we realize y'all's buttholes probably be tightening up right now because there's no *way* that progression ends with anything that isn't just bigoty as *shit*, right? Well, naw, we weren't going to say anything of the sort, but if that sweet little balloon knot of yours *did* pucker up while reading through those questions, then there's your answer, baby dolls.

To many outsiders, rednecks are just the worst. They/we never lost their/our racist and xeno/homophobic attitudes, and over the last thirty years outsiders emphasized a bunch more almost-as-bad stereotypes on top of it. We're dumb, we're inbred, we're sheep (we also like to fuck sheep, some assume), we're backward, we're regressive, we're hateful, and, worst of all, we're *proud of it.* Ugh. How disgusting we must seem.

And we get it. We don't blame yuns. It'd be hard *not* to feel that way, given how we've been portrayed in popular culture and by the more, um, vocal members of our group over the years. We fully understand why you'd feel that way. How do *we* feel, though? Well, since you asked . . .

16. **Sounds like an attraction at a theme park for hipsters.**

FRANKLY, MY DEAR

What does the word *redneck* mean to *us*? As for all groups of people, a lot of the stereotypes are true. But also like all other groups, we just want people to understand that the negative stereotypes don't define us. Maybe it would be easier if we broke it down this way:

What a Redneck *Is*

A redneck is, *usually*, a poor white Southerner, but a redneck can be rich. Say he wins the lottery. Somethin' like that. But if you grow up with money, in our opinion, it's pretty much impossible to be truly red. Yo ass is white. And that's fine. White people got a lot of great shit. Most of which they stole from other more-hittin' peoples, but still.

A redneck can also be black, believe it or not. We've lived in the South our whole lives—trust us on this one. Stick around, and you'll get a shining example of this phenomenon. (For the record, a redneck can be any other race too. Trae knew a red-ass family what adopted a Korean baby, and that sumbitch turned out red-assed as a goddamn baboon.) And lastly, though we're hesitant to admit it: a redneck does not *have* to be from the South. There are people who fit the bill in pretty much every region of this country. Though just speaking personally, we sortly wish those people would adopt a different title. *Redneck* is *our word*. It's not really okay for you to say it, see? But we suppose we'll let it slide, since we know y'all got redneck friends. So yes, there are exceptions, but *by and large*, a redneck is a poor white Southerner.

What Else Is a Redneck?

A redneck works hard and loves harder. A redneck is *fiercely* loyal to his people (and his animals). A redneck knows how to have a *damn good* time. Look, you can talk all the snobby shit you want, but if you think shootin' guns and muddin' and pontoon boats ain't fun *as fuck*, then us and you, well, we just two different kinds of people. A redneck loves

Porch Talk with Drew

I'm a hillbilly. That's just what I am.

I like hillbilly music. I like hillbilly food. I like hillbilly women (*one* hillbilly woman—sorry, baby). What we have in common with rednecks is that we're proud as hell and ready to fight about anything you wanna get cross about. We also value hard work and are mostly by definition white.

So I get called a redneck a lot, and in some ways I guess I'm that, too, but the thing I am most is a hillbilly.

Hillbillies are Appalachian. We're hill people. To me, the term means a hill person what likes to have a good time. His or her favorite things: music, the mountains, swimmin' naked, havin' a chip on his or her shoulder. Things he or she don't mind that other people do mind: mud and dirt, folks judging him or her, any and all rules (especially those relating to havin' shirts or shoes on). The term is best known as a derogatory way for city slickers to describe folks from my region who moved to cities for jobs. That's kind of a common thread with the words *hick, redneck, hillbilly*. People made 'em up to make fun of my people.

Hillbilly was meant to be an insult, just like *redneck*. One difference is that *hillbilly* hasn't historically been as associated with hate, racism, and social ignorance as *redneck* has. That's not to say there aren't racist hillbillies, but racism isn't essential to the definition of hillbilly, probably because at the places where the term was used most widely—city ghettos and factories—so many hillbillies worked alongside, associated with, and even lived with minorities.

Because of that, I've always resisted the term *redneck*. To me, it meant some things I for sure am: proud (perhaps to a fault), stubborn, and country. But *redneck* also meant a whole lot of things I ain't: ignorant, hateful, racist.

Of course, I *hate* that being proudly Southern (while being white) means that people assume you're ignorant and/or racist. Of course, I don't want to be associated with any of that and want all of these words to either mean something positive or go away. But the fact is, they ain't going away. I'm a hillbilly. And in truth, I'm also a redneck. My daddy is a preacher what used to drink and ride a motorcycle. My brother is in prison. My mamaw used to dip tobacco and cooked with lard. I am what I am, and people are gonna define me as they wish.

But those words no longer get to mean what people who ain't those words say they mean. My thinking used to be that redneck meant something hateful, something "other" than myself. That was because I'd let other people define me and my culture. No more. I'm country, Southern, and proud. I have always been a hillbilly. And from now on, I'll always be a redneck. A loving, accepting, intelligent, and proud hillbilly-ass redneck. *Skew!* Let's party.

DM

his truck, his ball team, his beer, his guns, and his momma. Do not fuck with a redneck's momma. Even if she's a pillbilly like Trae's. [17] A redneck neither wants nor needs help from anybody else. He's proud. He just wants to be left the hell alone.

Which leads us to what is in our opinion the single most defining characteristic of a redneck: a redneck don't give a damn. Not the very first one. A redneck's damn field is completely barren. You could fill the Grand Canyon with all the damns a redneck does not give about what you or anybody else thinks. Ort he wear sleeves to his mamaw's

---

[17]. Hell, *especially* if she's a pillbilly. Trae's momma been to jail. She will fuck you up.

funeral? Probably, but, hell, Junior won on Sunday, and she woulda wanted him to represent.

You don't like the way he lives? Don't give a damn.

You think he should act with a little more tact? Don't give a damn.

Countless scientists and experts agree that the exhaust from his truck is bad for the environment? Well, hell, ain't that something. Guess they'll have to grab a spot in the kiss-his-ass line. It's gonna be a long wait, though.

You ever notice how rednecks are pretty much the only subgroup of people left in this country that it's almost entirely socially acceptable to mock publicly? Why do you think that is? Well, we'd like to posit that it's due almost entirely to his lack of ability *to give a damn*. Over the years, every other group of people has (rightfully and appropriately) stood up for itself and said, "Hey, guys, listen: it's really not okay for you to talk about us that way. We're people, too. You need to stop." And people did. Mostly. But when rednecks heard they were being made fun of, it went more like this: "Do what?! Who's talkin' shit?! Oh yeah?! Well, you tell *everbody* that they can *kiss my ass*!!" And that was pretty much the end of that.

We generally feel proud of these traits. There doesn't have to be shame in being a redneck. Some of the most awesome people this country has seen have been rednecks. And on that note, before we tell you what a redneck is *not*, we want to take a moment for a very important aside:

Oh, man, we're so excited, y'all. We're gonna wax poet-y about some of our idols. (Note: since both Billy Carter and Jeff Foxworthy have already been covered at length, we're excluding them from this list. We are, after much consternation, doing the same for Lynyrd Skynyrd and all of the country music greats—with one notable exception—as they factor heavily in chapter 6, "Pickin' and Spinnin'.")

Anyway, without further ado, we give you . . .

THE TEN GREATEST REDNECKS OF ALL TIME

1. **Dale Earnhardt.** All right, first of all, moment of silence. Show some goddamn respect . . . Okay, thank you.

   With that said: *Skeeeeeeeeeeeewwww!!* Fuckin' Dale, baby! The Intimidator! Listen, y'all, if you ain't a redneck, you probably don't understand how much Earnhardt means to us. In fact, there's a common theory that Jesus has already come back, and we just called him Dale Earnhardt. Put simply, the man who wore number three was one of the baddest motherfuckers to ever run 'em, and that's sayin' a lot. He legitimized NASCAR, made a shit ton of money, had three smokin' wives (which may *seem* like a negative until you realize the importance of the number three to the man's mythos—and also, you just hush now!), and then in 2001 he died the way he lived: racing at Daytona International Speedway, smokin' it with both hands on the goddamn wheel.

2. **Also Dale Earnhardt.**

3. **Also Dale Earnhardt.** (This was the only way this could go. It was written.)

4. **Brett Favre.** This motherfucker here, y'all. *Shew-wee!* It's hard to even express in a paragraph how awesome Brett Favre is. An unassuming Mississippi boy with a thick drawl, a howitzer attached to his shoulder, and a true redneck's propensity for not even *thinkin'* about giving a fuck. Interceptions? Who gives a shit. Givin' a shit's for pussies. Chicks dig the long ball. We have seen Favre literally knock 250-pound men out of the air with a bullet pass. Did y'all know that Favre was, like, five years into his NFL career before he learned what a nickel defense was? Take a guess how much he gave a shit. Football superfans talk up field generals and surgical precision and reading defenses, but goddamn it, some motherfuckers can just flat-out *play the game*. And Brett Favre was maybe the best of said motherfuckers ever to do it.

5. **Levon Helm.** So we noted that we weren't going to do any country music greats because that could be a list all its own. But Levon Helm isn't covered by that exception. From small-town Arkansas and with the drawl and manner to show for it, Helm was a drummer-singer-songwriter most notably for The Band and then later as a solo artist. And he was a goddamn musical genius with the voice of a Southern angel. You ever heard "The Night They Drove Old Dixie Down"? Jesus H. Christ, it's like if heroin were a Civil War ballad. One of the most influential rock 'n' rollers of all time, beloved and revered by everyone who ever worked with him, Levon Helm was a Southern Man Done Right.

6. **Pat Summitt.** Nearly 1,100 career wins, eight national titles, a 100 percent (*100 percent*) graduation rate—Pat Summitt was arguably the greatest coach in the history of American sports. She changed countless young lives for the better, but she never changed who she was: a redneck country girl from Clarksville, Tennessee. Fuck Alzheimer's.

7. **Sergeant Alvin York.** This is one of them sumbitches what you wouldn't believe a word about if it wasn't all totally documented as fact. One of *eleven* children born in a two-room log cabin in rural Tennessee, Sergeant York got drafted to fight the Germans the *first* time around, in WWI—and that did *not* work out for the Germans. He killed 28, captured 132, and just generally kicked some Hun ass. All while being a goddamn pacifist. Like we said: he was somethin' else.

8. **Randy Moss.** Some people are confused right now. Those people don't know shit about retired wide receiver Randy Moss. Yes, he has a (bullshit) reputation as a dreadlocked "thug," but Randy Damn Moss is, in fact, about as red as they come. From the heart of coal country in West Virginia, Randy races trucks, has caught

more bass than he has touchdowns, and speaks with an accent thicker than Trae's. His most "red" moment was hittin' a cop with his truck and not gettin' shot. He's a redneck.

9. **Billy Bob Thornton.** "Mustard on ye biscuits, mmhmmmm." Billy Bob broke onto the scene playing a dimwitted redneck named Carl in *Sling Blade*. Well, the man damn sure isn't dimwitted, but he came by the redneck part honest. His momma was a psychic, and when he was born, he was the fattest baby ever born in that part of Arkansas. That's red *as hell*. Also: his fuckin' name is Billy Bob.

10. **Andy Griffith.** You can hear it right now, can't ya? Everybody can. That whistlin' theme song to every Southerner's childhood, no matter when that childhood took place. *The Andy Griffith Show* is an institution down here, and the character he played, unassuming small-town sheriff Andy Taylor, was one of the earliest examples in pop culture of a man being decidedly down-home and countrified while also decent and wise. Andy was belying our shitty stereotypes before many of them were even conceived. Rest in peace, Sheriff.

Whew. That was fun. So now let's move on to what a redneck is not.

What a Redneck Is *Not*

A redneck is *not* (necessarily): a racist, a bigot, a homophobe, a xenophobe, an idiot, a cousin fucker, a pig fucker, a methhead, a pillhead, a dumbass, a wife-beater, a Bible-thumper, or just a generally hateful piece of shit. Now, let us clarify: there are *plenty* of rednecks who are at least a couple of these things. But there are plenty of *most groups of people* who are these things. All we're saying is that a redneck is not *by definition* these things. Not to us, and we hope not to you, either. Which brings us to why we're doing all this shit in the first place.

How to Spot a Fake Redneck
Wears glasses at night to hide all the fucks he gives
Expensive "designer" camouflage . . . has never been huntin'
Belt buckle cost more than these work boots, which are clean
Keys to a very new, very expensive, very clean super duty truck; bottle opener is key chain
Dip ring in front, because sittin' on it "hurts"
CRAFT BEER
VAPE
GET TURNT BEER
GET TURNT BEER

Porch Talk with Trae

I was pretty surprised by many of the responses to my videos. 'Course, to be fair, I was surprised about damn near *everything* that happened as a result of those videos. One of the only things that *didn't* surprise me was all the hate mail I got. And the vast majority of it was your garden-variety Internet-troll keyboard-warrior bullshit: "Ur gay." "Bet you like wearin' dresses yourself you fuckin' pervert." "How can you make fun of Jesus? I'll pray for you, you stupid faggot." Shit like that. None of that surprised me, and none of that affected me. At all.

The hate mail that did surprise and affect me, though, were the ones that accused me of faking all of this. Fake Lord, have mercy, that shit got me heated. Which I realize may seem weird to people, to be so upset by someone thinking you're *not* a redneck. But it wasn't so much defensiveness over being a redneck—it was defensiveness over being anything other than *exactly what I am.*

I'm a lot of things, y'all, many of them not great. But I am *not* fake. I pride myself on being one of those what-you-see-is-what-you-get type of fellers. So that's why I got pissed off by those comments. But what *surprised* me so much about them was the fact that so many of those messages came from two very distinct groups of people, and they're polar opposites.

The first group was your more stereotypical shitty hick rednecks, and they were like "Y'ain't no redneck; no redneck likes queers!" Shit like that. That didn't surprise me. Fuck those guys. But the *second* group threw me for a loop. Because the second group was like . . . ultraliberal Portland baristas. Yeah. I mean, not literally *just* pretentious coffeemakers from Oregon, but that *type* of person. Buncha Salon.com motherfuckers. And the reason they had for not believing me was basically: "Well, clearly *this* isn't authentic. I mean, no genuine redneck *knows facts.* Everyone knows that's not a thing." See, they believed and agreed with the liberal views and points I was making. But it was precisely because they agreed with me that they did not believe I could *possibly* be a white-trash Tennessee boy. To these people, there was genuinely no such thing as a well-informed and open-minded redneck. The two things were mutually exclusive. And y'all . . . I really don't appreciate that.

Periodically, people like this will ask me, "Why 'redneck'? Are you really a redneck? Aren't you more of a 'good ol' boy' or 'country boy' or something? Okay, you're from the South, but you're not *really* a redneck, though . . . right?" Sometimes a person will even write, without talking to me, something like: "He calls himself a redneck, but I like to think of him as more of a Southern gent." Shit like that.

No, goddamn it. *No.* Those people don't get to tell *me* what I identify as. Growing up, I never *chose* to think of myself as a redneck. It's just what I was. It's what almost everyone I knew was. So when you try to tell me I'm something else, you're kind of implying that *you think being a redneck is a choice*. And that really demonstrates a lack of understanding and empathy on your part. You should really be more open-minded.

I'm not going to reclassify myself or all of a sudden just "admit" that I'm not actually a redneck. I'm not going to give these people that out. That's not how this works. I'm a white-trash piece-of-shit poor-boy redneck with a pillhead momma from Celina, Tennessee. I'm *also* a highly educated, nonreligious, open-minded lover of *all* people. And if anyone can't reconcile those things in order to fit their own narrative, well then, that's his problem, not mine.

Settin' It Straight

Even though the term *redneck* is polarizing and oft misunderstood, we chose to adopt it for ourselves because we want to continue what so many tried to do in the seventies and eighties and redefine this shit culturally.[18] Also, what choice do we have now that Trae got famous off a character that seems to have been named by a straight-shootin' eight-year-old? We like the word, in truth. We use the word.

Like many of our fellow young Southerners, the three of us all have chips on our shoulders the size of Stone Mountain. But those chips may seem to most people to be largely unearned, especially in the cases of Trae and Drew.[19] They were never doubted in their respective hometowns growing up. Hell, on the contrary. Teachers, parents, peers, respected old people in town—they were all pretty much in agreement that these two were goin' places, son. So why the attitude? Why the grudges? You gotta be a pretty big asshole to be all "Man, all those people that believed in me and encouraged me growing up, all those people that said I would never fail and always amount to something—I'll show them! I'll show *all of them* . . . just how right they were. Um. Yeah." What the hell is that? Who do they have to prove wrong?

Well, frankly, pretty much everybody else. Those people believing in us were Southern too, and mostly poor. (Small rural areas tend to be like that.) It's not about them. It's about the people in the other places. The people who hear our accents and immediately start talking more slowly without even realizing it. Who automatically assume that we're racist

18. **Look, we're pretentious rednecks too. Stay on board.**

19. **Corey mostly partied.**

Bible-thumping troglodytes just 'cause we like fuckin' sweet tea. By the way, how can y'all not like sweet tea?! Sweet tea *hits*, goddamn it!

Let us clarify something: we're not *offended* by redneck humor. We're comedians. We support making fun of literally everyone.[20] Keep making the jokes. That's fine. But what chaps our red asses is hearing from people who see us online or come to our shows and then, with complete sincerity, tell us things like, "Oh, you're like a *unicorn!*" or "Ya know, I genuinely did not believe people like you existed." Really, guys? Keep in mind that all of these people are self-proclaimed liberals, by the way, people who purport to absolutely abhor prejudice. They're open-minded; they don't judge. They hate racism and homophobia. They know that it's just flat *wrong* to judge a person based on one superficial characteristic—unless the person speaks with a drawl, apparently.

These same people will often look down their noses at the South as a whole, tut-tutting at us for our backward ways, all the while being completely blind to the fact that prejudice toward poor white Southern people *still counts as prejudice*, y'all. To genuinely not realize the fake-liberal hypocrisy of that is pretty astounding to us.

So that's why we want to show people a different side of our homeland: a side that many people apparently have no idea exists. And to do that, we need to get their attention. And maybe we're wrong here,[21] but calling yourselves Liberal Rednecks is a pretty damn good way to get people's attention.

So . . . y'all listenin'?

---

20. Even amputees. Yeah.

21. Please don't let us be wrong.

2

The Draw

The South is poor. Very poor. Just poor as hell, y'all. Of the ten poorest states in the United States, only New Mexico (number nine) lies outside of Dixie.[1] The only states below the Mason-Dixon line that are *not* in the bottom half in terms of median family income are Maryland (number one) and Virginia (number seven). But, hell, any Southerner knows that Virginia barely counts, and Maryland sure as hell don't. Rednecks don't eat crab cakes. A redneck eats a reheated salmon patty made with his wife's contempt, and he likes it, by God. To hell with Maryland. Only reason they're number one on the list is because that's where all the lizards what run this country hide their money. Talkin' bout defense contractors, y'all. *Wake up, America!*

The point is that much of the South is an impoverished land of limited opportunity. Which is honestly putting it nicely. Putting it not

[1]. Way to go, New Mexico. What kind of state allows themselves to be in the top ten? Oh, right. Our bad. Y'all keep on keepin' on, man . . . we'll get there one day.

nicely would be to say that much of the South is an economically desolate shithole that's utterly bereft of hope and prospects. Home sweet home! What makes the situation even worse is that these parts of the South operate like black holes for poor people:[2] they consume all light and are basically impossible to escape. You hear a lot of romanticizing about all the red dirt we got down here, but what people leave out is that shit turns to mud real quick. And despite what many of the songs of our people would have you believe, getting stuck in the mud ain't worth a damn.

WHAT THE HELL HAPPENED?

Most people are generally aware that the South is the poorest region of the country, but how often do they consider the reasons for that? The fact seems to be treated largely the same way that most unfortunate facts about the South are treated: "Oh, well . . . the South, amirite?" The rest of the country's expectations are so low that the attitude seems to amount to "Well, *of course* the South is the poorest part of the country. It's the dumbest and the fattest too! Who wants kombucha?!" People today essentially look at the South's issues and dismiss them with the equivalent of a hashtag.[3]

But why *is* the South so poor, then? Well, hell, we don't know! We're comedians! What kinda damn book you think this is, one a them fancy learnin'-type books? Goddamn, boy. There are scholarly articles and books by scholarly-type scholar fellers that will provide a much better answer to that question than we can here, but what it

---

2. **Not like the kind in truck stop bathrooms; like the space kind.**

3. **#JustSouthThings.**

basically comes down to is: that war really fucked our shit up, y'all. It's kind of a whole thing down here.

Now look, we were fighting for the wrong cause, and we *needed and deserved to lose*. You ain't gonna hear no "war of Northern aggression" talk 'round these parts. We were bein' dicks, and we got dealt with. That's it. But, having said that, if you're looking for explanations for the South's economic woes in the intervening years, you have to acknowledge the impact of the postwar period. The entire economy of the region was based on slavery, and, in our opinion, that's a fuckin' shame—a deep shame we still feel. Once the war ended and that "peculiar institution"[4] was so righteously abolished by Honest Abe, millions of people in the South, including the freed slaves, looked around and just kind of went, "Well . . . now what?" And it turns out, that was one hell of a question.

The Southern wealthy wasted no time in proving that a rich man doesn't have to legally own a poor man to subjugate and exploit the absolute shit out of him, and they substituted sharecropping and tenant farming to take the place of slavery in the South's fields. Listen, if any of you kids out there reading this has thought to yourself, "I think I'd like to be a sharecropper when I grow up," *don't do it*. Don't be fooled by Big Sharecropping. It's no way for a man to live. The system led to an endless cycle of debt: borrowing money to survive until you get paid and can pay back the money you owed before, and then borrowing more money to survive until you get paid again to pay back the— y'all get it. This is a cycle that will be painfully familiar to *any* poor person, Southerner or not. Y'all ever heard of payday loans?

The new economic system, though a step up from literal slavery, was not kind to those on the bottom rungs. Meanwhile, agriculture

4. By "peculiar," we mean fuckin' awful.

was becoming more and more mechanized, and even terrible share-cropping jobs were disappearing. At the same time that people were plagued by these economic issues, white Southerners just could not stop being buttholes. It's something we continue to struggle with. Race relations were . . . not ideal during the postwar years, with white Southerners constantly trying to pass new laws that would effectively treat free blacks the same as they were treated as slaves. Black Southerners, shockingly, were not altogether down with that. This led to constant tension and racial strife (and some pretty sweet music), often erupting in violence. Take all these factors together, and you have a region that's going through some pretty serious shit, and the simple fact is that the South has never fully recovered to this day.

IN IT TOGETHER

In case y'all haven't picked up on it, the South is poor. Did we mention that? Well, it is. But it would still be disingenuous to try to depict the experience of being poor in the South as a consistent one. This is being overly simplistic, but there are two distinct types of Southern poverty: urban and rural. City and country. Black and white. Of course, there are poor black people in the rural South, just as there are poor whites in Southern cities, but to make a general point, you can do worse than to categorize Southern poverty in this way.

So here's the thing. We, the authors of this book, are three white liberal Southerners. We're neither equipped nor inclined to try to speak for our poor black compatriots. Their experience is their own. However, we believe that (a) there are many aspects of growing up poor that *are* fairly universal (poor diet, shitty schools, substance abuse, wearing knockoff Nikes that used to belong to your older cousin, etc.) and (b) to rich people, it's all the same. If you're poor, you're poor, and that's it. Well, really, it's more like "If you're poor, you're lazy," but either way. What matters is that this is an endemic problem in the South,[5] and it's not doing any of us any favors. In fact, it's doing us the opposite of favors. People down here are ravaged by the lack of money and options, and oftentimes the coping mechanisms for dealing with it just lead to more problems. And the three primary coping mechanisms for poverty in the South are the draw, the bottle, and the Lord.

THE DRAW

Ever heard of "the draw"? If not, congratulations on your food stamp–free childhood; bet that was cool. The draw is welfare. Money from the government. And buddy, it's got a *lot* of devotees. In terms of fans, the draw makes the Crimson Tide look like a period. Receiving this income from the government monthly is often referred to colloquially as "drawing a check," hence "the draw." A lot of young Southern hayseeds probably assume there's a vibrant and thriving niche market for artwork centering around check marks:

"What's your daddy do?"

"He draws a check."

"What, like for Nike?"

"Naw, like for bein' crazy."

The draw most typically refers to the actual monthly check from the government, but the Supplemental Nutrition Assistance Program (SNAP), or "food stamps," are also a huge part of government assistance in the poverty-stricken South. The idea with food stamps is basically to provide poor people with a type of currency that can be used to buy only food, as opposed to something unnecessary or even harmful, like cigarettes or Kid Rock box sets. Well, it took our people

5. Much like the music of Jason Aldean.

CRAZY CHECK

★

We're big fans of all manner of checks. Checks hit. But if we had to pick a favorite type of check (aside from "ones with my name on 'em"), we would probably go with the infamous "crazy check." The crazy check is a species of government assistance that's native to the American Southeast but can be found all across this great land. It ostensibly refers to a type of government assistance that's granted to people who are mentally unfit to work, but really what it means is "That sumbitch draws a check, and it ain't a damn thang wrong with him." Basically, "crazy check" is a catchall for talking shit about your friends and neighbors on the draw . . . and a very succinct way to describe your uncle.

No job, walks funny, but never been hit by a van? Crazy check. Meanders around in a state not unlike that of someone who's been railin' Percocets for ten years but still (mostly) pays her bills? Crazy check. If somebody's spending money, and you don't know how they got it, it's one of two things: sellin' pills or drawin' a crazy check. Lotta times both.[6] That's what we in the South consider diversifying your portfolio.

What are the requirements for drawing a crazy check? Literally no one knows. Even the people who get a crazy check don't know. This is evidenced by stories of people like ol' Cross-Eyed Bobby Joe Spivey, who "has to take his clothes off and run down by the high school once a month to keep his crazy check." Goddamn it, there just ain't no way that's true, Mema. But at any rate, the parameters can't be *too* restrictive because these sumbitches is as ubiquitous as Earnhardt stickers in a flea market parking lot.

6. Important note: these are not mutually exclusive. See: Trae's mother.

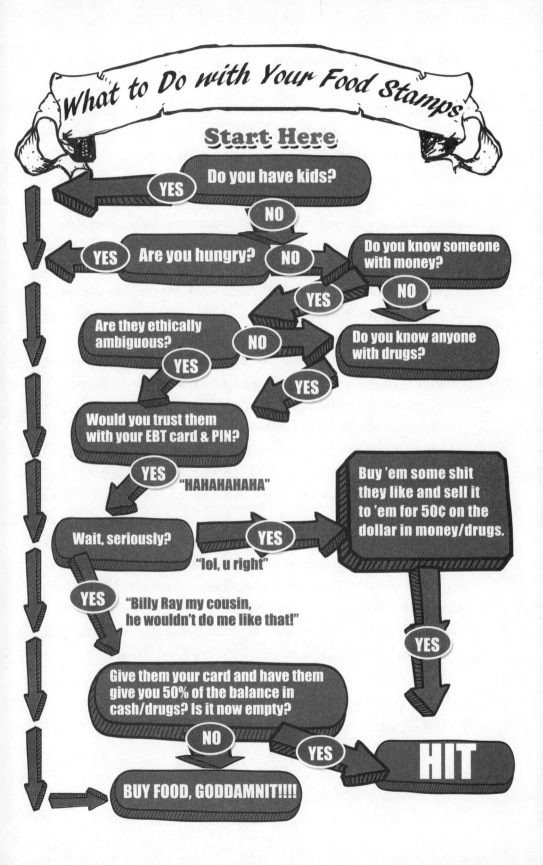

approximately zero days to figure out how to get around that shit. See, food stamps used to look like, well, stamps. They were actual pieces of paper that came in a little booklet. And those stamps could be used only on food—*or* they could be sold to someone else for cents on the dollar and thus converted into regular money, and you know what you can buy with regular money? Whatever you want, baby (read: weed). The government thought it could get around this by discontinuing the paper stamps and moving to an electronic system where food stamp recipients would have a food stamp debit card that could be used only for—you guessed it—food. Well, the people who came up with this clearly had not met many rednecks, because you gonna have to try a lot harder than that if you want to stop a redneck from making some shit work the way he wants it to work. Nowadays, what usually happens is that people swipe that food card for some other "fence"-type item, like cases of Mountain Dew,[7] and then turn around and sell *that* for weed/pills/commemorative-plate money. We're an enterprising people, y'all.

Now, don't misunderstand, food is bought too. People got to eat. But hell, after you done and spent half your freshly laundered food stamps (which was a modest amount to begin with) on a new tattoo of the Undertaker power bombing Satan (worth it), your options can get pretty limited. Chicken breasts and kale are expensive (and "super gay. Not like Doritos"). Canned meats and cheese spread are cheap as hell, baby. Easiest decision you'll ever make right there. And this is why poor people in this country are fat. Think about that next time you see a fat boy paying with food stamps and think to yourself, "Well, he don't look too hungry to me."

In places where work is continually hard to find and keep, and has been for generations, the draw can seem like the only viable option. And

7. **Goddamn, maybe we ain't worth savin'.**

in all honesty, for many people in these places, it is. You hear stories of women purposefully having more babies just to increase the amount they can draw, or people purposefully *avoiding* work because they're waiting for their approval for disability benefits to come through. Narratives like these are used by the rich and by right-wing politicians as evidence that poor people are lazy and entitled. (You know, the people who work on the goddamn roads these lizards don't want to pay taxes for.) This would be like using convicted killer Aaron Hernandez as evidence that all University of Florida football players are murderers.[8] But this idea that poor people are lazy is the only narrative that makes sense to people on the other side. More on that later, but the point is that—while the horror stories that Middle American parents tell their little future job creators about poor people before tucking them into their Ronald Reagan bedsheets are definitely overblown—abuse of the draw is a serious problem.

But that ain't the only thing we abuse, buddy.

THE BOTTLE

If there are two things we the authors of this honorable tome are about, it's country music and gettin' drunk. Ain't much better. And there are plenty of country songs romanticizing the process and results of pounding that sweet corn liquor. And they pretty much are all kick-ass.[9] So far be it from us to shit on the bottle.

Having said that, it's no secret that substance abuse runs rampant in poverty-stricken areas. Why is that? You know what sucks? Bein'

8. They are, though.

9. With the exception of literally anything that's been played on **CMT** in the past fifteen years.

Porch Talk with Trae

 A lot of people don't realize how interwoven into the fabric of certain communities welfare can be. In my hometown of Celina, Tennessee, government assistance is so ingrained in everyone's experience that people genuinely don't realize that not everyone receives it. When my oldest son was a baby, I was back home visiting with a friend of mine I'd grown up with. He also has kids, so naturally the conversation gravitated toward Dad Life. Being the insufferable whiner that I am, I started bitching about the cost of diapers, formula, etc. You know, baby shit. Well, not like actual baby shit, though we also talked plenty about that, I'm sure. Just the cost of having children. I noticed that he looked almost confused, and then this happened:

Good Buddy: Wait, you don't get WIC? [WIC stands for Women, Infants, and Children, and is a federal assistance program centered around providing for poor mothers and kids.]
Me: What? Naw, man. Hell, I wish.
GB: Dude, you should sign up, man. No reason not to. It helps a lot. We get milk, diapers, juice, all kinds of shit from WIC. All free. Makes a huge difference.
Me: I mean . . . I'm sure it does, buddy, but I don't qualify for WIC.
GB: What do you mean? Everybody can get WIC. You just have to sign up.
Me: I'm *pretty sure* that's not true.
GB: Just sayin', man, look into it. Also, you hear about Carla Cherry?
Me: Got some new titties?
GB: Buddy, goddamn.
Me: Skeeeeew.
GB: Skeeeeeew.

The next day, I went and looked up the WIC program even though I was 95 percent certain he was just as wrong as possible. Turns out, yeah, he was super wrong. For the amount of money I was making at the time (around $70,000 a year), I would have to have *seven kids* to be eligible. Now, don't get me wrong, that totally checks out for me. You shouldn't be able to *get* free shit from the government just because you want it, but I had to see for myself. Because that's the thing: this friend of mine is a smart guy and one of the best people I know, but he's pretty much always lived in Celina, and in Celina everyone *does* qualify for WIC because in Celina everyone is poor. He genuinely had no idea. This is how systemic poverty can be.

broke. Know what don't suck? Bein' drunk. Next question. But it goes a lot deeper than that. We're using "the bottle" as a catchall term here for "gettin' fucked up," and in the rural South, ol' Jim Beam gets his fair shake,[10] but the real party devil down here is "hillbilly heroin," that "Roxy Music," that "killer cotton."[11] Talkin' bout pills, y'all. Pills are such a problem—hell, such an *epidemic* down here—that we've devoted all of chapter 11 to them. But we would be remiss to fail to mention the issue in a chapter about poverty, because poverty and pills go together like . . . literally anything and pills.[12]

But before Big Pharma developed a way to chemically enslave

10. Just kiddin'. Beam ain't cheap enough. More like ol' Evan Williams or ol' Bobby's Uncle What Makes Liquor in a Radiator.

11. I made these last two up, but you can't tell it.

12. People don't ruin their lives on the shit because it *ain't* fun, all right? We're all adults here.

Porch Talk with Corey

I'm not going to even act as though I have any idea what it's like to grow up poor. Just wasn't the case for me. I guess it's because my parents loved me a little more than Drew's and Trae's. I mean, sure, I've been a "starving artist," but that was completely by choice, and it did *not* have to be that way. One thing I can speak on, however, is the crazy check. My uncle drew the fuck out of a crazy check, and I'll be honest with you guys: I think he deserved it. Trae talked about how a lot of times the crazy check was the one what was a little bit easier to get on account of just fudging some paperwork a bit, but my uncle? Goddamn, y'all. The man is something else.

Here's a story to show you just what I'm talking about.

One morning back in 2014, 'round seven o'clock, I heard a loud banging at my door. I was immediately alarmed because the company I tend to keep don't drag their worthless asses outta bed before noon unless there's a line for presale tickets to a Jimmy Buffett concert or some shit, and I *know* that after what happened last time, the Jehovah's Witnesses ain't gonna be fucking with me for quite a while. (Y'all ever paint your dingdong up like a frog and skip around the house looking for flies? Hits.)

I rolled over and wiped the sleep out of my eyes just confused as hell until I heard, "Open the goddamn door, boy! I know you're in there!" There's only one person in the world who sounds like my uncle, and by God, that was him. I went over and opened the door to reveal an even-more-pissed-off-than-usual Uncle Keith staring at me. As he was already halfway to the couch, I told him it was okay if he came in. At seven o'clock in the morning, what the shit did I have going on?

He sat on the couch and began to huff and puff as he was working the cap on a bottle of OxyContin. He took a handful, washed it down with an old, flat Coke I had lying on the table, and began to cuss up a storm. "Goddamn it, I swear on everything you just can't find no one wants to do shit anymore!"

"What do you mean, Uncle Keith?"

"The goddamn Supercuts over here ain't fucking open yet, and I need a goddamn haircut!"

I explained to him that *zero* haircut places would be open at such an hour, and then asked the question any Southern boy would ask his uncle in this situation: "What the hell you going to Supercuts for anyways? Don't Bill always cut your hair?"

Here we go.

"Oh, you just wait till you hear this bullshit!" he yelled. "I went down there yesterday, to Bill's, I walk in and say, 'Bill, I need a haircut.' That sumbitch told me I'd have to wait on account of he's got three people in front of me. *Three fucking people!*"

"Well, did he?"

"There was some folks in there, yeah. But that shit pissed me off. I ain't ever had to wait before. So I told him, 'You listen here, you son of a bitch. I ain't gonna have you do me like this. I've been coming here my whole fucking life to get my hair cut. And I want the sumbitch cut today.' Well, you ain't gonna believe it, but he kicked my ass out and threatened to call the law."

"I absolutely believe that," I said. "What I don't believe is that you're upset that he had other clients. I know you didn't have an appointment."

"You just don't get it! Goddamn, you just don't know shit, do ya?"

"Well, I'll be honest. I do not have any clue what's going on right now, no."

"You know how I like my haircut: high and tight! Same as I've been getting since Poppa used to take me."

"What does that have to do with anything?" I asked.

Uncle Keith went into a near fifteen-minute-long tirade

about how the high-and-tight haircut was going out of style. Something to do with goddamn political correctness and the fact that the clueless liberal media interpreted it as part of the uniform for white supremacy. He explained that Bill was giving in to the bullshit propaganda and instead of just facing my uncle like a man and explaining to him that he could no longer cut his hair the way he wanted it, he had instead orchestrated a conspiracy to keep my uncle out of the barber shop.

Couple side notes here on Uncle Keith's high-and-tight conspiracy theory: (a) No. No, that is in no way what happened, and (b) In case you have never been to a barber in the South, the only haircut they know how to give is a GD high-and-tight. They would go out of business without it.

After his rant, my uncle finally calmed down long enough to enjoy an open pack of peanuts he found between the couch cushions. He called me gay for sleeping in so late, and then he took more pills.

So, yeah, some people need that crazy check.

our people,[13] there was whiskey. Whiskey's still there. Whiskey will always be there for ya. There to tell ya, "You know what'd be awesome? Takin' your shirt off and ridin' the four-wheeler past the jailhouse," or "Hey, that horse is givin' you the stink-eye. You just gonna stand here and take that shit? That horse don't know you." Don't listen to whiskey, y'all. Don't *ever* listen to whiskey.

Look, when you're poor and they fixin' to shut the lights off on you, that crumpled-up $5 bill you got ain't gonna make a dent in the light bill, but it'll buy a bottle. And that bottle will make it all a little

13. Y'all woke yet!?

better, for a little while. Then you wake up, and shit's worse than it was before. Such is the nature of the demon liquor. It becomes yet another endless cycle. And this cycle infuriates people on the outside looking in. "You can't even afford to pay the water bill, but you can buy whiskey? *Not in my America!*"

To hell with that. We get it. Dealing with the crushing hopelessness of poverty is rough enough as it is. Expecting people to go through it *stone cold sober* is just inhumane. But at the end of the day, it definitely doesn't help matters. And speaking of not actually helping matters . . .

THE LORD

When it comes to coping, people down here usually go one of two ways: the bottle or the Bible. Sometimes one and then the other; sometimes both at the same time. But you'll seldom find a poor man what don't worship one of 'em. And if you're going to compare the two, it'd be pretty hard to argue that the bottle doesn't ultimately do more damage in the end. But, hell, at least there's some kick-ass stories along the way. When was the last time you heard somebody killing it around a bonfire with a story 'bout a prayer circle? "Man, you missed it at this last lock-in, son. Shit got *wild*." That don't happen. "Soon as you walked in the door of the rec center, man, *it was hos, it was weed* . . ." Naw. Not a thing. 'Course, to be fair, you also don't often hear about an ol' boy teein' off on his wife's face cause he had a little too much of the Holy Spirit.[14] There's pros and cons here, guys.

But still, something about the Lord appeals to poor people. Could be the promise of salvation after a lifetime of turmoil. Could be potlucks.

---

14. Guarantee they's been a fair share of drunk fellers who been slapped upside the head with a Bible, though, for what that's worth.

We don't know. The fact remains that Jesus has been a salve for the destitute since Day One of the Saga. That story rings especially true in the South. Slaves singing spirituals. Coal miners gathering to pray before making their daily descent toward hell. Jesus is and has always been a big deal down here, and for many people it's because He's just about all they got. And look, if faith makes you feel one iota better about your lot in life and keeps you away from the bottle or the scrip, then, hey, more Holy Power to ya. We ain't here to judge—that's Jesus's job, as we understand it—and we ain't gonna do his job for him. Lazy-ass Jesus, always lookin' for a handout. When we do it, we're freeloading vagrants; when he does it it's "tithing." Bullshit. Anyway.

While we understand the appeal of the Lord to those with little to nothing else, we question how much good it really does. People say to put your trust in the Lord, and He will see you through the hard times, but did the electric company start accepting quoted scripture or something? Did we miss that? Seems like a poor business model, if so. "Jesus, Take the Wheel" by Carrie Underwood was a catchy little ditty but absolutely *terrible* advice. You genuinely do that, and your ass is goin' in the ditch. Hell, does Jesus even *know* how to drive? He walked everywhere; that was, like, one of his things. Whatever. The point is that sending a message to people mired in poverty *to just give up* (and let God take care of it) is counterproductive at best and dangerous at worst.

So far, we've covered many of the facts surrounding poverty in the South. And those facts don't paint a pretty picture (which checks out; we mainly paint houses). Well, it's *not* a pretty picture, but we also don't want to come off as unsympathetic. Because facts are one thing, but now it's time for the truth.[15]

15. The truth is like facts, but it hits harder. You'll see.

Porch Talk with Drew

My father has been a preacher for most of my life. But he's been a railman for all of it. Working for the railroad meant food for his family; it meant being away from home a lot; it meant we were middle class in our tiny poor town (though we were working class by national standards); and it meant my daddy was a union man.

I don't know when the railroads unionized, and it don't matter when. It matters that it happened, and it was important. It was so important that when my father got injured on the job but was denied benefits because the symptoms didn't arise for nearly a year, the union and his contract allowed him to fight—solely because it, the union, existed. That winter, we ate deer meat that he'd killed and frozen earlier in the year. We cut coupons, and corners. We struggled.

But he won. He got back pay and his job back. Unions matter—so much so that my dad told me he often voted Democrat. Not always. But often. A preacher in Tennessee, of a Baptist church no less, would vote with the allegedly godless, soulless heathen party? "Of course," he'd tell me. "Most of those Republicans don't care about God. They pretend to. And these Dems may be just pretending to care about me, but when Democrats are in office, I get a raise."

My family clings to the Lord as tight as any family I've ever been around. But when my father sees preachers on television preaching "prosperity gospel" and living in mansions and driving nice cars, he has to change the channel so it doesn't make him sick. He's worked hard for every dollar he has ever earned, and I know for a fact he gives God all the glory for the opportunity to do so—but he is a shining example of how giving God credit doesn't have to mean givin' rich people votes.

DM

IN DEFENSE OF THE POOR

The aspects and realities of being poor in the South we've discussed up to this point have all been pretty stereotypical. Your typical Reaganite would read through this chapter with a smug look of satisfied disgust on his face. "I knew it," he'd think to himself before reaching for his Manhattan or whatever. Because, admittedly, this is all a little ugly and doesn't cast the Southern poor in a very positive light, but here's what's important to understand: generally speaking, *it's not their fault.*[16]

This is where our aforementioned Job Creator Friend spits out his Old Fashioned (seriously, we're not sure what they drink) in absolute disgust. "This narrative again? Typical freeloaders, making excuses, refusing to *take responsibility for their actions.*" Really, Chad? When was the last time you took responsibility for a goddamn thing? These are the same people that make deflecting their entire existence. When their stocks go down, "It's the market." When the girl presses charges, "She was asking for it." When the economy tanks because of two decades' worth of *their policies,* "It's the freeloaders." And they wanna talk about taking responsibility? Yeah, well, fuck that.

These people don't get it. They actively, forcefully, do not fucking get it. To be completely fair, it's hard to "get" something that you have never in your life even come close to experiencing. Chad looks at himself in his high-dollar job with his high-dollar house and his high-dollar leased Porsche, and he pats himself on the back. He deserves this. He's worked hard to get it. Then he looks at poor Randy—on disability in a trailer park with an old broken-down Ford—and Chad shakes his head. Randy deserves this. He should

---

16. The South is Matt Damon, we're Robin Williams. Y'all are the Academy. We'd like to thank you.

have worked harder. And for Chad, that's the end of the story. He knows all he needs to know. But that doesn't tell the whole story at all. Not even close. The whole story goes a little more like this:

THE BALLAD OF CHAD AND RANDY

Chad played quarterback in high school. He was all right but not quite as good as the kid who backed him up, but, hey, that kid's dad didn't pay for the new practice field. The private school Chad went to destroyed the similarly sized public schools in their region when they played each other because while they had the same enrollment, the athletic budgets were astronomically different. Chad gets pretty used to winning this way. He makes pretty good but not exemplary grades (his tutor is Chinese but nice enough otherwise). Chad gets his face in the paper and a partial football scholarship to Wake Forest. He goes to Wake but passes on the scholarship because he just wants to "focus on school." His dad happily foots the bill—school is important.

Chad doesn't work while in college. His dad forbids it. He tells Chad that he can work at the firm in the summertime, but during the school year he must focus on his studies. And Chad does. He focuses on his studies—and on railing sorority girls in the basement of the frat house and bragging to all the pledges about it.[17] Chad lightens his course load and changes his major a couple of times in an effort to "make the most of the opportunity" (read: milk this shit for all it's worth).

Ultimately, Chad graduates with a 3.1 GPA after only six and a half years. Way to go, Chad! He then goes to a work as an account rep for a firm owned by one of his dad's best friends. He goes golfing with

17. Let the record show that it ain't a damn thing wrong with railing sorority girls.

clients and takes them to football games on the company dime. They talk about immigrants and pussy. Chad establishes himself. He gets married to Brittney; she was on the homecoming court. They buy a house. He leases a Porsche. Chad knows that he's killin'.

Randy played football, too, at a tiny public school in the middle of nowhere. Randy wasn't the greatest athlete, but that boy could *hit*, and he always left it all on the field. Still, no scouts came to Randy's games. His school was known way more for being a punching bag for the region's private schools than for producing collegiate talent. Randy gets pretty used to losing. Randy's grades aren't great, but they aren't terrible. His momma doesn't care either way, though, and his daddy ain't around. Hell, his momma isn't around much, either. One of Randy's coaches tries like hell to get him recruited, but when Randy takes the SAT exam, there are math problems on that sumbitch from classes his school didn't offer. It had intended to but had to cut more teachers again this year.

So he doesn't have the grades, and he doesn't have the shine. But his coach, saint that he is, gets Randy an offer from a small college in West Tennessee. So Randy goes, happily. He is gonna make something of himself. He is gonna show his piece-of-shit daddy what a real man is. And Randy does well. After all, the boy can hit. He can't work on account of football and class taking up most of his time, but he gets some loans. Hell, it won't be nothin' to pay those back once he gets a good job with his degree. But then, halfway through his first year, Randy takes an awkward hit and tears his knee all to hell. The training staff rehabs him through the spring, but when he isn't bouncing back, his scholarship gets pulled. Oh, well. Randy thinks he'll just work now—he is a good worker anyway. He can pay his own way. But Randy has to wait for his knee to heal. Oh, well, one more loan won't hurt. Randy starts working, but between the hours he has to pick up and the pain in his knee (he thinks something is off with it but he doesn't have access to the trainers anymore, and he doesn't have health insurance so, hell, he'll be all right), Randy is struggling.

His grades slip, his bills rack up, and just like that, Randy flames out. He moves back home (where the hell else is he gonna go?) and starts working trimming trees with his buddies from high school. He has some hydro pills now to help his knee through it. He feels sick a lot, though, too. And even with his insurance, it's all he can do to afford the pills, especially trying to pay off those goddamn student loans. And then just last week, his truck breaks down. He doesn't have a way into work, but the boss ain't trying to hear that shit. Randy thinks he might lose his job. Then what? He could maybe get on unemployment or something for a little while, just until he gets on his feet. Randy feels like he's dyin'.

Now see, every word of that you just read was made up, but every word of it is true, too. Do you see the difference between Randy and Chad? Randy needed (and failed) to *soar* in order to be able to make a successful life for himself. Chad just had to not fuck up. Now, to Chad's credit, lots of shitty rich kids *do* fuck up, but that's the thing: even when they do, they get bailed out, time and time again. Y'all ever heard of a feller by the name of Jonathan Football?[18] Randy fucks up one good time? That's it, buddy. And as the narrative above illustrates, he doesn't even *have* to fuck up—one bad break is plenty enough. And you might think that blowing out Randy's knee in the story was a cheap trick, but it doesn't even matter. Even if Randy had made it all the way through, at the end of the day, he'd have a middling GPA on a garden-variety degree he got from a wholly unimpressive school. No references. No connections. Mountains of student loan debt. Fuck the country-song-football-injury

18. **Johnny Manziel. He's a professional rich douche who also played football for a little while.**

story. It's not necessary. The fact remains: the deck is stacked irrevo-cably against Randy,[19] and Chad is playing with pocket aces. Yet most all of this country's Chads look at the Randys with disdain. You know why? Because. They. Just. Don't. Get it. And they don't care to. It doesn't *matter* to them. Why would it? Not their problem. Know what *is* their problem? All these taxes they have to pay to take care of lazy asses like Randy, goddamn it. That's as far as their reasoning goes.

Whether the Chads realize it or not, the pure and simple *fact* of the matter is that for the vast majority of people, the single most important factor in determining whether you will have money or not is whether you were *born* with money or not. That's it. Statistically speaking, that's all that divides us: pure, blind luck. Chads don't like to hear this because they feel it detracts from all the hard work they've put in to get where they are. Well, sorry, Chad, but the numbers don't lie. So-ciological studies, including landmark cases from Harvard and Johns Hopkins, have all consistently found that, by and large, if you're born into a poor family, you will be poor, and vice versa. *Why* is this the case? Well, there are sociological theories on that too, but this is our book, and we ain't writin' a book just to talk about what some other sumbitches found out. So now we gonna give you *our* thoughts.

STUCK IN THE MUD

If you're poor, it's hard (really, really, *really* goddamn hard) to stop being poor.[20] You see, Chads think you just "stop complaining and

---

19. **And if Randy were black, it'd be even worse—there'd be no tree-cuttin' job.**

20. **There we go again, blowing people's minds with our revelatory insights.**

get a job," and if you work hard, that's all it takes. Well, that's really fucking stupid, Chad. We're starting to not like Chad much. Anyway. Every poor person knows that you can work your ass off and still get behind. Way, way behind.

First of all, the current minimum wage in this country is a damn joke and not enough money to actually survive on in most places. It's not our intent to open that particular can of political worms[21] right now, but it's just fucking math. Even if you have a job that pays enough for you to actually get by, then that's fine—until some shit happens. And we don't know if y'all have heard or not, but shit happens; that's just what it does. You need new tires on your truck, or God forbid something even worse, like a transmission. Or you hurt your back. Or you get a sick kid. These are all things that suck for anyone, but if you're poor, any one of them has the potential to literally ruin your life forever. As parents and Chads love to remind us, money doesn't grow on trees, so when these things come up, you have to borrow to pay, and when you're poor, your credit sucks. So now guess where you are? Back in that sharecropper debt cycle we talked about earlier. Borrowing money to survive until you can get paid and pay back the money you borrowed . . . and on and on. You spend the rest of your life owing money to the money you owe.[22] It fuckin' sucks, y'all.

Add to this the fact that being poor is expensive as hell. Overdraft fees, late fees, predatory interest rates—the list goes on and on. It costs a lot of money to have no money, and that sure as fuck don't help none. Conversely, if you *have* money, they literally just give you

---

21. **Arguably the worst kind of worms.**

22. **Shout-out to the National for their song "Bloodbuzz Ohio." They ain't red, but they still hit.**

more money. Interest rates, dividends, whatever the hell an ROI is, all this shit serves to take rich people's money and turn it into even more money. And look, there's nothing wrong with that. We're just saying: the system is not designed for upward mobility, regardless of that bullshit grown-ups fed you about the "American Dream."

For poor people, this shit's a nightmare. And add to it the fact that money management is a legitimate skill that poor people just don't have. They're never taught anything about how to manage money, because who the hell would teach them? No one around them knows shit about it either. So when they get older and finance some stuff they can't afford or max out a credit card or whatever, it's not always because they're stupid or careless. They're just ignorant. And now they know, now they've learned, but unfortunately, it's probably too late. One mistake like this, and their credit score—hell, their entire financial well-being—is well and truly *fucked*. For poor people, that shit's like your virginity: they ain't no gettin' it back.

So we reiterate to the poor people of the South: *it's not your fault.*

But that doesn't mean that we shouldn't do something about it. That doesn't mean it isn't a problem. Because it absolutely is. When people get poor, they get desperate, and when people get desperate, bad shit happens. Bad shit like crime, drug abuse, and violence. So it's not a stretch to say that the issue of poverty may be the single most important issue facing the South—hell, the whole country—today.[23] So what do we do about it?

Well, y'all ain't gonna believe this, but we got some thoughts.

---

23. **That and the music of Jason Aldean.**

STOP VOTING AGAINST OURSELVES

Poor people, *especially in the South*, consistently and heavily vote against their economic self-interest in every single election. This is infuriating—absolutely maddening. These motherfuckers enact policies that prey on the poor in devastating ways. They limit health care. They gut spending in order to give their friends in the 1 percent a tax break, and guess which programs go first? We'll give you a hint: not the fucking tanks. They take a hard line on drugs, packing private prisons (owned by their rich buddies) with nonviolent offenders, the vast majority of which are poor men. They make it their life's mission to bend the Poor Man over for the benefit of their fellow lizards, and every single fucking election, poor people line up in droves to vote them back into office. Why? Fucking *why do we do that?!*

Well, because of Jesus. That's why. It may seem like an oversimplification, but that's about the size of it, really. Sometime in the mid-twentieth century, the right wing initiated the frankly brilliant strategy of anointing itself the Party of the Lord. And it worked. Republicans now claim to represent the moral high ground, "family values," a "traditional way of life," and all that bullshit. Poor people hear these assholes spouting the same kinds of things that they hear their pastor spouting on Sundays and, *bam*, there you have it. Votes cast and fates sealed, just like that. And when you look at it this way, maybe the Lord *is* more harmful to poor people than the bottle.

We have got to stop this, y'all. Do you *really* think if Jesus came back he'd be hanging out with Ted Fucking Cruz? Ted Cruz's *wife* doesn't hang out with Ted Cruz.[24] How did these people make everyone forget that Jesus was a poor brown socialist hippie with long hair and sandals? He was *not* a fucking neocon. Look, Jesus was

---

24. **Ted Cruz is a skinwalker and a demon from the Nether.**

absolutely about the poor—it totally makes sense for poor people to be big fans—but for the love of the Him, stop conflating that reality with the fallacy of "the Christian Right." Stop letting these mother-fuckers lie to (and steal from) you! For fuck's sake! Stop it!

Seriously. Please. Stop.

LEARN STUFF

Hey, look, we get it: learnin's boring and dumb and "for queers." But, again, the numbers don't lie: it's hard as hell to break out of poverty, but education is far and away your best chance. The higher level your education, the more money you make, statistically, across the board. One of the issues with this though, is that the schools in poverty-stricken areas are not great. This is one of the major factors in the poor staying poor. So "getting an education" is easier said than done for a poor person.

So what can we *do* about it? Well, stop focusing on "the gay agenda" and "Mexicans takin' jobs" and all this other bullshit and start focusing on stuff that actually matters, including education reforms. Stop making poor kids think that sports or the army are the only ways out. Reading also can work. And, again, we admit that reading isn't as fun as scoring touchdowns or shooting the shit out of everything, but it's also way more practical and beneficial in the long run.

And also—and we're back to our own personal musings now[25]—the more you learn, the more you want to know. The more questions you ask, the more you realize just how much bullshit you have been fed your entire life. The more poor people who go down this road, the better.

25. But, again, this is our book, damn it.

Porch Talk with Trae

I grew up one of the poorest kids in one of the poorest parts of Tennessee. I talk about it a lot. It's a whole thing. But I was also one of the smartest kids there (not much of a feat, frankly). So they put me in the "gifted" program in school. The program for smart kids. But here's the (hilarious) thing: programmatically, "gifted" is considered a part of "special education" for budgeting and organizational purposes. Well, at my tiny, rural, poor-ass public school, due to budget constraints, "gifted" and "special ed" were lumped together into the same classroom, with the same teacher. She could teach only so much material, and it wasn't like the special-ed kids could do gifted-kid course work. So while I was put in the gifted program ostensibly to challenge me and enhance my abilities intellectually, what ended up actually happening was that I took special-ed classes. I colored molecules and shit. Now, look, that's objectively hilarious. But it's also pretty sad, and another pretty good metaphor for the systemic disadvantages of poverty.

So what can we do to improve economic conditions in the South? Put down the Bible for a minute and pick up some different books.[26] That would be a pretty good start. That and stop buying scratch-offs.

Seriously y'all. Stop buying scratch-offs.

26. **Talkin' bout gettin woke, y'all.**

Porch Talk with Trae

This chapter is extremely personal to me, for reasons that are probably obvious by now. I lived this shit, y'all. Firsthand. This was my life. So I tend to get pretty fired up about this subject, especially when I see people on the right talking about poor people being lazy and entitled and freeloaders and a drain on society and all that bullshit. It kills me because I know beyond a doubt that these people don't know a fucking thing about what it's like. They don't know shit about the struggle. Well, I do. And so I don't take kindly to having my life experience explained to me by people who demonstrably have no fucking clue what they're talking about.

I figure most people who read this book will probably be pretty much on board with picking up what we're laying down. But I'm sure there will be some people who read this who are not (and I appreciate y'all doin' that, for the record). And those people will read through much of this chapter with disgust. "Just more making excuses. Still no taking responsibility." Well, I would really, sincerely like to know what I have to make excuses about. Before the first video ever went viral, I already had an MBA and a job negotiating multimillion-dollar federal contracts. I have been completely financially independent since the day I turned eighteen, and I have never once as an adult taken money from the government—or anyone, for that matter. I put myself through college by waiting tables and with academic scholarships that I *earned*. I did things the right way, by their (Republican) standards. I'm the antithesis of lazy and entitled.

I'm the model of the American Dream, and I would have starved to death as a child if not for food stamps. I'm telling you (any right-wingers reading this) that *you are wrong*. I am living, breathing, job-creating proof that *these systems can work*. They're necessary. And, furthermore, the alternative is untenable. A civilized society looks out for its less fortunate members, for Fictional God's sake.

Yes, right-wingers, you're wrong about poor people. You know what makes sense to you and what you've been told, but you don't know the first fucking thing about the reality. Some of you will probably hear my story and say that I'm proof that it doesn't matter where you come from: if you take responsibility and you work hard, then you can succeed. Yeah, well, here's the thing. I'm an outlier. An anomaly. And I have absolutely no explanation for that. I genuinely don't. Sometimes people ask me how I rose above the circumstances of my upbringing, and I mean . . . I don't know. I just did.

My mother had one sister, and her sister had two sons, my first cousins. One of them, BJ, and I were very close when we were kids. I looked up to him like a brother. We shared much the same experience as children, and we had a lot of the same genes as well. We buried BJ in 2015. He overdosed after years of addiction and prison sentences. I looked at him in the casket and thought to myself, "Why him and not me?" Why did our paths in life diverge so profoundly despite starting off in roughly the same place? Because see, *most* people who come from the circumstances I come from end up dead or in jail, by a large margin. But not me. And I do not have a good answer as to why that is.

For the record, neither does sociology. But there's a phenomenon known as "resiliency." Some kids from highly disadvantaged upbringings are just resilient, and they don't know why. So at least there's a name for it, I guess. But my *point* with all of this is that I am in no way proof that anyone can rise out of poverty if they just put their mind to it. I'm the exception, not the rule. But since I have had the *extraordinary* fortune of being that exception, I intend to use my position to plead with people on the right to please, *please* take it from someone who lived it: *you're wrong about poor people*. You are. And your wrongness is dangerous.

Being born poor is a burden the likes of which is hard to quantify. It's so hard, no matter how motivated and disciplined you are, to truly break out of it. It took me thirty years to really catch up financially, and I'm a goddamn cultural phenomenon. So please stop acting like it's as simple as reaching for those mythical "bootstraps." Walk a mile in a poor man's boots, buddy, and then talk to me 'bout them straps.

And lastly, I wanna state for the record that I want right-wingers to stop shitting on poor people first just on principle but also because I just flat-out don't believe them. They like to rattle on about "personal responsibility" and how all they want is for poor people to take charge of their own destinies and rise above their station. They want success like that for everyone, they say. Except that, no, the fuck they don't. They don't want that shit for a second.

If every poor person really and truly broke the shackles of poverty and rose to a higher station in life, who would the right-wingers have to look down on? Who would they have to exploit for their benefit? Who would they have to blame when things go to shit? Rich people have billions of reasons to keep poor people exactly where they are. It's absolutely in their best interests to do so. So just think about that the next time you step in the voting booth. That's all I'm saying.

3

Let Us Prey

Jesus Christ!

He permeates every nook and cranny of public life in the South and most aspects of the private side. We pray to him before meals, in public, and at sporting events. We pray for people who don't believe the way we do. Sometimes we even tell 'em we're going to pray for them because they do not believe the way we do. That's actually pretty shitty.

Our culture is so wrapped up in Christianity that people outside the South call our homeland the Bible Belt. It's usually meant as an insult; sometimes it's a warning to anyone who'd think about visiting.

But what is so insulting about it? The Bible, however you feel about it personally, is a damn good book. The prodigal son is the theme of every single movie you liked as a teenager that didn't have titties in it. (*Joe Dirt*: great flick.) The story of Jesus has been rehashed in every generation. (*Matrix* trilogy, anyone?) And don't get us started on the Book of the Revelation.

Okay, get us started. If the Book of the Revelation came out today as a graphic novel, and then a damn movie, nerds would line up around the block for eight hours to see it. John the Revelator woulda been an

Avenger. That story has elders, scrolls, and a lamb with seven eyes doing some sweet occult shit. There is a dragon, a seven-headed beast, a Sea Beast,[1] and a pregnant lady in white robes. Gettin' hype yet? Well, there are also seven angels, each with a trumpet, what when they blow 'em, all manner of hell breaks loose: locusts, an army of badasses, and other shit we've had to block out of our psyche because our pathetic human brains cannot fathom the glory of such ridiculous fuckery. Finally, in the end, there are some bowls. Wait, bowls? The Apocalypse ends on *bowls*? What's so scary about bowls?

Well, these aren't regular bowls. They ain't even Tupperware bowls that've been in the fridge for too long and now hold moldy pork. Naw, way worse. These is like the Navy SEALs of bowls. One makes all of the ocean turn to fuckin' blood, and another makes the sun burn the godforsaken (literally at this point) earth like the piece of celestial garbage the earth is.

Did we forget anything? Oh yeah, the *four horsemen of the dad-blame*[2] *Apocalypse*, who ride different-colored horses out of the sky, respectively wielding a bow for conquering, a sword to "take peace," the scales of righteous justice, and, finally, on a pale horse, a rider literally carrying death. That's his weapon: death. As a concept. Naw, the Bible is metal as heck,[3] y'all.

So why is being called the Bible Belt an insult? The Bible hits. It's probably something to do with that second word: the *Belt* part. Belts

---

1. Sea Beast, incidentally, was also the nickname of one of Corey's college girlfriends.

2. We're trying to cuss less in this chapter—it being about the Lord and all.

3. This is gonna be hard as, uh . . . crap. We're definitely gonna fail.

are useful, sure. But belts are also oppressive.[4] They represent order and uniformity. They maintain the status quo and squeeze tight 'round ya guts when you went too hard at the buffet. Belts are boring and represent rules. They also represent ya daddy givin' you a little TLC and stripin' that butt with leather. Teenagers sag their pants and never wear belts because teenagers don't do anything not hittin', and belts ain't hittin'. Now, look, don't get us wrong. A nice belt to match your new blue suede shoes you wearin' to the Derby party is prolly purty nice. But when you have to wear a belt, it means someone died or your boss is a prick—and either way, it ain't hittin'.

Business men and women wear belts because it makes 'em feel like they have control over some aspect of their lives. Sure, Todd, your boss may hate you, and your marriage is failing, and, man, if this deal doesn't go through, you really might have to cancel Christmas vacation, but by God, these *pants will ride exactly as I want them to, just below my pudgy navel!*

And that, really, is why being the Bible Belt is so bad. The Bible itself, and the faith based around it, and its protagonist ('Sup, Christ?) aren't *necessarily* bad. But the way folks have *used* the Bible to excuse their power grabbing, their meddling, and their hatefulness, and, really, to squeeze culture like a belt[5] three sizes too tight has to change. The Church has always had a major role in the South. In good ways and in so many bad ones, it affects politics, family relations, social issues, culture, and even diet.

It's highly unlikely that its reach will relent anytime soon. In our

---

4. **The Amish people need to check their suspender privilege.**

5. **Okay, this metaphor is starting to get tired. But you know what metaphor is timeless? The Garden of Eden. Mankind was doing fine just walkin' around eatin' mangos and banging under trees. Then we had to mess around and *learn* some shit, and now everything sucks. 'At's the human condition in a nutshell (what you then wear over your nuts cuz you naked in a garden, Adam).**

lifetime, your sanctimonious neighbor is not going to stop offering, "Ya know, God has a plan," as an "answer" to life's tragedies.[6] There won't be a day anytime soon, despite Aunt Tammy's constant fears that she won't be allowed to pray out loud, that politicians don't claim to be following God's guidance in their civic duties (as well as in their decision to run in the first place). No, Jesus is here to stay. So let's deal with it.

What's that Mahatma Gandhi quote about Jesus being cool but his followers sucking a communion wafer? Actually, he said, "I like your Christ; I do not like your Christians. Your Christians are so unlike your Christ." However you feel about it, and *we know*, some of yuns feel a *lot* about it, you can't deny that at the very least, sometimes people in the South like to use Jesus as an excuse to be dickheads.[7] And, well, we gotta get to fixin' that. But first, let's acknowledge some of the good the Church has done in the South. As we heard a preacher say one time, "You gotta start the sermon out with love and hope. Then, ease 'em into hell and hardship." He raised a huge offering that day, so we're heeding that advice. First, we'll do some celebrating of the Church's positive side. Then we'll have our come-to-Jesus moment.[8]

6. Even if this were true, and "God's plan" was, for example, for babies to get cancer, well, then God has an awful plan. He prolly don't want you tellin' everyone He's responsible for that stuff, Tammy.

7. Fuck it. We can't not cuss.

8. "Come to Jesus" basically means you face the truth. At the end of a lot of evangelical sermons, the preacher invites sinners to the altar to ask forgiveness for their sins by saying "Come to Jesus!" This, in a Christian's world, would be the most important moment of facing the truth in his life. The phrase has gone on to mean any moment where someone has to face any type of truth. Yes, it's hella ironic that we're alluding to a come-to-Jesus moment about changing how our culture uses Jesus. It's subversive. We're geniuses.

BLACK CHURCHES AND CIVIL RIGHTS

Southern churches have played key positive roles. The most obvious example is the role of black churches in the civil rights movement. African American church leaders like Dr. Martin Luther King Jr., Fred Shuttlesworth, and Ralph David Abernathy became the moral and political leaders of the movement. Their religious doctrine became the movement's philosophy. Their congregations and others became the nonviolent protesters and boycotters. Their church buildings became the meet-up points.

Dr. King drew from the nonviolent teachings of Gandhi, but he also drew heavily from biblical scripture. Ending Jim Crow became not just a question of political right and wrong, but one related to a concept all Southerners are familiar with if not obsessed with: God's will. That claim was a bold one: God created all of us equal. God wanted all his children to have the same opportunities. God was on the side of desegregation.

Of course, some white Southerners (and white Southern preachers) fought this tooth and nail, but as we know, they lost—literally, in 1954's *Brown v. Board of Education*, the decision handed down by the Supreme Court that ended segregation in schools. And they lost culturally over the years since. Racism still exists, obviously, but you'd be hard pressed to find anyone who says that segregation is "God's will" who isn't considered a bat-shoot-freaking-crazy person. It isn't a coincidence that the Church played such a key role in changing the majority's cultural outlook (yes, in spite of what you may hear, *most* people in the South are decidedly against segregation). For whites in the South, hearing Dr. King, a preacher, talk about Jesus's mercy, and say it's God's will that Christian lives be fruitful and free, and that God's love is the right choice to make over hate—well, that was hard for them to reject for very long without also rejecting their own religion.

Of course, many Christians held on to that prejudice and hate anyway, because hypocrisy goes with church like gravy goes with biscuits. I guess those folks thought heaven would also be segregated. I don't know who the heck would wanna live in eternity listenin' to praise music without any black folk around, but, hey, whatever floats your whites-only boat.

So, thanks in large part to the Church's role in the civil rights movement, to be a Christian meant at least *pretending* to not be a racist. This is still on display at restaurants across the South on any given Sunday afternoon. Church ladies and overweight men with ties with crosses on 'em can be seen desperately trying not to say some Fox News shit to a Mexican taking their order on the Sabbath. "Now, Pedro, I ain't gonna speak nothing but English to you, and I expect the same back because this is an English-speaking country," a lady in a pastel dress will say to a man named Diego. She then pauses to consider words carefully, as she realizes that her pastor is two tables away. "But you should know God loves you in spite of what language you speak." Her smile beams, and Pastor Dan nods approvingly before ordering another dessert.

We desperately hope and pray[9] the Church takes over this leadership role again in the South for the LGBTQ rights movement. We won't hold our breath, but, of course, we do want to say thank you and great job to those churches leading the way with love in their hearts and on their gospel tracts.

THE CHURCH AS AN EDUCATOR

Back in the day, churches in the South played a large role in founding colleges, schools, and universities. Like most places, a lot of

9. Trae doesn't pray.

our best schools were started by rich people from somewhere else (Hey there, Vanderbilt!), but a lot of great institutions were started by the Church.[10]

We've gleaned from our research[11] on this topic a single common thread in the founding entities of these schools: they seem exclusively to be churches, state or other governments, and rich people. What do those entities all share in common? Access to gobs and gobs of money and power. A lot of this chapter will be about the Church abusing said power, but we figured it was important to point out that with schools, it was one instance where that power was used for good—mostly. We also got to consider Bob Jones, Liberty, Regent, etc. How you gonna name a university "Bob Jones"? Bob Jones don't sound academic—it sounds like the guy your Dad bought his huntin' truck off of.

DELICIOUS CHURCH FOOD

Another positive tradition, and one of us Liberal Rednecks' favorites, that's closely related to worship in the South, is eating delicious food. Church potlucks, whether they be at a homecoming service, on a holiday, or every fourth Sunday of every month just because, are some of the best times to be around the church house. We bond, laugh, plan, and, most importantly, we eat. A lot.

Homecoming service is a Sunday usually in the summer when church members who've moved, married, and joined their spouse's

10. Drew's alma mater, Maryville College, in Tennessee, is one such school. In spite of the price tag, he has good things to say about it. No, this book has not gotten him out of debt, so he still will not be donating yet. Go, Scots!

11. We did no research.

church or left in a fit of anger because Brother Daryl got to be the deacon and they didn't, get to come to their old church, reconnect with the old members, and eat fried chicken so good it would convert an atheist.

Sundy chicken[12] is a tradition all over the South, directly related to eatin' after church. It was annoying as hell when the preacher came over after church, because we knew we'd have to be on church behavior for a lot longer, and we weren't gonna be allowed to watch any of the cool cartoons like *Batman: The Animated Series* because it was "too dark" (though we watched the heck out of 'em when he wasn't around—y'all 'member that one with the maze and the Riddler? Amazing). But what hit about his visit was that we always had way better food. Momma had to impress the preacher man!

CHURCH MUSIC

Modern Christian rock is the worst sound on the planet in the history of the world. Its very existence is the biggest argument against the notion that a just and loving God exists and is engaged in our activities. However, church music in general must be celebrated. Gospel and its musical progeny have given us so much more than we deserve. There's some music that traces its lineage back to Sunday choirs—a few Ray Charles and Hank Williams Sr. records come to mind—where halfway through you're absolutely certain that God is real and talking to you through that speaker. He's saying, "Everything will be fine, deep down in your soul. Just close your eyes and dance." We'll celebrate this more, but we have to say: the Church gave us some great tunes. Thank God for that.

12. **Sundy chicken—we spelled it right. Momma makes it right, too.**

BUT...

Of course we can't state that the Church played such a positive role in race relations without mentioning that it also helped create a lot of those problems in the first place. We also can't mention the delicious food at the Sunday potluck without acknowledging that we have fat kids in the South or that maybe, perhaps, God meant that whole gluttony thing. We shouldn't talk about the Church founding educational institutions without addressing its central role as mayor of Dumb Dope City in the land of "Evolution is just a theory."

The Ku Klux Klan was ostensibly a Christian organization, and the Bible was often used by many in the South to defend slavery. We use our Bibles to hold open windows when we're cooking a pie and the oven gets a little smoky.

So now we get to the hellfire-and-brimstone portion of our sermon. Thus begins our come-to-Jesus meeting.

It's time to repent.

CHRISTIAN "OPPRESSION"

You get home. Change outta your work clothes into some ball shorts and a Skynyrd T-shirt. There's leftover steak. You don't microwave it, because you're not a freakin' communist. After heating it up with some potatoes in the cast iron, you sit down with a beer—something light but flavorful. You curse your boss for that thing you just remembered she said and then put it out of your mind. Then, in spite of how certain you are it will ruin your evening, you turn on the news. And there she is: another Aunt Tammy in all her glory. She's wearing her good white blouse and a crucifix pendant so big Jesus can see it from heaven. And she's just as upset as she can be. Her kid's school is doing a Charles Dickens play instead of a nativity scene, she explains, and this "is a violation of my rights."

Before you can change the channel and/or have an actual aneurysm, she has moved on to how it ain't fair that Muslims get to have mosques, but the Ten Commandments aren't written in blood above the state capitol building with a holy sword. As the camera pans out, we see her state representative standing proudly by her, smiling. "We gotta get back to following God's word," he says. Last year he was caught having an affair with an aid, and during his first campaign, he got into a literal fist fight with his opponent at a "Babies with Beetus"[13] fish fry event. Yet he continues to tell us, with a straight face and with no journalists calling him out, "The Bible holds all the answers and guidance for our lives."

Christians just *love* to feel persecuted in the South. Growing up, you'd hear tales of women being murdered in other countries[14] for following Christ, and then some old-timer would sigh and calmly say, "That'll be happening here before long." Christians are paranoid. We have lawsuits being fought over religious texts being displayed at government buildings, over prayer in schools, and over elected officials refusing to follow the laws of the land as upheld by the US Supreme Court because it "goes against [their] religion." We aren't sure if quitting and getting a new job where you don't have to uphold any laws

---

13. Diabetes.

14. It was never clear if the story was 100 percent true or even a recent one. We assume it often was true; people *do* die for their faith. But it always felt odd how some folk sure seemed to feel satisfied that some poor African or Middle Eastern lady had been beheaded for refusing to curse Jesus. It was as if they'd almost rather be able to say, "See, people hate Christians. Told you so," than live in a world where no one is murdered.

also is against God's will or not—we're still waiting on Mrs. Davis[15] to get back to us.

There is a somewhat understandable, though not justifiable, reason for this fear and paranoia. A big part of growing up Southern is growing up "other." (See our chapter on rednecks.) Yes, of course, this is not as protracted as growing up a minority, gay, foreign, or a Kenny G fan, but the fact is the media portray an America where Southerners fit in only as goofy "Aw, shucks!" buffoons, evil, racist Colonel Sanders types, or smooth-talkin', whiskey-sippin' mysterious gentlemen. Our women are even more invisible. In that landscape, there are almost no Southern Christians or evangelicals[16] portrayed. With one giant, glaring, Fox-y exception, the major networks don't put forth the agenda or perspective of the Southern Christian. This is *not* persecution, at all, but it also is the obvious reason there is such a defensive mind-set among Southern Christians. When you aren't portrayed nationally in a positive light, you either accept that identity or reject the whole damn system. And Southerners ain't really much for accepting anything we don't like.

The thing is: none of this has any bearing on day-to-day life in most small towns and cities across the South. A small business owner

15. We're talking about Kentucky Kounty Klerk Kim Davis, of course, who won't uphold the law she's paid by tax money to perform and issue marriage certificates to gay couples exercising their rights. We aren't actually waiting on her to get back to us. We're waiting on her to meet Jesus.

16. You can look up what that word means, but we use it mainly to mean those who evangelize—which sometimes means those who preach a very active and lively Gospel but which often means those who tell people how to live and are terrible to have at parties.

in Mississippi who is a Christian recognizes that in the cultural zeit-geist[17] of America at large, there is no spot for him and his faith. When he goes to his next prayer meeting and says he feels ostracized and unwanted, everyone there agrees with him. And when members of that prayer group individually go to work and PTA meetings and then another different prayer group and say the same things to people they already know are Christians, they also *all* agree with them. And so it spreads, to the point that you have a large majority of people who feel 100 percent certain that they're being ridiculed, persecuted, and picked on. What proof do they have? Just look how we're treated on the news!

And what do politicians like more than anything in the whole world (other than being awful lizard people who have no moral code, best we can tell)? They love a scared majority. Lord God, do they love a scared majority—the way that Corey's Uncle Chuck loves a good cas-serole.[18] Scared majorities win them elections. And that's how and why Christians in the South have become so darn political. Many of them are terrified. They feel certain everyone is out to get them and prevent them from having church thirty-two times a week and pretending not to see one another at the liquor store on Saturday.

But the irony here is that often what Christians do in response to this fear of being persecuted is vote to persecute others. In order to protect their "rights," Christians take away the rights of anyone differ-ent. And when they do, CNN puts the loudest, dumbest, most hateful one on TV and does a whole segment about how backward whatever county the fucking Yankee reporter can't pronounce is. Then "pro-gressives" in Seattle or Chicago watch it and go, "See, that's why the

17. Imagine a Mississippi tire shop owner whinin' about the cultural zeit-geist. "Naw, Randy, I'm tellin' ya, they got hashtags and everthang, son!"

18. And, really, who don't? Better have cream or cheese in it.

South is awful; they're *all* like that. Let's turn this off and go get some organic chutney and never think deeply about the South, Tristan."

We can't fix stupid anywhere. Neither Aunt Tammy nor Tristan the barista is gonna change. But their kids might. Their friends might. We can't save everyone. We're here for those who wonder if maybe, just maybe, things could be a little bit better. We're here for the reckoning. Let's get to it.

WHAT WOULD JESUS SUE

One thing Christians like to point out is that they aren't allowed to be as Jesusy as they want to be because they can't hold church at school or put the Bible up at public buildings. To be fair, it's not the whole Bible but the highlights they're after. Specifically, the Ten Commandments. In 2005 two cases came before the Supreme Court of this United States that originated in the South relating to putting monuments of the Ten Commandments up at state buildings. In *McCreary County v. ACLU of Kentucky*, the court ruled 5 to 4 that the proposed monument could *not* go up because it violated what is known as the First Amendment's establishment clause. Sweet Lord Jesus, did the poor downtrodden and oppressed *majority* of that county and state cry "Woe is me!" that day. Christians all over the South lamented how the country had changed (It had not. At all.) and was going to shit (true, but mostly because of their party).

What these crybaby Christ kids ignored was the undeniable *fact* that *if* the court had allowed the Ten Commandments to be placed at a state building, *then* there was *nothing* that it or the people of Kentucky could do to stop, for example, some Kentuckian named Usama (surely there is at least one) from also displaying copies of the Koran. And we ain't saying that would be a bad thing to us, in a vacuum. We're saying that would be a nightmare to deal with the shit storm of protests, hand-wringing, and crying from the more active churchy types who sure as hell would never let the brown man "come in our damn state buildings and spread that terrorist hate book."[19]

They were also ignoring that another, similar court case, *Van Orden v. Perry*,[20] came down that *same* day. In this decision, a forty-year-old monument at a state building in Texas that had the Ten Commandments written on it was *allowed* to remain on the property. Yes, you read that right: the same court, on the same day, looked at basically the same issue and decided that the Ten Commandments could stay in one case and not the other.

The vote came down to one justice voting one way on one case and another on the other. Justice Stephen Breyer stated that the main difference to him was the *purpose* of the displays. In the Kentucky case, the group setting up the Ten Commandments said unequivocally that the purpose was to celebrate the Ten Commandments as a legal document that showed *God was at the root of the founding of our country*. Read that again and try your best to pretend that the purpose was not overtly to make an argument *for* God being involved in government.

The second case, Justice Breyer explained, was one where the monument of the Ten Commandments had been donated decades ago by a secular civic club that stated the purpose was to honor the history of the law and the Ten Commandments' place in that history. Plus, no one had complained for forty years, so whatever religion Van Orden claimed was being established sure seemed not to have made anyone else notice.

19. **This quote attributed to various aunts and uncles and frat party goers we've been around all over the South.**

20. **Yep, Rick Perry. Yes, that one. The former governor of Texas. He's a champion for Jesus and for having a family hunting camp called Niggerhead (Stephanie McCrummen, "Rick Perry Family's Hunting Camp Still Known to Many by Old Racially Charged Name,"** *The Washington Post,* **October 1, 2011).**

In other words, the court assessed by a 5 to 4 majority in one case that the goal of one monument was blatantly making a stance about God's place in our history, and the other was simply acknowledging the history of the document as a legal text. Whether you buy any of that or not, one way or the other, it's unfathomable that a person could read the facts of both cases[21] and walk away thinking, "You know what? The Supreme Court really wants to oppress Christians and prevent them from practicing their faith." No. The Supreme Court's goal was clearly to prevent people from using the government building to promote one particular faith.

CHURCH CULTURE

And that's how these cases go. Christians are told they can practice their faith however they want, but they cannot do so publicly in a state- or government-owned building in a way that infringes on the rights of others. That's actually a reasonable rule.[22] The remaining question, then, is, Why do so many ostensibly sane, strong-hearted, and well-dressed-on-Sundays God-fearing people *feel* so darn scared all the time in their tiny li'l Southern towns where *everyone* in power politically and socially identifies as a Christian (or at least pretends to on account of fear)? Well, again, part of it is the national media actually shitting on these folks a lot, but another big part of it is just being isolated. Living in rural Southern areas can lead (as it would anywhere) to groupthink. Also, being at church literally all of the frickin' time means being around the same people most hours of your week.

21. Because Evangelicals always make it a point to supplement their arguments with case law.

22. "Yeah, if by reasonable you mean SATANIC."—Evangelicals, probably.

HOW TO GET OUT OF CHURCH

★

Southerners have church. *All the time.* This is one trait that seems to carry across most demographics. Whatever the race, denomination, income level, or type of area, if a congregation is Southern, it has church all the time. Does it get exhausting? Absolutely. If you find yourself a member of one of these churches, is there anything you can do about it? Of course, we wouldn't recommend lying (while effective), on the off chance that God is indeed watching, He probably wouldn't be too keen on you double sinning on a Sunday by missing church and lying to your family. The key is to have something else to do. Now, Liberal Rednecks, you're saying, "I can't do that! If I do that, eventually they'll say I'm choosing whatever activity I have planned over God, and that also won't work."

That's why you gotta plan many different activities, and you gotta make sure they revolve around the one activity that Southern Christians (though they'd never admit it) honor as much as they do being devout: makin' a dollar. This Sunday's surprise sunrise service makin' you upset just thinkin' about it? Take an extra shift at work. Not feeling the idea of a visiting preacher coming through because you know as soon as he's done, your pastor is for sure gonna have to do a set as well? Get a side job selling real estate or some other unstructured gig where no one can track your progress. Or just don't go to church if you don't want to. Either way.

Wednesday-night service. Thursday-night Bible study. Sunday morning. Sunday-morning second service. Sunday afternoon when the preacher comes over and Mom gives him the last soda *again*, and him and Dad talk about God for three hours, so it's basically church all over again. Sunday-night service.

Prayer before the football game. Prayer after the football game. Friday-night fifth-quarter service after the football game. In Drew's town, the coach told the players that if they went, they didn't have to run on Monday. Another clear example of how hard it is to be a Christian.

Prayer at meal times. Prayer before bed. A Saturday singing you forgot about where brother Daryl starts feeling the spirit and preaches for an hour.

This is the main reason Christians feel so darn oppressed. If you're around other people who also feel oppressed all the time, eventually you're gonna start to think the world hates you and all your friends and all your neighbors and all the people you know. And if you think everyone you know is hated by a "buncha libtards,"[23] maybe you should stop to consider that maybe, just maybe, since you don't actually know any of these libtards, and you've never even met them, you and your way of life are fine. So relax.

And it's not just church itself we have to go to. There are church trips. Church fund-raisers. Church barbeques. Vacation Bible School and lock-ins. Half of popular vacation spot Gatlinburg, Tennessee's annual revenue comes from youth church trips.[24] Some of us make

---

23. Autocorrect tried to change *libtards* to "libraries" three times, and we think that's the funniest thing in the world. Imagine a buncha libraries come to life, just persecuting and makin' fun of all these fear-mongering religious zealots. Poetry.

24. Gatlinburg is the capital of church youth groups. It's also the capital of pancakes, shitty Putt-Putt venues, and fat, awful people. It's also next door to Dollywood, Dolly Parton's theme park, and we wanna go on record as saying she might be the second coming of Christ (has anyone asked her?), and we love her and will fight you over her.

our kids go on these church trips even when it isn't Sunday and even when they'd rather do any other thing. And look, the Liberal Rednecks ain't gonna get anyone doing this to stop: The kids go away for a night or two in a safe environment to bond with other kids, and it's free or relatively cheap? Even atheist parents are going, "Well, I mean, they really do have to decide for themselves. One lock-in won't hurt." But it's probably time we were all honest about them. When you send your kid to Gatlinburg to listen to God-awful praise music and wear matching T-shirts "so no one gets lost," you're mostly sending them to eat at new and exotic buffets ("This one has a chocolate fountain!") and get versed in the ancient art of finger banging.

Yup, any place where teenagers are gathered, in the name of God or any other thing, they're gonna be feelin' a lot more than the spirit.[25] These are just facts. This isn't necessarily a bad thing, but it's something we figured might need to be addressed. The church youth night hayride? Finger banging! The overnight lock-in? Lots of finger banging! The trip to the creation museum? Feeling up under the bra at the Ark exhibit, and, hopefully, on the bus ride back: finger banging!

It's perfectly natural, to be fair. Puberty is a hell of a thing, and oftentimes kids from Christian homes haven't been given much of a warning or prep course on just how intense those feelings are gonna be. And who could blame the faithful for overlooking this important lesson with their kids? Truth is, they're scared. Jesus may have the kids' backs, but that first time they have sex, their hearts are no longer the organ they're most concerned with.

Which brings us to our next issue: the Church's backward-ass relationship to sex and how it affects us all.

---

25. For example, titties. In case you didn't get it, we meant titties.

"JESUS WEPT" (AND IT WAS A GOOD WORKOUT, APPARENTLY)

★

We gotta stop with the dirty-blond, fair-skinned, very ripped Jesus. The dude was a Middle Eastern Jew, so his eyes weren't blue, he wasn't pale, and that seventies rocker look he's sporting is *way* off. He was olive skinned, and he probably had a sweet Jew-fro. But aside from being embarrassingly inaccurate, the Mark McGrath Messiah we all grew up with is *overtly* sexual. I remember pics of crucified Jesus with an eight-pack so pronounced that the blood from where they speared him was running *through* his muscle lines. He looked like a Calvin Klein cologne ad. "The Savior, for Men."

Y'all, that's just plain creepy. No wonder Aunt Tammy been praying to that picture seven times a day, including at night when the kids is asleep. That pic is enough to make a closeted Republican senator hit his knees and beg. Let's tone it down, y'all. If we ain't gonna stop makin' Him look like a Swedish rock star, let's at least quit with the Christ's-body-is-more-defined-than-our-abortion-laws images.

LET'S GET HITCHED

All over the South, young folks are getting married for one eternal and undying beautiful reason: ~~true love~~ getting to bone without feeling religious guilt. And, look, if waiting till marriage means a lot to you, knock yourself out. But you can't look me in my eye and tell me that kids getting married at eighteen is a great idea. Kids gettin' a gym membership that lasts more than a month at eighteen isn't a great idea. Being eighteen is the antithesis of commitment. Being eighteen is to commitment as diets are to drunk people: it don't matter how much you "believe" in it, you're gonna fail.

But many *are* getting married, and the truth is, a lot of it has to do with religious guilt making sex before marriage a no-no and biology making sex a must.[26] We're not saying change all your beliefs and tell the kids, "Welcome to Bone City, population as many as you can get drunk!" We're saying that maybe, just maybe, divorce and the anguish it puts families through is a more intense and harmful "sin" than pre-marital sex, and we should teach our kids that gettin' married is a terrifying, intense, full-time job they're not qualified for and don't want yet. And the kids who don't get married to skirt the Bible will oftentimes do it in the butt, because that way they're technically virgins. Yes, this is real. Kids do this. Particularly the dumb kids, but still. 'Course, on the other hand, we're pretty adamantly pro–butt stuff, so never mind. The marriage thing, though? That needs fixin', and it starts with being more honest about sex and our bodies.

Better sex culture: do it for the kids.

Which brings us right smack into that territory yuns knew we was wading into and most of yuns didn't want us to, even if you know you're gonna agree with us: abortion. Talking about this topic is like watching a serial child rapist get executed on television. No matter how it goes, it just feels awful.

Look, we ain't changing a single person's mind about the topic. Forget trying. Forget even wanting to for now. Let's focus on one thing and one thing only: the amount of time and money Christian organizations have spent *not* on making abortions illegal but on making them and services provided by lady doctors harder and harder to get for poor

---

26. **Did you know that if you don't have sex at least once a year after turning eighteen, you *die*? That's a fact. Look it up. (Don't look it up.)**

people. For example, Louisiana recently passed "admitting privilege"[27] laws that closed down three of the state's five clinics that provided this *legal* service. Mississippi has only one clinic left because of these laws; Alabama was close to having only one because of them.

Along with those services being stopped, prenatal services provided to poor women who are *pregnant and planning to keep their babies* were also stopped. Think about that. Yuns are literally and inarguably *harming unborn babies* to "save" unborn babies. That's insane. And you're lying about it. You're saying these tactics are for "women's safety," but then admitting they're actually to stop abortions. The US Supreme Court saw right through this type of crap recently with *Whole Woman's Health v. Hellerstedt*, ruling similar tactics in Texas unconstitutional.

Christian and Church-backed organizations are going out of their way and spending massive amounts of money to block women from getting perfectly legal procedures, and in doing so are hurting the very precious life they say they're protecting. For example, a poor, uninsured Alabama woman who wants to have a baby goes to these same clinics to get prenatal and even postnatal care and to learn about being a mom and raising a healthy baby. In other words, they're throwing the fetus out with the bathwater.[28] And why? Really? Why not spend that money trying to make abortions illegal? "But we are." Ha! Got you! Then quit with this "safety of the mother" bullshit.

27. "Admitting privileges" refer to a doctor's right to admit patients at hospitals. Explaining this tactic is pointless because if it fails, it will be replaced by another. The main takeaway is that it was created to "protect women and keep them safe," and that's a total lie. No, it wasn't, not at all. I hear you. Abortion is a sin, but isn't lying as well?

28. Too far? Nah.

Christians who are pro-life know they lost. That's what's really going on. And instead of trying to talk women out of abortion, they're playing shameful political tactics and shaming people. You, the poor, underrepresented, downtrodden "oppressed" majority are blocking people from a legal right (whether you think it should be or not). That is the *definition* of oppression.

And you're doing it partially because you think sex is for married people who want to have kids and raise all nine of them in church (because condoms are a sin!) and teach them to be exactly like you, and, look, that's your right—just as it's just other people's right *not* to do that and to live a different way. And, we know, that makes those people "murderers" to you. Thing is, yuns don't get to decide who is a murderer or not. Yuns shouldn't decide who gets rights, either. Yuns also don't get to decide who is a slut or not. Stop shaming people who don't jive with your puritan ways. You think God don't want us boning outside of marriage? Sweet, keep that to yourself, and we'll keep to ourselves the science that suggests that whatever created us absolutely was intent on us crushing as much puss/dick as possible. [29]

HOMOSEXUALITY

Another classic example of Christians suffering oppression whereby they're oppressed because they cannot oppress people: the Church's views on homosexuality. The amount of political will the Church has expended in response to homosexuality is unbelievably staggering and mean. To understand the depths of the hypocrisy and downright hatefulness on the issue, we have to look no further than the timeless and horrendous case of one Kim Davis.

---

29. **Again, you die if you don't have sex a lot. Them is facts. (They're not facts.)**

Mrs. Davis and her haircut[30] made international news when she proudly went on television to proclaim that she would *not*, under any circumstances, keep her oath as county clerk to uphold the constitution of Kentucky and in conjunction with that sign marriage licenses when the folks being married were of the same sex. (You know [*whisper voice*], gay.)

And, sincerely, we respect her stance. The Liberal Rednecks are all about standing up for your beliefs even when they're hateful, bigoted, and go against everything your alleged Lord and Savior stood for.

The thing is, doing that would have involved quitting her job—but that's just something the four-times-married[31] mother was not prepared to do for her faith. Go on TV and be called a hero by powerful politicians who agree with her and her "stand"? Sure, that's fine. Have the Church pay for her legal bills and prop her up (instead of, oh we don't know, giving that money to the poor)? Yes, sir. But actually quit instead of breaking an oath (which, by the way, is a sin)? That's just something Jesus apparently wouldn't do.

Kim Davis is an analogy for Christians at large in the South. She was *not* oppressed. She was not *forced* to do anything. She could have quit. The truth is she did not want to quit her job as an elected official. She wanted to bend the political will of those around her so she could

---

30. We believe her haircut is a political statement in and of itself. She clearly hates gay men so much she won't let them or any women who hang out with them touch her head. This has led to the ugliest head of hair we've ever seen.

31. Only to three different men, though, so praise Jesus, that one don't count!

SAD CAMPAIGNS

★

Ya know, it's a good thing the pro-choice crowd has the Supreme Court (mostly) in their corner, because in the court of public opinion, their asses get taken to church, son. Pro-life absolutely dominates in terms of marketing and PR, at least in the South. But in our opinion, it kinda isn't fair, because they're playing with a stacked deck. Think about it. Every single pro-life billboard or ad you ever see features the same thing: a fat, cute-ass baby bein' just as fat and cute as it can possibly be. You can't touch that, y'all.

Seriously, how do you combat that? What does a pro-choice billboard even look like? A picture of a teenage girl *not* crying herself to sleep? Still having hopes and dreams and stuff? How the heck do you capture that? What, maybe instead have a stripper pole with a big red X through it? A welfare line with nobody standing in it? And the pro-life slogan . . . Jesus: "It's not a choice, it's a child." Y'all, you can't touch that. It's too good. What would a pro-choice slogan be? "Abortion: *it actually kinda worked out*." Yeah, good luck winning the hearts and minds of the people with that. Our hearts really go out to the marketing people over at Big Abortion. Talk about a thankless job.

prevent other humans from marrying each other because she didn't like the idea of it. That's not oppression—that's someone trying to use the inordinate amount of power they have (over the media and literally as the clerk) to affect the lives of strangers she disagrees with. Guess what that is? Yup. *That* is oppression.

Porch Talk with Trae

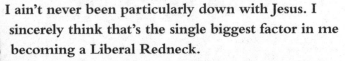

I ain't never been particularly down with Jesus. I sincerely think that's the single biggest factor in me becoming a Liberal Redneck.

Lotta rednecks vote Republican because Jesus is like Ronald Reagan's number-one homeboy. Beginning in the mid-twentieth century, the right wing started focusing on cornering the Christian vote, and succeeded with aplomb. I mean, it's brilliant, really: they have successfully convinced people who actually have *no* business voting for their platforms to fall in line by aligning themselves firmly with their God. Look, say what you want about Republicans, but them motherfuckers know how to win, at literally any cost. I mean, this strategy disgusts me, blatantly exploiting people's faith like that—but goddamn it, I respect it.

But that never affected me because I said to hell with Jesus early on. Why, you ask? How was I able to avoid the church-steeped childhood that Drew, Corey, and honestly nearly everyone else I knew growing up had to endure? Well, see, it's pretty simple.

My uncle, my dad's only sibling, is gay. I've known he was gay since I was roughly eight or nine years old, so pretty much ever since I first understood what being gay even was. I knew my uncle was gay, and I knew I loved him very much. He and my dad were extremely close as brothers, and my uncles (he and his partner) were always around when we were growing up. He's the best. He's absolutely hilarious, he's a phenomenal cook, he always gave us the sweetest gifts, and he's the only person in my family with good taste in clothes. (Like I said, he's gay.) And he hits. So hard. He's one of the sweetest, kindest, most genuine people you will ever meet. I loved (and still love) the absolute shit out of him *and* his partner. They were two of my favorite people on Planet Earth when I was a kid.

My dad was never religious (I imagine my uncle had a lot to do with that, too), but my mom, though no zealot by any means, came from a fairly religious family, and so my sister and I dutifully went to church early on. But once I got old enough to understand (a) what gay was, (b) that my uncle was gay, and (c) that the Church was *not* on board with that *at all*, I started to fall out of favor with the Lord pretty fuckin' quickly.

The church people would never say anything about my uncles specifically. They wouldn't be all, "And the homosexuals—for example, little Trae's *godless queer uncle*—are an abomination." It wasn't *that* overt, but they didn't hold back on the homophobic rhetoric that Southern churches are so well known for. So, very early on (I might have been ten), I started asking questions. And churches, they ain't much for people asking questions, particularly little fat boys. But I did. I would ask things like, "So . . . are you saying that my uncle is going to burn in hell for all of eternity . . . because of what he *is*?" And these people, being the way they are, they answer, "That's right, honey. That's what the Bible says." They look straight into a child's eyes and tell him that about someone that he loves. And they genuinely don't realize how insanely fucked up that is. I mean, seriously, that's *crazy*. And I knew that then. I remember thinking, "Well, *fuck that*." I saw my uncles every Sunday for dinner and football—I hadn't ever even *talked* to Jesus. Why the hell would I take *his* side?!

And so I walked away. I distinctly remember thinking, at ten years old, "Okay, even *if they're right*. Even if they're one-hundred-percent right about everything—if that's how their God operates, then He can go fuck Himself. I'll take my chances in hell." And I started telling people basically that and, *hoo-wee*, people where I'm from do not appreciate that kind of talk. But I never cared. And still don't. When it came to the Church versus my uncle, I knew then and still know now beyond a doubt where I stand.

Another glaring example of fake oppression is the current[32] Alabama Supreme Court judge who has told his state to ignore the US Supreme Court's gay marriage ruling and simply not honor gay marriages. Lord, Alabama, sometimes we think yuns are trying to end up on the wrong side of history so you can be the setting for the climactic scene in all documentaries about civil rights issues. Are y'all, like, counting the tourist money you get out of the civil rights landmarks and then thinking, "Why not go for the gay stuff, too?"

The point here is to consider what this man is doing and think more about all this "oppression." The head of the highest court in the state is literally ordering people not to follow federal law but rather to follow *his interpretation* of God's laws in order to *prevent* humans from marrying each other because he thinks it's wrong. This is a textbook example of oppression. Imagine if you can for two seconds that this was, again, a practicing Muslim judge in America who was ordering the people of his state to follow the Koran.[33]

Do you have that in your head? Are you picturing how that would look? When a judge can even suggest doing something like this and not only not be fired but be lauded, then you just *have* to admit that Christians aren't oppressed in the South. You can be a judge and, in the

32. Current at publication time (2016). We're not afraid of these examples being dated in the future because they're so bat-poop insane that they're timeless in their horrible glory.

33. We also hate that we keep using this example over and over, because it feels like it implies the Koran would be inherently worse than the Bible as a legal document (it wouldn't) or that it's some kind of boogeyman in the world of religious texts. It's not. We're simply pointing out how, culturally speaking, all these Bible-backed moves would be categorically rejected if they were coming from the Muslim faith. If you're a Christian and you think "That would be awful, to live under Islamic law," just realize that enforcing biblical rules as actual laws is just as insane.

name of following Jesus, try to force everyone to break a law upheld by the Supreme Court of the United States—and *nothing* will happen to you, apparently! That's stunning. That's sad. That's awful. And that means he's not oppressed.

FEAR OVER FAITH

Where do these political actions come from? What drives Christians to spend so much time, money, and energy on issues other than, ya know, being Christlike (a dude who seemed to hate being involved in politics)? We'd say fear. Fear is a powerful motivator, but it's not an appropriate one. Fear and hate are the Hall and Oates of emotions. They have a prolific and long career making music together, and it's really hard to tell them apart.[34] A lot of churches use fear as a way of convincing people to love the Lord. No wonder that same emotion convinces them to lash out at others.

LGBTQ politics in the South—all fear. Take gay marriage, for instance. The idea batted around for years was that it would ruin the sanctity of marriage. This ridiculous notion has finally fallen out of favor because everyone realized it boiled down to saying, "Ew, gross, they gonna get the gay on my marriage." Not to mention the divorce rate among straight Christians is already so high we all got at least four uncles and aunts what's been married five times. So maybe it's time we admit that the sanctity-of-marriage ship has sailed.

Then there was the "slippery slope" argument. "Well, if we get hommaseckshuls gettin' married today, then what's to stop a man from marryin' his *dawg* tomorra? Or his little girl? Hunh? Where DUZ IT END, DEVIL QUEERS?!" This type of argument is part of a specific

---

34. **And also, depending on your mood, they really hit the spot.**

Porch Talk with Corey

I'd like to tell yuns about the "Judgment House." Judgment House was an event held every year around Halloween (Satan's birthday), and its purpose was to scare the hell out of you. This isn't necessarily specific to my upbringing in church, as I know a lot of Southern Baptist churches had a Judgment House too. It's a play where you'd walk from room to room, and it usually centered around a teenage girl who, while a churchgoer, decides for one night to dabble in the dark arts of partying (you know: having *fun*) at the absolute most boring fucking party I have ever seen in my life. The party scene was basically just a couch and a table covered in empty cans—not beer cans, by the way. They were soda cans that the church ladies had put construction paper on and written the word *Beer*. For fuck's sake, my uncle Gordon went to that church. He'd-a gladly donated his stash from the night before; woulda been his ministry. There was a bunch of fake cigarettes, and I even remember the song they played every year at the party because it hit for me: "So Fresh, So Clean" by Outkast. It definitely did not fit in with the theme of a shitty party because that song is objectively righteous as fuck.

While at the party, the girl (being disgusted by all the hittin' sin that was about) decided to stay sober and then drive home. Well, as with any play worth its salt (*Lot's Wife*), there was a twist. See, there was a boy at that party who was getting turnt as a motherfucker ("We get it, Corey. You said Outkast was playing. Duh!") and decided that he needed to go get some more beer. On his way to the store, he wrecked into Little Miss "Fun Sucks," and they both died. Ambulance scene was pretty hilarious. If you ain't ever seen a bunch of shitty Christian actors trying to fake cry, you owe it to your life. It sounded like a grizzly bear trying to suck off a bobcat.

The next scene is the reading of the Lamb's Book of Life. Tina Tiny Tits, of course, gets called on by the Lord to enter heaven. She's been such a good, obedient, boring little twat that she's just a perfect fit to spend eternity with a bunch of older and more dead boring little twats. (Heaven has to suck, is what I'm saying. Not a hot take.)

Ol' boy what was drunk driving? Naw. He got sent straight to hell. The hell scene was just a pitch-black room and the "actors" middle-aged men from the church screaming and laughing into a goddamn megaphone: "You should have stayed in church, Donnie!" "Shouldn't have turned your back on the Lord, you little sinner!" "You're gonna burn forever and ever now, you abomination!" Screamed this to a bunch of eight-year-olds. Eight-year-olds, dude.

So, yeah, that all *may* have fucked me up a little bit. But I made it through, and now, "Ain't nobody dope as me."

phenomenon that sociologists refer to as "Being Very Stupid." What's the logic here? Gay people exist in great numbers and have done so for literally ever; how many of them are also pedophiles or, for God's sake, into bestiality? We've known exactly one feller what had sex with animals, and he was an old redneck feller named Walter, not a nice young gay feller named . . . Devon or whatever. But apparently to many Christians, gay stuff is a gateway sin. "I don't even know how it happened. I was just kissin' Donnie in the back of his Jeep one night, and next thing I knew, I was throwin' drug-fueled horse orgies in Pa's barn!" Thankfully, this argument, much like the sanctity-of-marriage one, has largely fallen out of favor.

Now the prevailing theme in gay-marriage issues seems to be "my rights." Christians are again *afraid* someone is trying to take away their rights by giving homosexuals rights. This is the most childish and fear-based viewpoint of them all, really. Rights aren't a bag of candy—we ain't sharing them. It's not like for every Terrance and

Porch Talk with Drew

When I was five years old, my mother, brother, and I attended church five miles from our house. We passed at least fifteen other churches on the way, so it seemed an odd choice. At the time, my father (now a sober preacher) was dealing with alcoholism and hadn't gone to church in years. I point that out just to explain that the hazy memories I have of this time period represent only a tiny fraction of my "church experience." Boy, was this time a doozy, though.

At Vacation Bible School, we were told to invite kids whose "parents aren't Christians." We were told to do "foot washings": a practice paying homage to Christ's washing Peter's feet and Mary Magdalene washing Jesus's feet with her tears. During our foot washings, though, the men were forbidden from washing the women's feet. And they showed us videos that they told us showed what hell was like.

Those videos were effective. I was "saved" that year. At five years old, I "gave my heart to Jesus to live with him forever." Looking back, perhaps five was a bit young to commit to a savior for *all of eternity.*

I remember most being scared. This is one of the main reasons I have such negative feelings about that specific church. I don't think that doing anything out of fear, especially as a child, is ever positive. Think about what we do out of fear: wear sunscreen, pay taxes, eat vegetables—all awful experiences. But the pastor wasn't deterred when he asked me why I wanted to be saved, and I said, "Because I am afraid of hell." He seemed to think that was a fine reason to act. Years later, he engaged me on Facebook and shamed me for being pro gay rights. He said I was not raised that way and told me he'd pray for me. I don't trust people who tell you they will pray for you when they mean to shame.

We left that church a couple of years later and found a very loving and beautiful congregation that to me represents everything a church should be. Many of the people there disagree with me on about every single issue and thought I have about Christianity. My own parents disagree with me. But every single one of them will hug my neck as hard as they can the next time they see me. They'll ask me how I've been, and when they follow that up with "I've been praying for you," they mean it. They say it sincerely and with love. On that church's wall is a sign that reads, "If every member of this church were like me, what kind of church would this be?" Taking that question seriously, to me, is the most Christlike thing a person can do. The people in that church are full of love. And that's the *only* reason I still go there when I visit my folks.

DM

Timothy we let tie the knot at a small ceremony in Myrtle Beach we have to disallow an Earl and Jenny from saying "I do" at her daddy's church in Tennessee. That ain't how it works. It has nothing to do with *your* rights. It's about *other* people's rights. Hush. All of yuns. Believe whatever you want,[35] but hush up about it, Methodists, Baptists, black churches, the Amish. (Do they have an opinion? Wait, they don't vote, so, actually, they cool with us.) *Everyone!* Gays getting married don't affect you. Hush.

Transgender issues ain't no different. Our boy Trae pretty well covered the hypocrisy and idiocy these bills was covering,[36] but the point is, it's also fear. Almost all of it is fear. All the issues about sex

35. **But your religion will dissolve if you don't catch up. Just sayin'.**

36. **If you ain't seen it, because you live under a rock: https://www .youtube.com/watch?v=Ov-ocQpQtrw. If you ain't know what the Internet is, well, buddy, that's okay. Thanks for readin'.**

and sex ed also come from fear. Those purity balls?[37] Fear (and also some sort of really creepy daddy-daughter sexual tension). Tryin' to get creationism taught in school? Fear. And this one really sticks in our craw. What are you so afraid of when it comes to science? *If* God created everything and planned this whole universe according to His master design, then any discoveries from that field and proof that we evolved from apes or have been around for longer than "a couple of thousand years" and the fossil record and carbon dating and even anti-gravity bongs—*all* of science glorifies God. If God did it all, then he gets *all* the credit. And frankly, making us from monkeys[38] was a fuckin' dope plan. Stop being so scared of science.

And what about fear and abortion? Many will tell you that *love* for the unborn has driven their crusade against ~~abortion~~ women, not fear. Truthfully, it's tough to argue here because we can't know their hearts—oh, bull, no, it isn't. You may want to protect the unborn out of love, but by attacking the way in which an organization—Planned Parenthood, for example—does business because you hate one (legal) thing it does rather than trying to get rid of that thing, you've made your fear transparent. It has nothing to do with love at that point.

37. Purity balls are yearly events in some parts of the South where daughters promise their fathers they won't bang anyone until they marry a man their father approves of. They wear wedding dresses, and the ceremony mimics a marriage—to their father. Yuh. We know. Everyone go shower and never mention this again.

38. Y'all ever seen that "monkeys typing in a room for eternity would eventually create the works of Shakespeare" quote? Well, one time Drew got high and stated, "Wait, that happened already. We're monkeys, and space is eternity, and we typed, and it happened." He insisted we put it in the book.

Yuns are scared. Pure and simple. And hey, man, we get it. One time in Portland someone offered us "vegan grits," and, to be frank, we nearly had a heart attack. We was halfway through calling our senators and organizing a march for our values when we realized, "Hey, wait a minute! We don't have to eat any vegan grits. And we can still make grits the way we like 'em." Isn't that a beautiful thing? And isn't that a nice gauge for oppression? Anytime you think someone is trying to make you eat vegan grits, just ask yourself, "Am I still allowed to make 'em with cheese?" If the answer is yes, then you aren't being oppressed, and you don't have to be afraid. And, again, we get why you're afraid. Christianity does seem to be slipping. It almost seems sometimes like it might be going away.

But we hope you see that a lot of what's happening to it is coming from within. We're relatively certain that the Bible even says something about this—about how the Church is responsible for the Church, not the world. That fear is killin' y'all. It's eating y'all alive from the inside out. But, hey, we also think the Bible offered the cure for that disease.

LOVE AND FAITH

And that cure is love. Just love people. Jesus said to do that. Stop telling everyone how they ort live their lives and how to be and just love.

THE FUTURE OF THE CHURCH

The Church's influence *is* fading in the South. Some feel this is because of the (nonexistent) persecution of Christians, or because so many people have "gone away from God" by accepting homosexuals as, ya

What Wouldn't Jesus Do?

WWNOTJD

- Have a third servin' at the buffet b/c gluttony is still a sin

- Have an AR-15 b/c "turn the other cheek"

- Say "I'll pray for you" in a snotty way b/c he was chill AF

- Hate gays, or anyone else

- Vote for rich assholes (He hated them—it was a whole thing with him)

GOD HATES FIGS

Holier-Than-Thou
BIBLE
King Rick James Version

Cru-ci-fix Chikin

know, decent humans who ort have rights. Others think it's because we as a country are falling apart as we career ever so quickly toward the inevitable Apocalypse.

If the Church were a person, these fears would be the crazy, paranoid talk of an old and out-of-touch papaw who just can't seem to wrap his head around the Internet and doesn't wanna face his own death or, even worse, his own insignificance. The Church's problems, like most people's, are internal. If anyone reading this damn book is somehow still here and engaged but is also a lover and follower of Christ and gives a damn what we think (and you probably don't, we know), we'd say it's time to adjust. Hide those antigay Bible verses in the same mental room where you've put away the verses about slaves, beating women for going outside, and eating shellfish. Stop suing everyone who wants to get married or eat a fucking cake. Jesus didn't sue anyone. And stop playing the fucking victim all the damn time. Was Jesus a huge pussy? We don't think so. So be more Christlike and stop being a pussy yourself.

"But wait. Aren't you guys tellin' the Church on one hand to stop tellin' folks how to live, but, like, at the same time, by doing that, tellin' them how to live?" Well, we feel that we're telling people to leave one another alone and to love, not "how to live." But at the same time, yeah, man, we're total hypocrites in some ways. But hey, no one is perfect. Except Jesus. Right, Christians?

Guess yuns ort pray for us, then. *Without* tellin' us about it. Just do it, Aunt Tammy. Just bring us over a casserole and then pray for our souls on the way home. In your car. Alone. Amen.

4

Y'all Hungry?

The boiled peanut (spelled P-Nuts) stands of South Georgia that line the road like a runway to Florida. The mom-and-pop produce stands filled with locally made jellies, jams, preserves, butters, and sorghum. The smell of smoked pork cascading through the air of speed-trap towns. Waking up to sizzling bacon, cathead biscuits, and thick sausage gravy. Eatin' at two buffets in one day.

Everyone loves food. But few have a love affair with it quite like us Southerners. Throughout history, humans have eaten to live. Folks below the Mason-Dixon, however, have fine-tuned the art of living to eat. Be it a bucket of chicken after church, a pancake breakfast from the Lions Club to raise money for the football team,[1] or a spread of quartered tea sandwiches at a Ladies' Club luncheon, mayonnaise, grease, and sweet tea[2] are the glue that binds the Southern

---

1. Who *will* win State this year, by God.

2. Mamaw's well whiskey.

family. Join us on a walk (or a motorized scooter ride) through the history of Southern food as we celebrate all that's good (most of it) with a side of all that's bad (diabetes) about our peculiar eating habits here in God's country.

SOUL FOOD, BABY!

This country was built largely by slaves.[3] And along with that, the slaves also shaped the way we eat here in Dixie. The slaves were the ones in the fields harvesting okra, sugarcane, sweet potatoes, corn, watermelon,[4] black-eyed peas, etc. They also raised the animals—pigs, cows, chickens[5]—and were responsible for the white man's eating.

This was before the microwave. This was before granola bars. This was before fucking kale. (Well, kale was about, but it would spend years as a garnish under fried shrimp on a plate at Shoney's before it would wind up fucking up a smoothie.) Things had to be cooked on a stove or over a fire, and you weren't just feeding a family of four. Matter of fact, after the slaves would cook for the entire family (usually at least fourteen *assholes*), they would then have to cook for themselves, typically getting what was considered the less desirable fatty meat, while the white man got the "good" meat. This is where we get fatback[6] to cook beans. (And that's as close to a silver lining as slavery in the South will get: fatback hits.) This is also the reason we have

3. This is not the popular opinion of most of your old, white-haired Southerners.

4. A lot of people named Uncle Keith just made a joke.

5. We get it, Uncle Keith. You're hilarious.

6. Pork heroin.

chitlins,[7] cracklins,[8] collard greens, catfish, ribs, and mac and cheese.[9] Slaves perfected these less desirable ingredients and pieces to feed themselves. If that alone doesn't make racism sound stupid, then we're sorry, but you're hopeless.

You can attempt to dissect it any way you want, but the reason that Memphis, Kansas City, all of North Carolina, and Texas are legendary for their BBQ is a direct result of black people being forced to cook for the white man. When you're eating a plate piled high with chicken, mashed potatoes, turnip greens, and mac and cheese, and for a brief moment, all your troubles seem small, the weight of the world doesn't matter, and it feels like you took a syringe of opium through one of your butt cheeks, thank black people. Their contributions to our cuisine completely shaped the uniqueness it's now celebrated for and have made cooking in the South as much of a pastime as it is a priority.

THE DEPRESSION ERA

The Great Depression was a dark time. Really, the only thing good that can be said about it was that fat people were considered wealthy and thus attractive. (Corey would have had to beat women off with a stick[10]—if he wasn't using the stick to stir a vat of butter.) Chipped beef on toast, grits, oatmeal, biscuits, and buttermilk—these were all staples in a poor Depression-era home, as they were cheap, filling, and sustainable. What vegetables weren't sold at the market were eaten by

7. **If you don't already know, then don't ask. Trust us.**

8. **Pig popcorn.**

9. **CoFo's kryptonite.**

10. **Not really.**

Porch Talk with Corey

GRANNY BAIN

My Granny Bain, born in 1920, grew up in the thick of the Depression. She used to tell me, "Well, we was poor before, so we didn't know much else—just that now everyone else was poor, too." She and her seven brothers and sisters worked the fields from sunup to sundown for their abusive papa and always-sickly momma. They had no money for entertainment, so at night they played a game called Nosy Poker. It was like Go Fish, but at the end, the person with the most cards got to stack them up and hit everyone else in the nose with them. She says they got so good that they could nearly draw blood every time.

I've always taken sugar and butter in my grits, to the chagrin of many of my Southern contemporaries; salt and pepper seems to be the proper method here in Dixie, but that never checked out for me. Grits was always sweet as a kid, and I can't fathom them any other way. Hell, I put sugar in my cheese grits. (Gross, I know.) Me and Granny were having grits one morning, as we often did, and I asked her, "Granny, why are we just about the only ones I know who take sugar in our grits?" She looked at me, confused. "Your friends don't eat sugar in their grits?" I said no. "Well, when I was a little girl, this was as close to dessert as it got for us. So maybe that's just an old-people thing."

Well, goddamn if that didn't put my whole life into perspective. Granny had to sugar her grits just to get the thrill of dessert. That broke my heart. She started naming a lot of other things they did back then, which made me realize how the Depression has shaped my diet over the years. I love tomato sandwiches, and cornbread and buttermilk was one of my favorite snacks (you break up the cornbread in a bowl of buttermilk). When there wasn't cornbread and buttermilk, me and Papaw (born in 1907) would crumble up crackers like cereal and eat them with milk. This was all standard practice to me, but over the years, friends would point out that it was weird.

It's just now becoming clear that *most* of my friends never had a ninety-five-year-old grandma. Mine taught me to put fatback in beans, make perfect biscuits, and lick my bowl clean before I dared get a second helping. I dig eating like a poor rural farmer.

Here's a recipe of hers. I love you, Granny!

GRANNY BAIN'S SWEET PEPPER RELISH

1 large head of cabbage, chopped
3 large onions, chopped
8 peppers (whichevern's you like the best), chopped
½ cup of salt
1 tablespoon celery seed
1 tablespoon mustard seed
5 cups sugar
1 quart vinegar

1. Combine cabbage, onions, and peppers with salt in a large bowl. Add enough water to cover it. Let it stand for 2 hours, then drain thoroughly.
2. Add celery seed, mustard seed, sugar, and vinegar, and let stand in a cool place for 3 days, stirring occasionally.
3. Pack in jars and seal.

Makes 5 to 6 pints.

the family, and in the event of a surplus, they would then be canned[11] and saved for the winter. Roadkill was picked up off the streets and eaten because, hey, you gotta eat, cuz. Wanna know the best way to make the taste of possum what has been hit by a Model T not be "awful as ass"? Fry the shit out of it, bayba![12] This era is what brought about our love of fried bologna, baked apples, creamed corn, and tomato sandwiches. If it was cheap, that's what's for supper!

Depression-era food is still prominent in our culture because, more often than not, simplicity is magnificent. The Krispy Kreme dough-nut was invented as a result of the Depression and, hell, we got an app now that tells us when the sign is blinking. What a time to be alive! Say what you will, these red-ass, rural, and downright backward folks' backs were against the wall, but they figured it out. Their cre-ations still live on today, some in high-class cuisine. You think shrimp and grits started out as a $15 brunch to be had with a woman who doesn't really love you? Hell, naw. That's Depression mess; that's slav-ery mess. Much like blues music, we derive most of our beauty from a sea of pain and anguish—and then rich white folks appropriate it and make millions of dollars on it. It's the American way.

HUNTING

What used to be a necessity for all mankind is now basically a great excuse to go out in the woods and shoot shit (hits). If you don't enjoy hunting, that's fine—still, you have probably benefited from it. Ain't a redneck on earth only hunts enough to fill up his own deep freezer (the

---

11. **You know how you rich white women put salads in a jar because of Pinterest? Well, this is not that.**

12. **This actually works for most problems: just fry the shit out of it, bayba!**

one they got using little Johnny's college fund, but, hell, let's face it, at least deer meat is an actual possibility), so usually that stuff gets passed around the neighborhood—so long as you'll go pick it up.

Deer steaks, deer sausage, deer jerky, and a personal favorite in the South, deer chili. Venison may not technically be the official meat of Dixie, but we all know it to be true. No one had to tell us to like Sky-nyrd either—some things come natural. Ain't nothing more soothing than sitting down in front of a warm fire with a cold beer, the remote, and a bowl of deer chili. Toss some sour cream and cheese in that sum-bitch, and you can spread it out for days.

Getting up at four in the morning on a cold and dreary day to put on a full-body suit of camo, dab a splash of deer urine behind the ears, and march into the woods to climb a tree and wait for something to happen doesn't seem like the best way to spend a day, but Lord bless the ones that do. Winter wouldn't be the same without staring at ten pounds of deer butt next to a tub of ice cream we can't eat anymore on account of getting the sugar.[13]

FISHING: HUNTING, BUT DRUNK AND ON A BOAT

It's ninety-five degrees in the dog days of summer in North Georgia. The mosquitos buzz around to the tune of a church bell that's ringing to signify dinnertime.[14] The jingle from an ice cream truck is drowned out only by the sirens from a fire truck racing to put out a blaze caused by a dropped cigarette in a bone-dry hayfield. You call your uncle

13. **Mamaw talk for diabetes.**

14. **That means lunch to old folk.**

Porch Talk with Drew

Southern women know their way around the kitchen. Used to be that hard livin' made division of labor a necessity. Women had to be able to prepare hearty meals with limited supplies and time. Even as times have changed and women work outside of the home, the expectation remains. However you feel about the reasons behind this, it sure creates a lot of amazing cooks. Both my mamaws could cook something fierce. My momma's potato salad is something I'd fight for. I have eight aunts still living, and all of them but one can cook her ass off.

But the absolute best chef in my family is hands down, without a doubt, my dad. And I don't just mean he can run a grill, though of course he can—and his work in smoked meat is artistic. I mean the man can cook. Anything. Well. And with love.

His biscuits and gravy are better than anyone's in the country. (If there are gravy biscuits outside the country, please someone tell me about them.) He'll make a soup that you eat every day for a week and only want it more as the days pass. On huntin' and fishin' trips, he cooks around the campfire. In high school, he took home economics, probably because he thought it would be easy or to be around girls. He won the Betty Crocker award for best baker. Y'all, he was a record-breaking tailback with a ponytail—and he was in home ec bakin' A-plus apple pies.

The best meal I have ever had in my life was one he made me when I was eight years old. We were staying in a cabin by a river in the mountains on vacation, and I'd been tubing that day. Before that, I'd played as hard as I could. Before that, I'd gotten up early to go fishing. I was hungry. Dad made baked potatoes and steak on an open fire. I had to sit there and watch him cook the meat, slowly, smelling it for what felt like hours, while he explained to me how you tell if a steak is done. You gotta poke it with your finger, he said—if it's not a little firm on the outside, it's not done, but it *has to be* soft in the middle.

Since me and Pop both like 'em rare, it couldn't have been too long that he was talkin' and showing me where to poke the steaks. But I was so hungry that I was salivating by the time I got to eat. I will never forget how good it tasted, and how happy I felt with my family, eating by the river.

And that's what's so damn special about food cooked with love and our food culture in the South. I ain't the first to say it, but I won't be the last, either: food brings us together.

DM

Terry to see if he's gonna come over later for homemade peach cobbler because it's Aunt Nelly's birthday, and it's hard to rustle up all the cousins like this—peach cobbler is about the only way to do it. There's no answer.

Do you call back? No. Do you worry? No. You know what's going on. He's on the lake. Or the river. Or more than likely, one of his buddies' papaw's pond. He's fishing, and he will not be bothered by the outside world before he catches his fill, drinks all his beer, or it's dark out—whichever comes first (the beer).

There's fishing all over the country, and the world. It's not primarily a Southern thing. But goddamn it, we have legendary angler Bill Dance, and yuns ain't the ones petitioning for it to be made an Olympic event.

We watch fishing on TV. We listen to fishing *on the radio, for God's sake,* and we spend our life savings on fishing boats that we then can't afford to put gas in. Wanna know something funny, though? A lot of people just throw the fish back. That's right. Rednecks act as head-shop lip piercers to fish and then send them back on their merry way. It seems like an odd practice, but to those for whom fishing isn't a necessity for survival, it became a safe haven for relaxation. Fishing is as close to yoga as a redneck will get.

Taking a boat out on a lake and just getting shit faced might make it seem like you have a problem, but take a fishing pole and you're a hunter-gatherer! Isn't that great?!? (I really don't know why people talk so much shit about us; we're awesome.) Not *all* we do is get shit faced and throw fish back—they's plenty of us that keep them. And Lordy, Lordy, when we do, a fish fry is about to go down!

Take it from us: fish fries hit. Breading up a catfish in some cornmeal and tossing it in that bubbly, boiling hot grease (the primordial soup from which the Southern man arose) while snacking on some of Mamaw's hush puppies[15] is just about as good as it gets. Wash all that down with a sweet tea and some homemade strawberry ice cream, and you have had you a day, son.

Hot damn! Forgot how much fish hits. We gonna come cook y'all some fish. Send us your addresses (and a blank check), and we will get to ya when we can! In fact, just send us blank checks, generally speaking.

THE GREAT BBQ WAR

In the West Indies, they have a word—*barbacoa*—that means to slow cook meat over hot coals. Much like our life expectancies, we decided to shorten that. Let's discuss the different types of BBQ and rate them accordingly.

Memphis. Memphis-style BBQ is typically pork only, usually consisting of the ribs and the shoulders. Some like 'em dry (no sauce), some like 'em wet (yeah they do, *mmm*). Instead of being tossed in the

---

15. **Cornbread testicles.**

sauce, however, the sauce is usually brushed on afterward. Kinda like pig ketchup. [16] The sauce is made with a dealer's choice of spices, tomatoes, and vinegar. It's typically thin and sweet, with a little tartness.

Famous establishments: Rendezvous, Cozy Corner.

LR Rating: 10 out of 10 biscuits.

Carolina. Typically considered the original style of BBQ (also happens to be all our favorite), Carolina BBQ can be pulled, shredded, chopped, and even sliced. They slow cook the whole pig in pits over slow-burning oak or hickory, mopping it with a vinegar-spiced liquid during the cooking process. If that doesn't make you want to head on over right now, you ain't got a pulse. And that's fine. We'll take your portion. Hot damn, that sounds good!

Famous establishments: Stamey's, Allen & Son BBQ, Red Bridges Barbecue Lodge

LR Rating: 2 (burnt from fireworks) thumbs up.

Kansas City (Missouri). Somewhere in the late eighteen hundreds or early nineteen hundreds, Henry Perry, a Tennessee native and true Southern OG, decided to throw BBQ in a pit and then cover it with a thick molasses sauce. The rest, as they say, is history. Kansas City BBQ is so good that, to this day, we still let them pretend to be Southern. Unlike Memphis and Carolina, KC uses *all* the meats, baby! Chicken, pork, beef, mutton, fish, and often turkey [17] are slow smoked every day in one of more'n a hundred BBQ restaurants in Kansas City alone. So good they even got a sumbitchin' tater chip named after 'em. That's a stamp of approval here in the South.

16. **Corey has his pants off right now.**

17. **Turkey, of course, hits as a meat (we ain't been to the country), but substitutin' it for another meat, like in the case of turkey bacon, is an abomination against God.**

Famous establishments: Joe's Kansas City Bar-B-Que, Fiorella's Jack Stack Barbecue, Arthur Bryant's Barbecue.

LR Rating: 10 out of 10 red-asses recommend it.

Texas. SAT scores aside, everything is bigger in Texas. The Texans cook their meat until it falls off the bone. Then they chop it up and serve it on a bun with a pickle and onion relish—very different from the slaw you'd get on most any other BBQ, but hittin' all on its own. Texas BBQ has absolutely perfected brisket. Typically, it's known as the cheap meat, but the way they do brisket in the Lone Star State makes any meal fit for a king. Oftentimes it's cut right in front of you on a butcher block and served on deli paper that you carry to your table, and you eat right off the paper. If you're too fancy for that, then you don't deserve Texas BBQ, or happiness. Fuck plates. We can bet money that a great deal of it is gone before you get there. They use a tomato-based sauce, but the way that tender meat melts in your mouth? Hell, you really don't need it.

Famous establishments: Black's BBQ, Kreuz Market, Smitty's Market.

LR Rating: *T* for Texas, A-plus for Texas BBQ.

OUR OTHER HITTIN' MESS

BBQ isn't the only thing the South is known for, y'all! Charleston, South Carolina, is home to some of the finest seafood on the planet. Apalachicola, Florida, ships its oysters nationwide, and a certain colonel decided one day to start hocking buckets of chicken in the Bluegrass State. Yessiree bob, we have a vast array of delicacies here in the South that we take much pride in. From the best pecan pies you'll ever have in the Peach State of Georgia, to the beautiful invention of mayonnaise-based BBQ sauce in Alabama, all the way to the only thing our grandparents think the French ever did worth a fuck: Louisiana gumbo! Now, the French aren't *exactly* responsible for the type of gumbo it's evolved into today, but they're certainly responsible for how cool the Cajuns sound when they talk about it, and that hits for us.

We've got the best fruit and vegetable stands, dairies full of fresh cream and butter as far as the eye can see, and we've got muscadine vines growing wild so's you can just grab some of nature's candy on your way to Mamaw's house out in the woods.

So many things we do here in the South are just so purely Southern. For our beloved Yankee friends out there, here's some stuff you need to try (very aware y'all have some of this, but you don't do it like us—we just have the market cornered on some things: banjo music, toothless women, boots that don't look gay,[18] truck stop hand jobs, and these dishes).

Fried Bologna. This is the perfect blend of poverty and decadence. If that was the theme of some fancy-ass New York fusion restaurant, the fried bologna sandwich would be its signature dish. Best served on toasted white bread with mayo, pickle, a slice of American (lol) cheese, and a splash of your favorite hot sauce.

Pimento Cheese. No baby shower in the South would be complete without stern gossip, a monogrammed onesie, and a solid helping of pimento cheese. A mayonnaise-based (what isn't) cheese spread filled with pimentos, a bit of cream cheese, and seasoned to taste (add a little sweetness for prime hittery), you'll find this at ladies' luncheons, PTA meetings, and swallowed whole by grown men on golf courses during the turn. Best served on untoasted white bread, cut diagonally. No condiments needed. It's all in there. Skeew.

Biscuits and Gravy. Often called "skeets and gravy," this is a tradition unlike any other in the South. Nothing gets you up in the morning and makes you want to lay back down quicker than a good helping of B

---

18. **For the record, boots that do look gay hit.**

Porch Talk with Corey

When I was growing up, my best friend Kris and his four brothers and sisters (also my best friends) lived a couple miles away from me. There was a field in between their house and their mamaw's house across the way. We had video games back then, but this is before they were as popular as they are today. So we actually played outside most of the time. We'd get up early in the morning, and Kris's momma would cook us your standard Southern breakfast: eggs, toast, bacon, sausage, and biscuits. The adults would drink coffee, and betwixt the six of us, we would kill a gallon of milk.

We'd go down to the basement (which is currently *my* bedroom) and catch a couple of cartoons before heading out to the woods. The woods in back of Kris's house wrapped all the way around the property and came out near his mamaw's house. The goal, every day, was to get to Mamaw's for a snack. We'd tear out through the woods, not giving a single damn one that vines and thorns were slapping us in the face. (We were eight years old—shit like that didn't hurt.) We'd swing from vines over ditches and beat the hell out of each other with sticks . . . I sincerely miss doing that.

Along the way, there was a muscadine vine. This was a big deal to us because we thought it was magical. We almost believed it was the forbidden fruit of the Bible, and, much like that dumb butthead Eve, we ate it anyways. It was delicious. When I eat muscadines today, I'm immediately taken back to that period in my life when I still believed in magic—when there was, um, aw shit, what's it called?

Oh, yeah: hope.

We'd recharge at the muscadine vine because from there, in accordance with the long, dumb route we always took, we still had about an hour of jumping over logs and fucking up our knees so that the older versions of ourselves could cry when it rains. We'd hit the edge where the woods met the field and . . . there was Mamaw's house! We'd take off in a dead sprint and wouldn't let up until we reached her sliding-glass door. She would be standing right behind it, waiting for us, then she'd greet us with a smile and a pat on the head, and we'd head straight for the kitchen table, where there would be a bottled Coke and an oatmeal creme pie that she'd already set out for us.

It's funny that now when I want to have a good time, my brain goes straight to booze and live music. But my fondest memories as a child involve food: running through a field to get an oatmeal pie and a Coke. What a South I grew up in.

and G. Some folks do it with brown gravy (hits), some with chocolate gravy. (Do I even have to say it?) But every Southerner knows that the right way to enjoy it is with that thick, white, sausage gravy that globs down your throat like a freedom slug on its way to belly heaven. Best served with a nap afterward.

Sweet Tea. Often referred to as "the table wine of the South." It ain't a mamaw on earth what don't have one of them old warped pitchers of hers full of this mess at all times in the icebox. To many, it's a bit too much. But to most Southerners, you simply can't get it too sweet. To put into perspective how much we love the stuff, anytime a Southerner gets back from a trip up north, first thing they do is tell a story about a waitress looking at them funny for ordering it. Every time. Best served very, very cold and after baseball practice.

Fried . . . Anything. Chicken is probably the most popular (and hittinest), but we don't stop at fowl when it comes to our frying endeavors. Pork chops, okra, squash, green tomatoes, cookies—y'all, we figured out a way to fry *Kool-Aid*—tell me again how we're behind in education. Maybe so, but maybe that's cuz we was busy doing hittin' stuff. You name it, we will batter it up, throw it in some grease, and go to town on it. There ain't a thing wouldn't be improved by frying it. And that's okay—every now and then. But you ort not make a habit of it. (We'll get to that in a second.) Best served in a big-ass tinfoil pan on a table filled with assorted covered dishes and pies.

CONSEQUENCES

To write this chapter, we decided to gorge ourselves on our favorite Southern cuisines. And that's great . . . but there is a downfall. See, now Drew can't fit into his sweet-ass leather pants, Trae almost broke the railing on his porch during his last rant, and we're fairly certain that Corey is gonna have to spend a week at the Mayo Clinic. This stuff is bad for ya, y'all.

Moderation is fine, but when was the last time you heard of a redneck half-assing anything but an alimony check? Don't often happen. See, a lot of our food habits are a direct result of what we have discussed in this chapter and many other chapters: poverty. It used to be (during the Depression) that the bigger you were, the healthier you were. Well, flash forward several years, and with the advent of dollar menus, five-dollar pizzas, and whatever the fuck Monsanto has going on, that's not the case. The less money you spend on food, the fatter you're liable to be. Hell yeah, potted meat and crackers is cheap as fuck, but that processed "meat" is full of sodium that will bloat your ass and stop your heart, and them crackers turn plum into sugar once they get digested.

A bottle of water and a Coke are the same price? Which one do you think little Randy Red-Ass Rogers is gonna get when he goes to the store? If sweet tea is the table wine of the South, Mountain Dew is

Food Map of the South

1. A. The Home of Chocolate Gravy!
   B. They also eat possum corndogs everytime a family pet dies

2. If you put your ear up to a crawfish shell, you can hear someone wreck a truck into a titty bar

3. A. Mississippi Mud is the hittinest pie of all time #GOAT
   B. Until 1978, chocolate pudding had to be sold in a separate store

4. Think peanuts are a vegetable & Reese's Cups count as a serving

5. A. Undisputed KING of Fried Chicken
   B. Mayonnaise was first used here as toothpaste

6. A. White BBQ Sauce — cause mayo ort be in everything
   B. Best Chicken Taffy IN THE GAME

7. Peaches, Pecans, and Peanuts, and another P-word: Pre-diabetes

8. A. Vinegar-based BBQ (CoFo's FAVORITE)
   B. Mustard-based BBQ, however, has to use a different bathroom

9. A. Shrimp 'n' Grits! (Charleston Hits, Y'all)
   B. Many natives put heroin in the cole slaw

10. A. Ramps … smelly-ass but hittin' onion
    B. Traditionally WV meemaws mash potatoes with their feet

11. Smithfield Ham is literally protected by law — this is Virginia's only law.

12. A. Boiled peanut stands everywhere
    B. Boiled peanut farts everywhere

13. These are not real people — they only eat rice cakes

the house vodka. We've got hardworking people down here who, after paying their mortgage, insurance, cell phone bill, and, Lord willing, slap aside a bit for their kid's college fund—well, yeah, frozen pizzas seem to be the best alternative because a dwindling bank account is more immediately scary than the thought of hypertension, diabetes, or gettin' a new swimsuit (besides, we was just gonna cut off some old jeans or whatever anyway). And that's how we think as humans: What about now?

DO WE CHANGE?

It ain't gonna be easy. And it's gonna have to be a personal thing, because Lord knows rednecks ain't gonna listen to a goddamn thing you tell them to do. For years, old Southerners have been trying to get the government to force schools to teach the Bible, but then when Michelle Obama tries to get them to eat a goddamn cucumber, all of a sudden it's "You can't tell our kids what to eat! Stay out of the schools!" Gee . . . wonder what the difference is?

For us adults, our health might be too far gone, but there's absolutely no reason to pass that ignorance and ill health on to your kids. We live among some of the most fertile farmlands in the country—remember them vegetables you fried up? Did you know that you can just eat them raw? Or hell, roast the sumbitches! Crazy, right?! Tomatoes hit on a catfish sandwich, yuh. But they're also good in a bowl with some salt and pepper on 'em.

Sweet tea is great. It really is, but how 'bout not every day? Can we try that? Y'all know you can get water from the sink, right? "But that's where the government puts mind-control drugs so they can come take our guns from us!" Okay, but wouldn't fighting a tyrannical government be a bit easier if you were fucking hydrated?

The South has the highest obesity rate in the country—and the highest poverty rate! So we're fallin' behind financially but eatin' better? Do what, now? Yeah, turns out that while we may have less expensive houses or clothes or may not have as much money for health care, we sure as shit ain't cuttin' the calories. 'Course the whole problem there is that high-calorie food often *is* cheaper . . . we're just forgoing nutrition, the source of which grows around us naturally all the time. "But raw vegetables and salads don't taste as good." Maybe not, but they do when you're stoned. So the next time that little bill comes up, how 'bout you march your hypocritical church ass down to the polls and vote to legalize marijuana? You might think it's a sin, but so is gluttony, Linda. Legalize pot, give some of these poor farmers a chance to make a little more income, economy starts booming again, we have more money for hydropon-ics, and the next thing you know, we've got a surplus of hittin'-ass fruits and veggies to put in little Timmy's lunch box instead of pro-cessed ham and Gummy Worms. Timmy grows up healthier and more financially successful as a result of it, and then he can afford to put you in a better home when the sugar ultimately takes your leg . . . then to treat the pain, you smoke nature's little herb to forget about how much you loved Ricky with his red Mustang convert-ible that summer your husband worked out of town, and everybody wins!

Fried food is amazing. Sweet tea is amazing. Indulgence, by defi-nition, is something we love doing. But for the love of God, if you want to have longer here on earth to enjoy all of the delicacies that our great little region has to offer, you have got to stop enjoying it as fre-quently. And you see them hittin'-ass mountains we got going? Take a run through 'em! You'll sweat out the grease!

Eat a vegetable, y'all!

Porch Talk with Trae

How can anyone not understand that Sunny D, liquid orange sugar (hnnnngh), could be bad for you? Well, I didn't know. And plenty more people plain don't know. Or don't give a shit. Or a little bit of both.

I've had many little moments of clarity over the years when I realize how markedly different my upbringing was from that of many Americans, and the realization that I was never taught a single goddamn thing about eatin' right was one of the most illuminating. Seriously y'all, it's just not a thing. Or at least it wasn't when I was a kid. Maybe some rural areas are doing better now, but prolly not—if for no other reason than to spite Obama's ol' lady.

So everybody back home just ate like complete shit most all of the time. Don't get me wrong: it was straight-up *delicious* shit, but still shit in terms of health. When I was about eight, my uncle, a trained chef, opened up a deli in the middle of town. Now, being a gay chef, he actually *does* know about nutrition and eating right and all that. He's also a little bit of a hippie, so he's about alfalfa sprouts and tofu and all that, too. Hell, he's even a vegetarian! (The horror!) I did not take after him in that regard. So his deli, the New Day Deli, was pretty much the crunchiest, hippest food that town had ever seen. Gazpacho, veggie kebabs, some mess called "Tiger Food"—you name it. Motherfucker had herbal tea and all in there. I know what you're thinking: "Well, clearly *that* didn't pan out. Who the hell would think they could sell rednecks on a damn healthful bistro? Especially if it was owned and operated by a *gay vegetarian?* No way that was ever going to fly. Hell, they probably tried to burn the place down, right?"

Naw. Ain't how it went down. Them red-asses ate
that shit up. Maybe it was the novelty. Maybe it was his
reasonable prices. Or maybe it was the fact that my uncle
is a goddamn *virtuoso* in the kitchen. You could give him a
bull's sphincter, and he'd make a *fire* bull butt risotto out of
it. Either way, people lined up for it. It was awesome.

And then the factory that was the center of the town's
economy moved to Mexico, and everything in the whole
damn county went to hell. My uncle, like most of the other
local businesses, had to close his doors. I honestly believe
his deli would be open to this day otherwise. My point is,
we have it in us to eat better down here; we just have to
be shown (a) how it works, and (b) that it *doesn't have to
suck.* Maybe the answer to the South's obesity problem is a
government program assigning gay chefs to rural areas. But
whatever the solution, there is hope.

5

Mamaws and Papaws

Mamaw, Papaw, Meemaw, Peepaw, Granddiddy, Neenee, Granny, Gran, Pop, old bald lady. No matter what you call your grandparents, one thing is consistent: they're more than likely your favorite people in the world. "Y'all come back now, hear?" "Put your feet up, stay awhile." "Y'all don't hurry on!" These are just a few expressions you will hear from the typical Southern grandparent as you attempt the post-chicken-and-dumpling exodus from their house. Standing at the screen door and watching you drive off as the lightning bugs[1] flicker through the evergreen leaves of a magnolia tree, they're never quite ready for you to leave. And, as guilt is the fuel on which old Southerners run, they have to let you know it.

Funny thing is, it wouldn't matter if you stayed eight hours a day, seven days a week—you'd still hear this one as you were leaving: "Come see me sometime!" That's a mamaw and a papaw in a nutshell: someone who always wants you around. When our grandparents are

---

1. *Fireflies* **is what pussies say.**

gone, specifically our mamaw—well, that's it. The last person on earth who thought you were perfect is no longer around to make you feel that way, if only for a moment. The last person who, through all your faults, through all your worldly transgressions, still feels as though you hung the moon. Once they're gone, you've got to settle back into the cold and unforgiving world without your safety net. That's why we love spending time at Mamaw and Papaw's house: it's a safe haven from reality. No matter how much you try on the outside, it seems that people are never satisfied with your performance. You could do ninety-nine things right, but your boss will focus on the one thing you did wrong. Not a mamaw and papaw—hell, with Mamaw and Papaw, something as simple as fixing the channel changer[2] will win you a week's worth of praise and a few grilled cheese sandwiches.

Speaking of food—my God, is that a big deal for mamaws and papaws, and in their own very specific ways. You see, we Liberal Rednecks consider ourselves feminists,[3] so in no way do we expect dinner to be ready when we get home. Hell, have you met the women in our lives? Wouldn't *dare* suggest it. We'd be limping to gigs for a week straight with a frozen T-bone on our nads, guarantee it. But our papaws? The greatest generation on earth? You damn right they 'spected[4] that stove to have three or four pots going when they crossed the threshold of the house that they built with their two bare goddamn hands. And, look, we aren't saying that's what made them the greatest generation on earth. You can decide that for yourselves, but that's the way it went down.

2. **The remote. The clicker. The thing that shuts up Nancy Grace.**

3. **In the South, this means "I mean, we don't hit 'em or nothing . . . hell."**

4. **We don't know why this is how we say "expected," but then again, we don't know why Keith Whitley had to die. If you don't know who we're talkin' about, shame on you. JFGI.**

To hear old folks tell it, the man would go to work all day (the days were longer back then, from what I hear), bust his ass for the man, and on the way home—driving his Ford Mercury and listening to Faron Young on that one little speaker in the middle of the dash—he'd be thinking two things: (1) "Sure wish I didn't need a church key[5] to open these beers; be a whole lot easier to kill this six-pack while driving without havin' to use that damn thing." And (2) "I swear to God if that chicken is cold when I get home, I'm gonna take it out on my kids and cause a ripple effect of abuse that will one day lead my great-grandson to do some weird performance-art project in a warehouse in Savannah about how his dad never told him he loved him. Sure, he'll *say* it's about war or whatever, but we'll all know."

PAPAWS

Papaws are most assuredly a different breed than mamaws. They love ya—Lord, they love ya—but they ain't as forgiving as their better halves. A papaw is definitely one to try to spoil the grandkid, but from what we've gathered over the years, it seems that he does this mainly to piss off his grown kids and get them back for years of heartache. Years of your backing the family car into a tree. Years of replacing school clothes because you burned cigarette holes in all your button-ups. Years of college tuition that was wasted on a kid who, instead of attending class, decided to follow the Grateful Dead for thirteen weeks until their tour ended in Seattle, and you met a boy named Theo who promised he could sell enough grass between there and Denver to get you both off for a year until he was busted in Salt Lake City, and you

5. Beer opener, bayba. Watch *Cool Hand Luke*, ya Yank!

Porch Talk with Trae

 My dad's dad, Johnny Crowder (Pa), was the true patriarch of my life growing up. My dad was the single most important person in my life, and we were supremely close, but when asshole cops in my hometown of Celina, Tennessee, pulled me over, the threat was, "Now, don't make me call Johnny, Trae." By the way, one time one of them smarmy motherfuckers made the mistake of *actually* calling my pa, who proceeded to tell that cop just exactly what he thought of his ass, which was that if he spent a little more time chasing down meth dealers and a little less time harassing teenage honor students, the Celina PD might actually be worth a damn, and, by God, if he didn't like that, he could call Jerry (the sheriff) and see what *he* thought about it.

They let me go.

When I would stay with him and Mema (his wife, more on her in a second), every night before bed he would have a *mixing bowl*—yes, a mixing bowl—filled with iced Coke, and he would never let me have any of it, which used to irritate the shit out of me, as I was a portly little fat-fuck kid. He would tell me I couldn't have any because "this has got Pa's medicine in it." It took me until I was at least twenty before I realized that sandbaggin' sumbitch was drinking whiskey during Leno. But that was just his way. He was smooth as hell; it didn't occur to you to question the man. One of my absolute favorite memories of Pa actually happened *years* after his death (it's not as weird as that makes it sound). I was talking to Mema about how we thought my oldest boy might have a hearing problem, and, hand to Fake God, this is what she said:

"Oh, you know what, honey, I bet that's it! Hearing problems run in our family. You know your Pa had a hearing disorder."

"What? No . . . no, I never knew that. What kind of hearing disorder?"

"He couldn't hear women talk."

"Wh—what?"

"Yeah, strangest thing. He could hear men's voices just fine, but he couldn't hardly hear women talk at all; somethin' 'bout the frequency."

Y'all, when I say I died . . . Jesus Christ! My pa, the absolute fucking legend, had convinced his wife and God knows how many other people that he was *medically incapable of listening to a woman.* Y'all, goddamn it, feminism, sexism, and all that shit aside, if that ain't some of the most Don Draper, OG fuckin' shit you've ever heard, then you can kiss my ass. Pa hit.

He died in 2004, right before I was set to leave Celina for the first time to go to college, and that shit shook me to my core. As a child, I had been motivated more than anything by not disappointing Pa, and now he was gone. Just like that. And it was stupid, too. He was such a hard-ass old alpha male that he ignored all of the signs of the widowmaker heart attack that killed him, thinking he would just "be all right, hell." In his defense, he survived getting shot with a sawed-off shotgun at extremely close range through a car windshield when he was twenty-two, so you can see why he would think a heart attack was for pussies. But at any rate, I had just become an adult, and my whole world was flipped upside down.

It fucked me up pretty bad initially, but then, probably two or three weeks after he died, I had a dream where he picked me up in a fuckin' *sweet* '68 Mustang. (Pa built, raced, and sold cars his entire life. He was as big a car guy as you'll ever meet.) In the dream, we rode around, and he told me, "The last thing I would ever want is for you to waste your time crying over me, not when you have so much hittin' left to do. And all I want you to do is hit, so stop worrying about me and just keep hittin', boy." I might be paraphrasing a bit here. But still. And look, I'm not a religious, superstitious, or paranormal type of guy, so I'm not saying that the spirit of my dead grandfather literally came to me in a dream to give me some of the best advice I've ever received in my life—*but that's exactly what happened.*

Even in death, Pa was teaching me what kind of man to be. I still miss him, and I always will. Even if he was a racist. (Look, as we point out, they all are, so what the fuck I'm 'sposed to do?)

TW

spent two weeks pawning off that sweet nasty[6] of yours in exchange for tractor-trailer rides toward the East Coast. Oh sure, you felt alive for a moment, but the highs couldn't hold a candle to the comedown you faced in Arkansas when you came to in a truck stop bathroom facedown in what you were praying was urine . . .

Okay, Jesus . . . went a little far there. Point is, the papaw deserves his hard and rugged exterior—he's earned that shit.

For the sake of staying on one track here, let's just assume that when we say "the typical Southern papaw," we're referring to a sumbitch who was born between 1920 and 1942. We're very aware that we've got some superyoung papaws out there, what with all the running around our generation has done, but "papaw" in this sense is more of an age than a title. Your typical Southern papaw comes clad in a pair of old straight-leg light-washed blue jeans, an oil-stained white T-shirt tucked into them aforementioned jeans, a trucker hat denoting exactly which war his ass is a veteran of, and one of them old metallic-green thermoses full of coffee that's stronger than

6. One a ya holes.

cologne on a New Jersey bellhop. He wakes up at four fifteen on the dot every morning, and even though he has been retired for fifteen years, he still goes straight to his shaving kit to get ready for the day: a day filled with porch talks, sausage biscuits, the sports section, and barbershop philosophy.

Here's a rundown of a typical day in the life of a Southern papaw:

4:15 Rise and shine and give God the glory.

4:18 Get false teeth out of the Dale Earnhardt[7] edition jelly jar they've been soaking in all night.

4:22 Slip on jeans, T-shirt, and the official papaw edition white New Balance tennis shoes issued at the beginning of every year at the Mason's Lodge.[8]

4:45 (It takes awhile for old folk to get dressed.) Splash some form of green aftershave liberally (the only appropriate use of this word for Papaw) to face, neck, and underarms because you "ain't buying two things to do one goddamn job."

4:50 Walk outside to take the trash out to the road and grab the paper. On the way to the mailbox, notice that your neighbor hasn't mowed his grass in several weeks. Call him a lazy good-for-nothing communist sympathizer under your breath, invoke Dwight Eisenhower's name three times like a yoga mantra to calm down, grab the paper, and head in.

4:55 Flip through the entire paper to get to the obituaries.

5:05 Wake up your wife to tell her that Freddy Holcomb has passed away. Hear her insist that she doesn't know him. Slowly

7. **Pour one out. Right now.**

8. **An accepted form of the occult in the South.**

realize that she's right, you were thinking of Steve Holcomb, and he has actually been dead for three years. You missed the funeral.

5:25 Brew a pot of coffee that will be done by the time you get through reading the funnies.

5:30 Think to yourself that if you were Dagwood[9] and the heir to a goddamn railroad fortune, you probably wouldn't take so much lip from Blondie.

5:35 Enjoy coffee from the mug your granddaughter made you during arts and crafts at kindergarten, the one that matches the ashtray your son made thirty years prior—when things were simpler.

5:55 Hop in your truck, which, whatever brand it is, is vastly superior to the other two brands of trucks and, by God, Marvin Dewberry can kiss your wrinkled ass for thinking otherwise.

6:10 Arrive at Waffle House just in time to have a cigarette outside with the rest of your army buddies and complain that due to Obama's political correctness, you can't enjoy a cig anymore the way the good Lord intended it: next to the hash browns.

6:20 Order your All-Star Special breakfast and remark to the waitress, "As soon as you leave that no-good husband a yours, me and yuns is gonna run away together!"

6:50 After a thirty-minute meal filled with pointless banter about the weather, why the Braves suck, and how old everyone is getting (especially Harold: hahahaha, fuck you, Harold), fire up one last cigarette and hop in your truck.

9. Hittin'-ass comic strip. Ask ya paw.

7:03 Quick gas station stop to buy a scratch-off,[10] more cigarettes, and to say hello to the Indian clerk named Shrey, who, even though that's not a hard name to pronounce, you call "Monty."

7:15 Pick up the grandkids at your kid's house to take them to school. They nearly convince you, like always, that y'all should just go to your house and eat cheese and crackers all day. You resist.

8:00 After you see that the young 'uns get into the building safely, you cruise down to the local muffler shop where your best friend Earl's son runs the joint. There is a bench out front with your name on it.

8:15–9:00 Sit on the bench and wait for Earl. He said he was gonna be late this morning on account of a doctor's visit. His bowels, or something to do with a polyp. Hell, you can't remember, but when he gets here, you and him are gonna have coffee again.

9:05 Earl shows up. Reminds you about the exploratory surgery on his bladder. Bladder—that was it.

10:30 After joining Earl in a brief moment of prayer to proposition the Lord into making the breeze blow a young mother's skirt up as she walks past, you and Earl head to the meat-and-three[11] to grab a quick bite.

12:00 After two cups of coffee to speed up the digestion, you joke to the waitress that since she didn't leave the bill on the table, "it must be free this time then!"

12:30 Arrive at Bill's Barber Shop to get the same goddamn haircut you've been getting since you were twelve, thank you very much!

12:38 As you're waiting for a chair to open up, you discuss high

---

10. We get that you Northerners just have money, but we need the lottery, goddamn it.

11. Southern diner what has meat from last week and fried veggies. Hits.

school football with the chief of police, who is also waiting on a haircut. While on duty. With the car running in the parking lot. You don't think the boys have been worth a fuck, 'specially since they started making people on motorcycles wear a helmet. Buncha pansies. "Only helmet I ever wore had a bullet lodged in the side of it! Woulda got Johnny too if I hadn't a stuck my neck out there. To this day, I don't know which Korea it was. But both of 'em can kiss my wrinkled ass for good measure."

1:30 After the haircut, you stop by the produce stand to pick up some okra for the ol' lady. You end up buying a few jars of sorghum and a sackful of peppermint and clove candy.

2:00 You get home to find Mamaw on the porch shucking corn and breaking beans. You join her for the length of a glass-bottle Co-cola and then retire to the den to watch Judge Joe Brown and nap on the recliner.

4:25 Mamaw wakes you up just in time for you to get washed up for dinner. You hobble to the seafoam-green back bathroom and wash off the dirt and the top two layers of your skin with machinist-grade pumice hand soap. Another splash of green mess on your face, and it's off to the supper[12] table.

5:15 After finishing the lemon icebox pie you had for dessert, it's off to the porch to watch traffic and listen to the june bugs rattle.

8:00 Bed 'er down, Pops. You'll need the strength to do it all again tomorrow—and every day until you fall and break your hip in the Piggly Wiggly.

The papaw is a creature of habit, and no one will tell you that quicker than a papaw himself. For some reason, it doesn't seem to matter what

12. Dinner is supper and lunch is dinner. Don't know when we stopped that.

Porch Talk with Drew

My Mamaw Flo came to live with us when I was younger because she got Alzheimer's, and we didn't have any of that—what is it, where you don't have to take care of folk because others will do it?—oh, yeah, money.

Her husband left her when she got Alzheimer's, but to his credit, he left her to a group of people he knew would take care of her better than he would ever be able to (especially with that new girlfriend he had, amirite, Papaw?). He knew my mother and her siblings would figure out a way to care for their mother.

And they did. My mother and some of my aunts rotated whose homes Mamaw Flo would live in. Basically, their plan was to have one person keep her till that person essentially broke down to the point that she was as crazy as my dementia-having mamaw. Then someone else would pick up the mantle and carry it for a little while. Hey, it wasn't the prettiest plan, but it was the best one. I remember some fighting here and there about things. I remember her being in a nursing home briefly. I remember pain and grief and fear and resentment and despair.

But I mostly remember love. They made it work, and they supported each other. I remember one of those uncles staying in our house and helping out my mother immensely. I remember a lot of people pitching in what they could—emotionally, financially, and time-wise. I remember that most of all. That, and how absolutely hilarious Mamaw Flo was sometimes. Y'all ever lived with a crazy person? Man, it's a trip.

On my sixteenth birthday, all my friends were over, and she was certain, in her disease-addled mind, that the party was for her. She was cracking jokes, clapping, thanking everyone for comin', and singing nonsensical gospel songs. She was on fire. Toward the end of the night, people were saying bye to her and huggin' her neck. It was destined to be a favorite memory of my life.

Then, for a cherry on top of my birthday sundae, in front of half my class, she grabbed my friend Doug's package, looked him right in his teenage eyes, and said, "Well, you're a pretty little girl, aren't you?"

If you think sixteen-year-olds didn't lose their collective shit over that, you ain't met sixteen-year-olds. It's still easily the best I've ever seen someone do at making people laugh, and I've been doing stand-up for most of my adult life.

I am so grateful for that moment, my mamaw, and the love and network of a family that led to it. Any goodness in me comes from stories like this: of all my aunts and uncles supporting their mother and each other, and us hillbillies gettin' by the best and only way we ever have—just barely, and carrying each other every step of the way.

DM

type of personality you had in your youth; by the time you're a papaw, you're a ritualistic curmudgeon who just wants the shade of a tree and a cold glass of sweet tea.

MAMAWS

A mamaw is a bit of a different story.

Here's a day in the life of a typical Southern mamaw:

24/7/365 Love you.

That's it. That's all a mamaw does. Of course, there are pies and fried chicken and all that jazz, but it all boils down to love. If someone calls you stupid, "They're just jealous." If you don't make the basketball team,

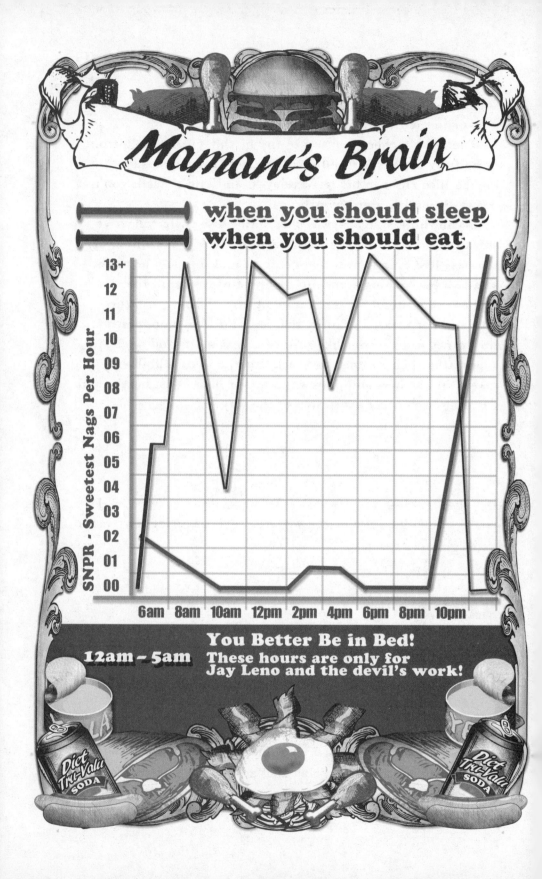

"The coach must've not wanted you to embarrass the other players."
If someone calls you ugly, "Well, you tell them that your mamaw said
that your butt would make them a Sundy [13] face!" Mamaws always have
a loaded answer to anything you can throw at them, and their wit and
wisdom are rooted in making you feel like you hung the moon—which
they genuinely believe you did.

That older generation of Southern woman is absolutely something else, buddy. The speed in which they can throw together a
chicken casserole or sweet potato pie in the event of a death in the
family or an unexpected family gathering is unparalleled. Like Doc
Holliday and his six-shooter, a mamaw's whisk and mixing bowl
seem to always be within arm's length—an arm you damn sure
don't have to twist to get her to use them. It ain't a mamaw on the
planet that will let boy nor beast starve in her presence. Thought
you was gonna just march on home after one sandwich? Think
again, Bryson. You must not know shit about old women. That first
sandwich is merely the trailer preceding the Tarantino movie of
food you're about to encounter.

I use Tarantino as an example because of the distinct parallels between his work and a typical day of food at Mamaw's: there's always
eggs, but sometimes they will be deviled, sometimes boiled, and
sometimes scrambled on a sandwich. (Though they all play different
roles, Tarantino typically uses the same cast.) Sometimes it doesn't
make sense. It's not uncommon for a mamaw to serve you a bowl of
Rice Krispies with a side of sliced homegrown tomatoes. (What's in

13. Not a typo. That's how you say "Sunday."

the goddamn briefcase?[14]) It can drag on for *hours* (looking at you, *The Hateful Eight*), and probably, most notably, you're going to hear the N-word a bit much. (Sorry, Leo.[15])

This last bit is a part of the history of mamaws and papaws that's definitely not something we've been looking forward to writing, because Lord knows, the last thing some good ol' boys want to do is disparage their elders, but goddamn, if this ain't addressed, we're just lying to ourselves and, most importantly, to y'all.

PRETTY DAMN RACIST

This is not just a Southern thing, but that's kind of the theme we have going here, so we'll stay within those parameters. Let's just get it out there: mamaws and papaws can be racist. Well, anyone *can* be. But, like, they're sometimes pretty damn racist. And look, you could say, "Well, hell, racism ain't got an age," and you're not wrong. However, no one does racist quite like the white-haired Southerner.

Everyone has stories of those little racist things their mamaw would say. Everyone has an older relative who still refers to black people as "colored." Everyone has a papaw who all of a sudden relates to an orange billionaire reality-star bag of shit.[16]

"Look, I ain't got nothing against black people, it's just in my day they knew their place."

"Hey, I'm not racist, I just really don't think we ort be mixing."

14. *Pulp Fiction.*

15. *Django Unchained.*

16. Come on, you know.

"Look, the country was founded by and *for* whites. I ain't telling no tale out of school; that's just the way it is."[17]

These are real examples of things old Southerners have said that were deemed "cute little innocent quips" by their grandchildren. And look, they may be cute and innocent—*to other white people*. But that behavior and language are damaging to other people and to a society that attempts to show pride in being a cultural melting pot. That systemic racism has put people of all color ('cept white) at an enormous disadvantage in this country. Even if this country *was* founded by white people, for white people, guess what? We ain't the only sumbitches here now.

Hell, when black people started whooping the shit out of us in basketball and dunking over our goddamn heads, we didn't just say, "Well, that's the way the game is played. Guess they win." Fuck, no. We invented the three-point shot to even shit out a little bit. Sidenote: I'm *very* aware that historically the best shooters in basketball have all been black (save for Larry Bird, who is legitimately the whitest person on the planet—sumbitch looks like the side of a fiberglass pontoon boat that just got pressure washed with bleach), but that's the one thing we have: shooting. Very rare that you see a big-ass white guy who can just dominate in the paint. Hell, it got so bad that we tried to pretend Yao Ming was white just so we could get credit (the only instance of "Well, they ain't black, so I guess they're white" in sports history).

Something we would like to talk about is not so much *that* old

---

17. When we hear someone say this, we can't help but think, "Well, Papaw, not really; remember those red people the white people had to kill to make room for the black people they was planning on shippin' in and subjugatin'?" This country has never been all white—and who would want it that way? If Kenny G were the only music to shake your ass to, women all over the country might well never have shaken their ass.

Porch Talk with Trae

Fair warning: this story is not going to be very pretty, but I always thought it summed up the mentality of the racist Southern papaw. So, yeah, here goes.

My papaw, who I called Pa, was one of my favorite people on earth, and I respected him probably more than any other man I've ever known. He was just a classic salt-of-the-earth, tough-as-nails, hardworkin', no-complainin'-ass motherfucker. He was *also* racist. But the thing about it is, to me, most of the racism you encounter today is fairly deliberate. People know exactly what the hell they're saying and why. They're wrong, and shitty, but it's very much intentional. With my pa, at least, it was just . . . ingrained.

He genuinely didn't mean anyone any harm or even see how what he was saying was in any way wrong; in his mind, it was just the way it was. This is true of most papaws, in my experience. Nothing he said sums up this mentality like the exchange we had one day in his office after two of my fellow high schoolers, a black kid (Mikel) and a white kid (Ryan), had gotten into a pretty goddamn sweet fistfight the night before in the middle of town. It was all anybody was talking about. And Mikel whooped Ryan's *ass,* son. I mean he went plum smooth in on that cracker. I was there because I hit, and every kid what hit was there, and so Pa asked me about it. This was the exchange:

Pa: So why was they fightin' for anyhow?
Me: Well, I ain't sure about this, but I reckon Ryan called Mikel a n—— to his face.
Pa [*totally incredulous*]: Well, what in the hell did he want him to call him, *Chinese*?!

Okay, that reaction is terrible, but he genuinely couldn't fathom why a black kid would be offended by a white kid calling him a word that was such a part of Pa's language and culture that he didn't even know it was offensive—even though Mikel and other black and white kids knew it was offensive. I know that sounds like a stretch. I'm not at all defending this mentality or his using that word. And I'm not saying Pa didn't harbor some prejudice. But that was his and other old white Southerners' outlook at the time. Today, it'd be impossible to believe that any white person doesn't know the word is offensive.

Tuv

white Southerners are so racist but *why* they're so racist. A lot of this is going to come off as us trying to defend the backward-ass thinking of a group of people, but that isn't entirely it. You can make points to defend almost any heinous act if you throw flawed argumentative bullshit at it. "Well, you know, the Nazis were just following orders," or "Hey, a lot of those Johnny Rebs were just fighting for states' rights!" or my personal favorite, "Look, Garth Brooks was just not given enough time to develop Chris Gaines [18] as an artistic concept!" Argue till you're blue in the face, Terry, but them are still shitty things no matter how you spin it (and then someone will hate you for being a blue person, and you can maybe get why racism sucks).

In order to get where we're going (progress), we must know whence we came (buncha old shitty white people who *didn't want to pay taxes* or pay for the labor of thousands of Africans who would manifest the goddamn destiny that the white folk had prayed to the Lord about). Before we had the Internet, before we had twenty-four-hour news channels—hell, before we had TV and radio—every form of communication was

18. It's heritage, not shitty music!

hearsay; even the written word was often just opinions, because without video or photographic evidence to dispute your claim, hell, back in them days you could just throw shit at a wall and call it a fact. (See: the Bible.) It's very easy for folklore to be adopted as cold, hard truth when you lack the education to see otherwise. And that's really the problem here: a lack of education.

A large majority of old Southern white folks who are still kicking it today grew up either during or at the tail end of the Great Depression.[19] This was a time when rural folks had no choice but to drop out of school and work the fields for their maw and paw—and we ain't talking college, we're talking elementary school. There weren't any laws against it back in those days (good ol' days—LOL), and, being honest, even if there was, we don't think it would've rightly mattered to those folks. Nor would it to us in this day and age, really. At the end of the day, starvation trumps conformity.

Children of all walks of life were forced to feed themselves and make sure that the family farm didn't get taken by the bank—a huge responsibility for anyone, but an absolutely insane one to be placed on the back of someone who hadn't even sprouted nut hair yet. From the time their feet hit the floor till the time their ass hit the bed (more than likely shared with six brothers and sisters), they worked for next to nothing just to make sure that every other day they could possibly afford a pot of beans to go with their cornbread and buttermilk. With plowing, picking, shucking, shelling, hulling, hoeing, and tilling, there was no room for education, abstract thought, and, from what can be gathered from old photographs, combing your goddamn hair.

19. **Didn't hit, from what we've heard.**

See, when you're having to steal cardboard from a dumpster to put in the hole of your shoe so that you don't get a blister while you're walking three miles carrying a bushel of corn to the market, algebra don't mean a goddamn thing. That's why we won World War II. Didn't have shit to do with Eisenhower or Patton or a fucking nuclear bomb. You just legitimately had a shit ton of folks who were better off at war. They preferred it. Hell, man, they got food, a place to sleep (albeit a scary one), a little spending cash, and back in those days (again, the good ol' days—LOL), they didn't have to answer to any women. Not sure if you're aware, but that's a poor Southern man's utopia. Once the war was over, for the ones who made it back, that meant coming back home, spending what little of a GI Bill they had on a cheap rancher to raise the baby their wife had while they were overseas (assuming it's theirs—remember, lots of folks didn't grasp math), and then it was right back to working to provide by returning to the workforce with virtually no education. So the cycle repeats itself.

Living paycheck to paycheck to barely scrape by while still being eaten alive by the pride a man has to make life better for his kids is not a breeding ground for opening your mind. You believed what you believed, and, honestly, even if you were open to interpretation on some things, by the time you got home and scarfed down the chicken and beans your wife made, you were too worn out to give a shit.

These are hardworking, salt-of-the-earth people we're talking about here, which is why it's extremely difficult to shit on them for ideologies that swelled up from ignorance. But that's what it is: ignorance. "This is what my daddy told me, and his daddy before him, and his daddy's daddy before that, and goddamn it, that's what I believe!" The Southern man is extremely stubborn. The *uneducated* Southern man (redneck) is almost stubborn beyond repair.

US VERSUS THEM

In a situation where you're basically a survivalist, it seems natural that one would develop an us-versus-them mentality. It's primal. But that doesn't make it right. Hell, we're an evolved species. (We are, dum-dums. It's not up for debate.) And for Christ's sake, we should act like it. The us versus them in question here was obviously (primarily) whites versus blacks. A very large portion of the population in the rural South subscribes to the thought that the abolishment of slavery made us all square. That's *absolutely* ridiculous, but lots of folks believe that.

"Hell, what more do they want from us?"

"We freed them, for God's sake! What more can we do?"

"Right—heard that. *Pffft!*"

Of course, while slavery was technically abolished in 1865, black men were not given the right to vote until five years later (women would have to wait until 1920, if you forgot how we've historically felt about them[20]), but due to Jim Crow laws and other actions put in place by white politicians, African Americans didn't truly receive full voting rights until 1965 (give it up for LBJ, y'all). But sure, racism and oppression basically ended with Abraham Lincoln's John Hancock on the Thirteenth Amendment. Are you shitting us, racist white folk? Goddamn, boy, come on now! But again, to the greater point, do you think that the average rural farmer in the late 1940s knew about any of this shit? No. Like we said, this is before the bombardment of media. Most of these people couldn't even afford a radio, so it really wouldn't have mattered whether or not it was being widely talked about in the world at all. They knew what they knew, and there wasn't much room for growth. "Eat or be eaten." "Get to fighting or get the hell out." "Fuck your freedoms, I've got kids to feed."

20. **Brooms with titties.**

When you work with only one race, live with only one race, mingle with only one race, and get *all* of your information from only *one goddamn race*, it's pretty easy to develop what we call "an ignorant-ass, shitty-as-fuck" bias. And when that's all you pass along to your ignorant-ass kids, you can understand why that becomes a huge societal problem. With the rise of the carny-handed mango man Donald Trump, we've reached the precipice of an anti-intellectual movement what's roots can be traced back firmly to the uneducated man's response to the thing he fears most: something different.

We're very aware of how sexist this next part is going to sound, but hell, we're talking about the goddamn 1940s, 1950s, and 1960s, which were sexist back then: the reason the mamaw's racist origin story (hittin'-ass movie that would be) hasn't really been explored here is because, well, the mamaw was pretty well conditioned to just do as her man said—and if a lot of these snake-handling, Bible-thumping assholes had their way, that would still be the case, and I mean, hell, we'd be willing to hear their arguments on that one. As was pointed out earlier, she didn't even have the right to vote until 1920, so forming an opinion was fairly moot during this period. Fret not, though: the Southern woman is worthy of a chapter all to herself. Mamaws fucking rock.

So again, let us stress: we ain't mad at your mamaw and papaw for saying backward-ass racist shit—ours did too. But we've got to move past this. We've got to stop forgiving things due to ignorance. Once, sure, but if you're not willing to at least *try* to fix your ignorance, well then we got news for ya: you're gonna have to get the fuck out of the way, because in the name of progress and equality (battles that, though slow, we *are* winning), there just ain't any room for that bullshit. Educate yourself. Get out there, man. See the world. Next time someone tells you that the [insert random race of people here] are ruining the country, ask him to name the people of that race who he knows. We'll just about guarantee you that he'll start stuttering.

That's our main problem with race relations: we don't know or give a fuck to know how the other half lives. Meet these people. Hang out with them. Show one ounce of goddamn empathy. Leave your hometown,[21] if only for a while. Read a goddamn book. Education is the only way to bridge the gap between our illogical differences. Even if it's self-education. Quit being a fuck-ass. That goes for us too. We can all be better.

POSITIVE NOTE

Let's try to get out of here on a positive note:

1. Sweet potato pie
2. Casseroles
3. Hand-me-down pocket knives
4. Fishing trips
5. Timeless wisdom
6. A lap to sit on
7. An ear to listen
8. Grilled cheeses
9. A bottomless supply of hard candy
10. Unconditional, unmatched, and undeserved love

Mamaws and papaws are mostly good. Remember the good things. Love your mamaw and papaw. Hold them close because we get them only for a while. But do us and the world a favor: let's grow up to be the grandparents of a new South.

---

21. But come back and holler at some strange on occasion.

Porch Talk with Corey

You get four grandparents if you're lucky. Due to divorces, remarriages, and a plethora of other family squabbles, I ended up with about seven of 'em. By age six, that number was down to four. Of those four, I liked only three—two of which were actually related to me, and one of those two wasn't really ever around, but we idolized him anyways. That was Papaw Larry, one of those "local mafia" types. Rumor has it that he used to work for the teamsters and would frequently tote Jimmy Hoffa around when he was in town on business. One night, right outside the Georgia line in Alabama, he took a bullet to the belly while trying to steal an air conditioner out of someone's window. Legend goes that he drove himself nearly an hour, while bleeding, to his veterinarian buddy's house, where the vet performed unassisted emergency surgery on him so as to avoid interaction with the law. They couldn't get out the bullet. Papaw let me touch it once.

The only truly good thing ever came out of him was my momma and her siblings. I mentioned earlier that there was one grandparent I didn't particularly care for—well, Larry married her. I know it sounds awful to talk about your mamaw and papaw like that, but you gotta understand that those titles carry weight with them, and if you ain't able to lift it, you don't get the honor.

When my momma was a very little girl, Papaw Larry and Nanny Trish decided to give her up. Neither of them wanted the responsibility or burden that came along with raising a child, and I am more than certain that the great state of Georgia probably agreed that, due to the red-carpet-length rap sheet my papaw had going at the time, it was probably the best move for all parties involved. Luckily for them, for my momma—and hell, for the world—Papaw had a mother named Edna—Granny Bain, as she would come to be known.

Edna Arlene Bain (maiden name, Edna Arlene Potter) was born on July 21, 1920, the daughter of a poor sharecropper named Charlie Potter and his wife, Mattie McDaniel Potter (who lived her life with a case of the vapors), in the rolling hills of northwest Georgia. As the youngest girl in a family of eight (Edna, Mack, Charles, Netty, Gordon, Marvin, Irene, and Frank), she had to, like her brothers and sisters before her, put aside her own interests for the betterment of the family due to the backlash of the Great Depression. This meant dropping out of school as early as sixth grade in order to dedicate the brunt of their childhoods to working the fields with Papa.

She had a tough life, but she was without a doubt the happiest person I have ever met. I suppose when you've lived a life full of heartache and grief, when you make it out alive, you're just happy to be here. When I was a kid, Granny took care of me when Momma and Daddy were at work. This was not a burden on her, and it certainly didn't upset me, neither. I never wanted to leave. We would spend the mornings watching *The Price Is Right*. Once a week, I would watch it at the beauty shop while Miss Vickie perfected every inch of Granny's beehive. It was a modern marvel. The afternoons would be spent on the porch—our sanctuary. We would break beans, shuck corn, drink bottled Coke, and play yella car. Yella car's a game where you point out yellow cars as they drive by. First one to shout out "Yella car!" gets a point. That's all there is to it. I used to think that I was just a lot quicker than Granny. Seems I always won.

Between watching the Atlanta Braves and the Grand Ole Opry, our evenings were spent in front of her television (which sat on top of her old television—Foxworthy nailed that one). Between innings, I would stand in the corner of the room, and Granny would throw me ground balls from her blue recliner. Don't worry, it was a Nerf ball. I would field the balls and zip them back to her as quick as I could. She'd laugh and call me Chipper Jones—which always made her dog perk up on account of that was his name.

Green beans, cornbread, mashed potatoes, hominy, creamed corn, mac and cheese, lemon icebox pie, and grilled cheeses—she'd make all of this at the drop of a hat anytime I wanted it (all the time). Granny made the best grilled cheese in the world. She would put a slice of tomato on it and her signature touch: bread-and-butter pickles. Sounds odd, but you owe it to your life to try it.

Granny used to always tell me that when I got older I wouldn't want to spend as much time with her. She was wrong, and I know she was glad of that. When I got my driver's license, the thing that excited me the most was that I didn't have to rely on Momma to take me to Granny's anymore. The first trip I made in my truck was over to Granny's house to show it off. We then went to get a hamburger and a milkshake. She was the best date.

As the years went on, my visits with Granny never ceased and were always my favorite part of the week—more often than not, several times a week. Eventually her mind started to go, and my visits became a bit easier because she moved in with us. That was bittersweet. It's very tough to see your favorite person dealing with such a horrid disease, but boy, what a blessing to have her in the same house. I no longer had to drive to share my biscuits and gravy with her; I just had to walk her to the table. As it goes, though, she got progressively worse and had to be moved to a nursing home. She needed twenty-four-hour care, and we couldn't provide it. A million thank-yous to the fine folk at NHC Healthcare in Fort Oglethorpe, Georgia, for the care they showed my sweet granny in her final years. It meant and still means the world to me.

My last visit with Granny was tough. On June 21, 2016, around one thirty in the afternoon, my sweet Granny Bain took her last breath. I was there. And I saw it.

Momma had just come in from seeing her and told me that

she was stable and that the doctors said she would most likely hang on for a few more days. It's not that I didn't believe her—I just had a funny feeling. I hopped in my truck and hauled ass down the road. I had been with her the day before and most every day for the previous few weeks, so I was not driving out of guilt or desperation; I was a damn good grandson. I just had a strange feeling. Me and Granny had a bond like that.

I got there, and Granny was like she had been for the past week or so: lying in bed, unresponsive, and with her eyes half-closed. Or half-open, to all you silly positive people. (Hope is a lie. Accept it!) I had already come to terms that even though my grandmother was still alive, I would never speak to her again. I would never hear that sweet laugh. I would never hear my favorite words: "You sure are a purty thang!" That's what she said to me nearly every time she saw me. She's the only woman who ever meant it.

I walked into her room right as the hospice nurse was administering another dose of morphine. (Ain't gonna lie: that's the first time I've been jealous of a dying ninety-five-year-old.)

As I said, Granny was unresponsive, *but*, as much of a "man of science" that I am, I was raised Baptist, and I still have some leftover spirituality harbored inside me somewhere, so for some reason, I still maintained that somewhere in there she could hear me.

Her mind had been gone for a while, so she would forget most everything I told her. It had been a difficult past few months because my career had been taking off, and there was no one I wanted to share that with more than her. This was, in my opinion, my last chance.

I sat at the foot of her bed and told her everything. How great the tour was going, how I was able to eat at actual restaurants now, how my girlfriend wasn't supporting a worthless loser anymore (now a worth-*something* loser). Hell, I told her some things I can't tell y'all. I broke the fuck out of some nondisclosure agreements. So sue me! (No dear God, please don't, I'm bullshitting. I'm grieving. My granny just died. Show some compassion, you heartless Hollywood lizards!)

Granny's breathing started to get a bit more labored. The nurse came in and told me that her oxygen was down to about 75 percent, but she felt sure that she was okay for now. I don't know why, but I still didn't believe her.

I told the nurse to leave us alone.

I walked over to the side of the bed, and I took my Granny's hand. After I cried the hardest tears of my life for about five minutes, I leaned into her ear and said, "Granny, it's Corey. I love you."

My Granny had not moved in a week aside from the nurses flipping her over to prevent bedsores; she had also not opened her eyes fully. When the words "I love you" left my mouth, I swear to you my Granny tilted her head just slightly, and her eyes flickered at me. I lost it.

I looked at her once more and said, "Granny, this is Corey. I love you, and it's okay if you go now."

She took one breath and died.

That's something I thought happened only in the movies, but it's true. It's a real thing. My grandmother was waiting on me. She needed to know it was okay. She needed to know that I was okay. I am not, yet I am.

The legacy that my grandmother left me is not unlike the legacy left behind by most of our great older Southern gals: love, work, and smile as hard as you can. You ain't got control over the rest.

We were writing this chapter when my grandmother passed. It made it difficult, but more so than that, it was cathartic, and I really needed to do it. Perhaps she somehow knew that. Perhaps that was her last gift. I will miss you, Granny Bain. You are my angel.

6

Pickin' and Spinnin'

Country, Southern rock, gospel, bluegrass, blues, jazz, hip hop, soul, R&B.[1] The South has an impressive footprint in the history of music. We invented or perfected a lot of types of music. We jam, we croon, we pick, and we grin. We rap, we beat, we wail, and we spin. We do it all, and we do it all well.

A simple chapter on our region's musical history cannot possibly do it justice. Entire books can be written about each genre. Hell, legendary country music institution the Carter Family has inspired at least nine books alone.[2] We ain't gonna cover it all—we can't. What we can do is pay homage to the Southern beginnings of some of the

I. Yes, soul and R&B. Fame Recording Studios in Muscle Shoals, Alabama, which we will get to, is responsible for some of the most famous soul and R&B music in the world.

2. We Googled this and stopped countin' at nine.

world's greatest music and discuss why it is we seem to make such good, unique music down here.

Music is one the most mysterious activities that humans enjoy. Seriously. Scientists still aren't super sure why the brain responds the way it does to music, but they've figured out that it does so from the same parts of the brain that respond to sex and food (believe the scientific term is the "hit center"). Sex and food are necessary for our survival. Perhaps music is too. We're gonna say yes. Music brings people together, makes 'em dance, can move you to tears, and, according to some Republicans, can even incite people to commit crimes.[3] It's a true force. We love it. Like, a lot. When we're on tour, one of our favorite things to do is go to concerts and music festivals on our off nights. Trae and Drew saw singer-songwriter Chris Knight[4] together in a tiny bar with about twenty other people—one of the best concerts they've ever been to. Both cried. (Nah, shut up! We just *got something in our eyes!*[5]) This year, Corey and Drew went to the Bonnaroo Music and Arts Festival together. There were tears there too, but it was mostly over all the beautiful hippies runnin' around naked.

Music is one of the best things on the whole damn planet. What else is that much fun and don't make you wake up hungover or ruin your marriage? There's nothing like music. Let's talk about how we do it in the South.

3. "I'm sick of people blaming economic and social factors for crime in black communities." And in the next breath, they say, "Eminem and Marilyn Manson are to blame for these school shootings."

4. Country music—the real kind. Ort be famous. Look up "Down the River."

5. And that something was *raw emotion.*

COUNTRY

Any talk of Southern music, in our minds, begins and ends with country music. There's a lot of talk over what is "real" country these days. Real country is any music that makes you wanna cry over a lover whilst fist-fightin' your cousin.[6] It may not be the most important or best, though arguments can be made, but it is the most visible and most viewed by the world as "Southern music." Country evolved from folk, blues, and western-style music in the southeastern United States—specifically Appalachia.[7] In fact, it was originally called hillbilly music, named after the region's people.[8]

Those people, the hillbillies, were white, proud, working-class Appalachians whose ancestors had brought with them culture, religion, a "fuck-the-man" attitude, and from-the-soul music.[9] Traditional Irish and Scottish musical structure got morphed, blended, twisted, and integrated into folk ballads, and the rest is sweet, sad musical history. Heading to Atlanta for work, Appalachian musicians took their instruments with them and played in bars and clubs as a way to make money. A few enterprising promoters and record companies later, the sound of the South was born, sometime in the early 1920s.[10]

In 1925 the Grand Ole Opry, a weekly musical show that would become an institution in the South, started airing on the radio in Nashville. Back then, for rural Southerners especially, the radio was a window into worlds they could not experience otherwise, and into the

6. It includes other stuff too, but this is accurate.

7. It's pronounced "Ap-uh-latch-uh."

8. This was a way better name.

9. Sounds like some cool cats to us.

10. Relax, historians. We're close to right.

Porch Talk with Drew

BONNAROO

One of the biggest music festivals in the world takes place in my home state of Tennessee, less than two hours from where I grew up. Bonnaroo, a four-day, multiple-stage festival spread out over an old farm in Manchester, Tennessee, has been an annual tradition for the last fifteen years. I have been there five times and always have a blast.

Some people shy away from festivals where there's camping, "for dirty hippies," they say. Thing is, I like dirty hippies. I've never been around more sincere or unafraid-to-be-themselves white folk than any group referred to as dirty hippies. They talk about love, music, the earth, oneness—and, if you can suffer through all that sophomore-year sustainability talk, they will share their drugs with you. Hits.

I really like dirty hippies. I got one to share her life with me. (Side note on "smelly" women: we're all animals, and there's something primal about a woman what ain't bathed. Pheromones are like titties for your nose—they get ya goin'. I recommend everyone get down and dirty with a dirty hippie at least once.) Her name is Andi, and she's the best damn dirty hippie of all time.

We truly fell for each other at Bonnaroo. The heat, the partying, four nights in a small tent, all the music, and enjoying each other's company the whole time—it became clear to me that we could hang out together forever. We've been back to Bonnaroo many times since, and each year has its own special memory.

What's special about Bonnaroo is that (a) you cannot possibly experience all the acts because of overlapping sets, heat exhaustion, and gettin' too turnt, and (b) by essentially living there for four days, it becomes home. So you cannot plan to see everyone you want to see, and you cannot leave. You lose yourself a bit, but in the best way.

The first year we dated, Andi dragged me to see an at-the-time unheard-of band out of North Carolina called the Avett Brothers. I discovered them in the realest, most organic way: I went to a field with three hundred strangers and just watched and listened. Me and her danced our hearts out. The Avetts went on to sell out arenas as one of the biggest bands in the world. They've remained a favorite of ours. That's another good thing about dirty hippies: they know about cool bands early on. But not in an annoying hipster way.

One year, Andi got sick at the main stage waiting on Kanye West to start. He was late. Very late. And we were tired. She lost her lunch, chugged some water, and rallied so we could dance to everyone's favorite musical villain genius. We've seen Radiohead, Metallica, Elton John, an amazing and weird set by South African freak rappers Die Antwoord. We've danced at the Silent Disco tent (imagine hundreds of people dancing their asses off in silence—the DJ plays music people listen to on wireless headphones) and laughed at the comedy tent back before I had the guts to admit that stand-up is what I wanted to do for a living. We've stayed up all night for late-night sets and passed out in the cinema tent, only to wake up in a haze realizing we'd missed a band we wanted to see. It never gets old, and the excitement never fades. Sittin' in the traffic waitin' to get in, we always feel like something special is going to happen there, and it always does.

Some years, because of scheduling and expense, we've gone without each other. I chuckled to myself on the last solo trip, thinking I smelled a dirty hippie and wondering if Andi had somehow made the trip to surprise me. I looked around, only to realize that I'd just smelled myself.

DM

Porch Talk with Corey

SLAMMIN' SAMMY

One time, me and several buddies decided to get supremely drunk and go to a Sammy Kershaw concert. We decided that often, but on this particular night, Slammin' Sammy was actually in town. Kershaw's voice is authentic and unapologetically honky-tonk. I don't know what it is, but I swear on my life that whenever "Queen of My Double Wide Trailer" comes on, my throat gets just a skoach wider, and the beer runs down it quicker than a trailer baby rolling down a hill of poke salad[11] after a rain. (We'd love to sing this one at your wedding if you'd have us.)

Country music is absolutely as much of a feeling as it is a sound. Anyone can pay someone to add a little steel guitar to his or her track, but if that shit ain't authentic, a true country fan can spot it a mile away. Ain't nothing not country about Slammin' Sammy Kershaw. He is from the bayou, gets piss drunk on shit beer, and in accordance with the rules of 1990s country music, he used to bang country singer Lorrie Morgan. All us in my hometown have always loved Sammy. There were zero farm parties that didn't have someone doing a rendition of Sammy's "Vidalia" acoustic; he was our absolute favorite to try to imitate because of how fun it is to try to sound how goddamn country he just naturally is. He sounds like a grizzly bear farting through a bicycle horn. Twang for days.

No good Southern concert would be without someone smuggling moonshine in some way or another. (This time it

---

11. Also known as *poke sallet* and *pokeweed,* this is a wild leafy plant that grows all over the South. It's poisonous, but you can eat the leaves if you boil them long enough. You can eat kudzu too.

was twenty-ounce water bottles full of booze hidden in the bras of the two girls with the biggest titties. Hits.) Our drunkenness grew exponentially as the night went on. So did the hollering.

There was a lady running around the front of the stage the whole time with a VIP necklace badge on holding a rag. 'Bout every second song, Sammy would lean down, and she'd run over and wipe the sweat off of his very leathery and furrowed sweaty-ass drunken brow. I let this go on for a while, just watching, and after proceeding to get even more drunk, decided that this lady needed a break. I went up to her and said, "Hey! Give me the rag!" She did. At the time, I assumed it was because I was charming; looking back, it was probably because at the time I was a six-foot-tall, 240-pound sweaty beast yelling drunkenly at her. But either way, I got the Kershaw rag.

I went down front, and as Sammy was leaning in to a guitar riff on one of his chart toppers, I wiped the sweat off of his brow. He looked up and gave me a wink and a thumbs-up. That was the greatest thing that had ever happened to me.

I took the rag back to my friends, and you ain't ever seen a group of more jealous rednecks. These are guys who could never in public admit that another man was attractive, on account of how firmly they clung to their heterosexuality, yet they wanted to touch the Sammy rag stat. That's music to a Southerner. Sammy wasn't just a sweaty drunken dude—he was a country music god, and this cloth held the perspiration of a man bigger than all of us: Sammy fucking Kershaw.

Night went on, and we got drunker, and the rag kept getting passed around. Eventually we lost it, as drunks are wont to do. If I had held on to it, it would be framed and hanging on the wall in my office right now: "That's Sammy Fucking Kershaw's sweat rag." Long live real country music.

best country music of the day. A North Carolina tobacco farmhand traveling to Nashville in the 1920s for a concert would be like us takin' a plane to China today to eat a dumplin'—technically possible, sure, and Corey would wanna do it, but it ain't practical. In a time when no one had cars, they also didn't have vacation pay. Or interstates. So trips were out of the question, movies weren't available in rural areas, and some people were trying to make beer illegal. Trust us when we say the radio was the easiest way to escape.

The Opry has now been around for almost a century and has hosted some of the most talented and famous musicians in the world in country music, western music, [12] and bluegrass. Though these genres maintained distinct features and stars, their blending created a new culture of people and music that would come to be referred to as "country."

Over the years, the music would evolve and become many different things to many different people. Outlaw country, [13] pop country, Garth Brooks creating what we call arena country, giving way to country with more rock 'n' roll elements—it all began with hillbilly music. It's become a phenomenon, and now Nashville, with its recording industry, stands as one of the longest-running, most famous "industry cities" in entertainment. Paris has fashion, Los Angeles has movies, New York has Broadway, and Nashville has country.

When done well, country is some of the best music around. It's pertinent, and often devastating. You ever been halfway through your

---

12. Western swing, honky-tonk, and Oklahoma and Texas cowboy music, and years later the Bakersfield sound, would come from outside the South to heavily influence what is known as country music today. We don't focus on these histories here, as they're not part of our story. But they're a part of country music's story, so it ort be mentioned.

13. Our favorite.

fourth or fifth beer, burger finished, with empty thoughts and a full belly, and George Jones's "He Stopped Loving Her Today" comes on? The ol' Possum's voice comes through. Rich and deliberate. The beer suddenly tastes better. The buzz you got going gets deeper, and so does the profound sadness lodged firmly in the furthest reaches of your soul. But ya know, in a hittin' way.

The pain in that voice—the solitude, the depths of loneliness—it's all real and heavy. The protagonist of the song dies alone. He's been alone for years. You can hear it in George's voice. He tells it all. And whether you've had a good day or a bad day—whether you feel okay with how ya life is going or you been thinking a little too much lately about warshin' your mouth out with a revolver—something about the fact that the damn song exists and the guy in it loved that lady his whole life makes you feel more resolved. Shew, goddamn! We need a beer.

Country Music Playlist

1. "Fancy"—Reba. If you need her last name, then you need to go back to school and learn somethin'. We will take some liberties with the definition of country music on this list, but "Fancy" ain't one of those examples. It's a song about a young girl goin' from abject poverty to bein' a diplomat's wife—through prostitution (which her momma sold her into). Y'all, if that ain't country, I'll kiss your ass.

2. "Just Let Go"—Sturgill Simpson. In the current climate of "drinkin'-all-the-beers" and "America-kickin'-the-world's-ass" country music, a song about tryin' to kill your ego is good fuckin' medicine. Sturgill Simpson for president.

3. "Elephant"—Jason Isbell. If Simpson is our preference for president, then we want Isbell to be king. A lot of his music is categorized as something other than country, and that's okay, but for us, this song about death and alcoholism and cancer has everything a country song needs, and Lord, it hits. It's devastating.

4. "Jolene"—Dolly. Try to find a Southern woman what don't identify with this song. Just try.

5. "If You're Gonna Be Dumb, You Gotta Be Tough"—Roger Alan Wade. It's all in the title, really. Hits.

6. "Highwayman"—The Highwaymen. Waylon, Willie, Johnny, and Kris got together, formed a supergroup, and sang a song about the death and reincarnation of a man on a horse, sailin' the seas, building giant dams, and riding a spaceship through the universe. Johnny and Waylon are gone. If we had a time machine, this is the one concert we'd have to go see.

7. "Burn.Flicker.Die"—American Aquarium. We've been American Aquarium fans for a long time now. We've seen 'em in tiny bars with almost no people, at festivals, and now in larger venues as they grow in popularity. No song captures pursuing a life in music (or entertainment in general) quite like this one.

8. "Joey's Arm"—Sons of Bill. The Sons of Bill are the sons of a University of Virginia English professor, and this song opens with a line about Joey's arm having only two tattoos: the rebel flag and one that says "Born to Lose." *Skew*. Hits.

BLUEGRASS

Bluegrass music, most recognized probably by the rolling twang of a banjo and the high, lonesome vocals to match, is decidedly Southern. Like country music, its origins are mainly Appalachian. The mountain folk whose people came from Ireland, Scotland, and England carried on traditions of jigs, reels, and ballads. The "bluegrass ballad," a common type of bluegrass song, is essentially just poor white people being sad, set to music. Many of these songs originated as folk ballads from the motherland and got a mountain twist put on 'em by the folk in Tennessee, Virginia, North Carolina, and Kentucky.

Now, you could reread that last paragraph and replace "bluegrass" with "country," and it would still make some sense. Country music and bluegrass have similar beginnings and have been confused many times by ignorant Yankees and even some radio programmers. Who could blame 'em? As we said, it's mostly white folk being sad, set to music.

Well, a key difference is, of course, instrumentation (banjo), but a main distinction is the way bluegrass often features melody "breakdowns" where musicians take turns improvising the melody on their respective instruments. This practice was adopted from jazz music—in this way, African and Southern black music traditions have influenced bluegrass music to make it what it is today. Bluegrass isn't as old as it seems (it's often called old-time music); bluegrass got its name from the band the Bluegrass Boys, formed by the father of bluegrass, Bill Monroe, in 1939.

Some people don't like bluegrass. The main gripe always seems to be that the banjo sounds "like a cat dying from throat cancer who hates everyone and is also crying." Well, fuck those people. Bluegrass uses washboards, moonshine jars, and goddamn *spoons* as instruments, so them naysayers can go plum smooth to hell.[14]

Bluegrass Playlist

1. **"Foggy Mountain Breakdown"—Flatt and Scruggs.** The quintessential bluegrass song from the quintessential bluegrass group.

2. **"Rocky Top."** Best fight song in the country. Go, Vols.

3. **"Uncle Pen"—Bill Monroe.** The originator of the name and the genre, Bill Monroe crushes. This song is one he wrote about his uncle and musical mentor Pendleton Vandiver. Honoring the past is a Southern thing.

4. **"Cumberland River"—Dailey and Vincent.** This is Trae's personal

---

14. If you came down here to this footnote to read an apology or some sort of backtracking, well, we tricked ya. We meant it. Fuck those people.

favorite bluegrass song for a lot of reasons, the least of which is not that it mentions his hometown of Celina, Tennessee.

5. "Wait So Long"—Trampled by Turtles. Modern bluegrass outfit what ain't from the South, but we had to put 'em on the list because this song just crushes.

6. "O Death"—Dr. Ralph Stanley. The Stanley brothers are iconic. Carter Stanley passed in 1966, and his brother would go on to win Grammys, become an ambassador to a culture and music, and write "O Death" before leaving this world fifty years later.

GOSPEL

Gospel music emerged in the South from Negro spirituals and slave work songs. Good-hearted slave owners would set aside time for their workers to create music and have a space to express their inner turmoil through song. LOL. JK. Those fuckin' assholes were the worst. *They owned humans!* What happened was that some slave owners were so far down the hypocritical rabbit hole they thought it was their Christian duty to convert their slaves to their religion (but not, like, never rape them or anything). After converting them, they had to allow 'em to worship on their own because "Ew, gross, we can't pray with the blacks. Heaven is segregated, don't you know!"[15, 16] Left on their own for very brief periods of time to

---

15. Direct quote, we assume.

16. We have generalized here. Some slaves weren't allowed to worship or congregate at all. Others had slave owners who actively tried to discourage Christianity among them because they were afraid that bible stories like Moses leading his people *out of slavery* might inspire the wrong kind of Christlike behavior. As despicable as that is, at least these owners were honest about how awful they were rather than pretending to care about black folks' souls.

socialize, congregate, and worship as they wished (unless they wished to do so as not-slaves, of course), these enslaved black people created worship music that adhered to their own traditions and musical sensibilities. Gospel evolved from this tradition as well as slave work songs. This was the only other time slaves could sing—when working—presumably because the owners thought that besides propping up the entire Southern economy, their slaves should also entertain them. The rhythm of the songs made the grueling work perhaps more tolerable and efficient. Slaves sang to escape the mental anguish of slavery, and they sang in codes to plan escapes and communicate other messages. This history is sad and awful, but it's also a beautiful testament to the unyielding will of the human spirit. Sorry to be corny, and please don't think we're being flip, but art created from oppression is always the best and most inspiring.[17] Which brings us to our next genre.

Gospel/Hymn Playlist

The gospel playlist is just gonna be a list of our favorite songs without particular artists, as most of them have a million versions and adaptations; sort of the point of modern gospel (other than, of course, spreading the gospel of Jesus) is that any choir or band can take the hymns and add their own take. Any version of these will probably hit—bluegrass or black church choir ones are our recommendation.

1. "Wayfaring Stranger"
2. "I'll Fly Away"
3. "By the Mark"
4. "Do Lord"
5. "Amazing Grace"

17. We ain't sayin' slavery was worth it or anything. Lord God, no.

6. "Down to the River to Pray"

7. "Shall We Gather at the River"

8. "I Saw the Light"

9. "At the Cross"

BLUES

Do we really need to tell y'all what the blues is? It's a type of music what comes from the depths of a black person's soul living in the Deep South in the 1920s, when being a black person in the Deep South was at the very least . . . *difficult*. At its most basic level, the blues is music about that experience. Singers repeat lines, telling their personal troubles and how "blue" they feel, while playing blue notes that sound like the guitar or piano is crying. We looked up "blue notes" to try to define them, and, well, like a lot of hittin' things, they're tough to describe. Basically, it's a note sung or played slightly lower than expected,[18] and that by being lower, just sounds fuckin' sad.

Blues riffs gave us B. B. King, the Rolling Stones, and hell, rock 'n' roll as we know it. It's the foundation, musically, upon which a whole lot of music was built. Listening to it makes you feel sad, and then somehow better. It's kinda like exercise for your soul: it feels bad, but then you feel better after. Of course, you can't drink and cry while exercising.[19] So it's way better than exercising.

18. Expected by whatever part of your human brain that expects notes to sound a certain way—look, we told you music is wild as hell. We don't know why your brain "expects" notes to sound a certain way, just like we don't why restaurant managers expect us to wear shirts. Life's mysteries.

19. Corey claims you can but offered no proof other than repeating, "That fuckin' treadmill was *all she left.*"

SOUL

Soul music, which came from R&B, was created by American black folk. Its beginnings probably owe as much if not more to the North region of the country as the South. The soul music that was coming out of Detroit and Chicago[20] is the most famous and well documented.

However, Memphis had its own influence on the genre with Stax Records, which was the recording home of Georgia native Otis Redding—maybe you've heard of him.[21] He also recorded at Muscle Shoals's Fame Recording Studios. There, and later at Muscle Shoals Sound Studios (founded in 1969 by the original Fame musicians), some of the most famous soul and R&B albums ever produced were recorded. Aretha Franklin made records there, as did Wilson Pickett. So while Motown may be the heart of the genre, and Chicago may get the (well-deserved) credit for being where soul and R&B singers were discovered, the South is where a lot of them came to make the records.

SOUTHERN HIP HOP

Rap, or hip hop, was not invented in the South, but we have put our own spin and imprint on it. Southern rap music—most prominently that coming out of Atlanta—has its own place in the hip hop world.

Atlanta rap specifically has put its mark on the national scene. In 1995 André 3000 of Outkast began and ended his now famous acceptance speech at the Source Awards with the phrase "South got something to say." He proved to be prophetic. Atlanta, once an outsider in the rap game, is now an epicenter for the genre, producing as many if not

20. Which also had a heavy influence on the blues.

21. You been livin' under a rock?

REDNECKS AND RAP

★

Yes, we're huge hip hop fans. Always have been.

"But yun's say you're country folk?"

Absolutely.

"Do what now?"

It's actually really easy to understand. See, our moms and dads had the 1960s, and outlaw country, and the greatest rock 'n' roll band of all time, Lynyrd by God Skynyrd (don't dispute us) to speak to them and their plight and their feelings and perspectives. Johnny Cash was making country music with Kris Kristofferson when our parents were coming up; of course, they leaned in to it.

We, on the other hand, had nineties country as kids. While it was chock-full of some amazing artists (Garth Brooks, anyone?), it was a decidedly different tone. Then that gave way to whatever the hell started in the 2000s, where every single song was about a truck at the river with beer and havin' a good time, and, well, we sort of checked out.

See, when you're a teenager growing up in a trailer as Trae did, or with a drug-selling brother as Drew did, and/or you're too poor to afford a truck, and songs about drinkin' in your truck by the river don't appeal to you that much because last time you partied at the river everyone was gettin' fucked up on pills, and two boys nearly drowned because they were so high they fell in and there wasn't a damn thing fun about it, that manufactured and manicured "beer-truck-farm" bullshit don't appeal to you that much. Sure, you may listen to it in your car when you're in a good mood, but sometimes you need music that speaks to the darker and realer shit in your life.

Well, that wasn't happening in country. And *most* people our age where we're from love rap for this exact reason.

Only rap was talkin' about what was real. Sure, we maybe never seen crack in our life, but "trap music" (loosely defined as rap about sellin' drugs) sure does paint a *similar* picture to what it's like to have friends who sell meth or pills. When rappers talk about the projects and wanting to get the hell out, as a kid in a small, jobless, prospectless town, we sure identified more with those songs[22] than the ones where the guy in the video owns a work truck that ain't never been worked out of.

Also the songs about big ol' booties; them spoke to us too. So we gravitated toward rap, and rappers.

22. We ain't even a little trying to compare rural poverty to urban and/or black issues. We're simply acknowledging that rap music speaks to redneck kids too.

more hits, new acts, and new producers than anywhere else. Memphis (Three 6 Mafia) and New Orleans (seems like folk sometimes forget Lil Wayne is from there) are also big-time players. Run the Jewels's last album was one of the best in years, of any genre, and one half of that duo (Killer Mike) is from Atlanta.

We can't say this enough: we fuckin' love rap. For reasons covered above, we identified with it growing up. Plus, like so much black American music, it *hits* so fuckin' hard. There's little in the world as satisfying as a great rap song addressed to one's haters. Is that one of the whitest sentences ever written? Absolutely. But it's true.

Hip Hop Playlist

1. **"Rosa Parks"—Outkast.** This is just one of many Outkast songs that we coulda mentioned. It made our list because it references the

civil rights icon from Alabama, has one of André 3000's best verses of all time, and has that harmonica-led, handclap blues breakdown at the end that sounds like something out of the 1930s Deep South. Beautiful.

2. **"Close Your Eyes (And Count to Fuck)"—Run the Jewels.** The album is an instant classic, and this song crushes from top to bottom. Killer Mike is the anchor of the duo and since he's from Atlanta, we count them as a Southern group.

3. **"Shot You Down"—Isaiah Rashad.** Chattanooga's own signed with Kendrick Lamar's label and immediately dropped this gem. The theme is heavy on self-reliance, risin' above your surroundings, and celebratin' your own success—what's more Southern than that?

4. **"King of the South"—Big K.R.I.T.** How was a song that opens "Grew up on the country side of town . . ." not gonna make the playlist? You already know.

5. **"It's Hard out Here for a Pimp"—Three 6 Mafia.** Tennessee's most famous rap group, Three 6 won the Oscar for this song on the soundtrack of the 2005 movie *Hustle & Flow*. They did this before Leo or Scorsese won theirs. These are the same people who made "Slob on My Knob" and "Sippin' on Some Syrup." They, those people, won an Oscar . . . and it was *fucking beautiful*.

JAZZ

Jazz is difficult to define as a genre, which is sort of its charm. Spanning over a century, the music is loosely described as an improvised swing-note song with polyrhythms and syncopation.[23] Its beginnings are traced back to one of the South's crown jewels: New Orleans.

---

23. **Hope that clears it up.**

There the black musician community created a musical genre that has shaped the very culture of that city and is still one of its most important and highly celebrated facets. We *absolutely love* New Orleans, and the music is a big part of it. Yes, we'd be lying if we acted like we were big jazz fans or aficionados. We ain't. This is probably because growing up, our main interaction with it was a watered-down commercial[24] version of the music what was in elevators at hotels we couldn't afford and just awful. The only other experience we had with it is that phase of Drew's sophomore year when he quoted Marx and pretended to like it.[25] So it never really took with us.

But not mentioning jazz as an awesome and soulful product of the South would be wrong. Like the blues, jazz was invented and cultivated in the earlier stages entirely by black American musicians who were the direct descendants of slaves who had brought with them their own respective religions, music, and traditions. In New Orleans, these traditions melded into a rhythmic and improv style of music all its own. We can't say enough how proud the South should be of this one-of-a-kind genre of music. Of course, like so many things in the South, that pride must be accompanied by a dose of humility (and even shame) at the same time. Slavery, of course, created the situation in which the people who made this music, as well as the blues—and then, by extension (arguably), American rock 'n' roll—came together. We could say black Americans were the genesis for nearly every major—or perhaps *every* major—musical industry/genre in the United States.[26]

24. Read: white.

25. Embarrassing, sure, but he says the ladies dug it.

26. Probably not heavy metal and not really country music, though indirectly even there the connection exists (and country musicians would "cover" R&B tunes sometimes without giving any credit or money).

SOUTHERN ROCK

A brief history of Southern rock: Lynyrd Skynyrd. The end.

Southern Rock Playlist

1. **"Simple Man"—Lynyrd Skynyrd**. Drew's momma used to sing him to sleep with this song. It's amazing.

2. **"The Southern Thing"—Drive-By Truckers**. Lord God, sweet baby Jesus, this song hits. Nothing captures the pride and shame of the South like this song. It's angry and sad at the same time, arrogant and humble. It's the "duality of the Southern thing."

3. **"Joe's Head"—Kings of Leon**. Back before the arenas and the rehabs and the model wives, before they went pop rock, and then country, the Kings were just a family of red-ass kids who'd grown up in Oklahoma and Tennessee. This song is from that time, and it's about catchin' a man with your woman and killin' 'em both. Skew!

4. **"Ramblin' Man"—Allman Brothers Band**. There's some contention that the Allman Brothers were simply a rock band. Either way, this song has a Southern twang and an outlook that's steeped heavily in their northern Florida (aka the South) roots. Get drunk and dance to it.

5. **"The Ballad of Curtis Loew"—Lynyrd Skynyrd**. What? You thought we'd say "Freebird"? This track is about a black blues musician the protagonist's parents don't want him hangin' out with, but he does anyway. Blues, race relations, his momma whuppin' him, and breakin' rules—this song is Southern as shit.

WHY IS IT SO-OOO GOOD?

The South has made some of the best music in the world, and we've barely even covered it. Other regions make great music too, of course. But we've put a hell of a stamp on the art form. Is there something special about the South that makes it so good at music? Yes. Southerners are special. Are we more musically inclined than other places for any specific reason(s)? Perhaps . . .

Church

In the more religious cultures of the South (which is to say all of them), you ain't really allowed to have a lot of fun. Drinkin' is wrong, sex other than on a strict schedule with your spouse with the lights off is wrong, drugs is definitely wrong, and if you think too much on it, you'll believe fun is wrong.

But most churches have music.[27] A piano sometimes, perhaps a band, almost always a choir—church music has always been the one place Christians have been allowed to let loose, be free, and not worry what some self-righteous asshat says God thinks about it. Aretha Franklin sang in church before becoming a superstar. So did Hank Williams. Can you imagine a service ending with one of them singing at the end? We might consider gettin' up early on Sunday and going if those were the usual acts.

Elvis and James Brown also sang in church. So did Whitney Houston. Al Green. Ol' Georgia boy Ray Charles? Yup, church. Turns out, when you got a large population of people who are pent up, held back, and someone's controlling their behavior, but they have one specific outlet through which they're allowed to express themselves judgment free, real magic happens. It's almost as if the inability to live free in life because of all of the church's dumbass rules makes the art better. On that note . . .[28]

27. There are some exceptions. Some churches think music is the devil's doin'. This is absolutely the worst argument for not worshipping the devil we've ever heard of.

28. Get it? Like a musical note. LOL, we're professional comedians.

Porch Talk with Drew
LYNYRD SKYNYRD

When I was a kid, the *only* band my father would listen to was Lynyrd Skynyrd. That's just how it was.

What we said about them being the entirety of the history of Southern rock is how it feels: true. I do fuckin' love the Drive-By Truckers, though, and in college I was obsessed with Kings of Leon. Both them bands are pretty Southern and pretty rock, but the fact is, I don't think I'd draw a distinction between rock and Southern rock if it weren't for Skynyrd. They created the genre just by existing and being such a force of nature.

I knew every song line for line growing up, and still do. In college, when I'd meet other Skynyrd fans, I'd ask them to sing "The Ballad of Curtis Loew" with me, and if they couldn't, I would shame them as fake Skynyrd fans. (I am a Lynyrd Skynyrd hipster, it seems.) Before my father started preachin', he had at least four Skynyrd concert T-shirts that I can remember; Dad would cut the collar out of them but not the sleeves because they was his nice clothes. I'd give anything to have those.

Dad does still have a sweet Skynyrd belt buckle. But, like most Skynyrd apparel, it has the rebel flag on it. In that way, the band really does represent the South. I love them, I'm proud to associate with them, and they produced greatness—but I'm still just a little ashamed of some of their traits.

Next time you're at a rock show and some smart ass yells out "Freebird!" to the performer, remind him that half the band died in a 1977 plane crash, and the other half survived but had to watch their brothers and bandmates perish in front of their eyes. Then tell 'em to put their fucking hand over their hearts when they say that word.

DM

Oppression

Goddamn, oppressed people make better music. We don't know why that is, but it is.

Music born out of slavery and/or the Jim Crow South, created by black musicians living under the oppressive and openly racist culture of the time, expressed their anguish, fears, desires, and perseverance. Now, we ain't sayin' that makes it all worth it—naw. But we're thankful for the music that come from it.

"White" music—country and bluegrass—though influenced by African and African American music of the time, was made mostly by poor Appalachian whites. Those folks weren't exactly Southern gentry, practicing on their guitars in the afternoons after having tea on the lawn of their father's plantation. Hell no. They were miners and farmers and the kids of miners and farmers. Poor people. And while being poor and white ain't exactly like being black, it's as close as you can come. [29]

Poor people make great music because it's all they have. The slaves, former slaves, sharecroppers, miners, uneducated railroad workers, and down-home barefoot folk of the South (white and black) made great fuckin' music because they weren't able to do anything else great. It was their mark on the world. They had no businesses to expand. They ain't have a chance to donate a library or start a university. Many of 'em couldn't even read or write. But a lot of 'em could play and sing. Some of those who could play and sing invented new ways to do it, and a very precious few of them got money and fame off it. Which brings us to another issue.

[29.] Again, this is why rednecks like rap a lot—they feel like they and the rappers have something in common.

Appropriation

Appropriation is a word that gets thrown around a lot these days, mostly by thick-rimmed-glasses-wearing white folks whose favorite pastime is telling other white folks that they're bad people who appropriate things. It kinda feels like white people have now appropriated complaining about appropriation.

As comedians and performers, we have borrowed and emulated and copied and pored over countless other acts, of all backgrounds, in order to form our own voices and routines. We think this is an essential aspect of any art and should be encouraged.

However: stealing and profiting off the works of others, *especially* when the others are the very minorities and disenfranchised groups who most need art as both an escape *and* a means to make a living—well, that's fuckin' deplorable, and it's very real. We can't talk about Southern music without mentioning this aspect of the South's musical history. We can't list all the instances because (a) the book would be too long, and (b) we can't claim to know 'em all. But go back and look at the traditions of slaves or poor black Southern artists in the time of Jim Crow and segregation. And that's why so many Southern black companies and individuals own and control these respective music industries. Oh wait, no: we were thinking of a different universe. And look at country music, where the poor people who invented bluegrass owned the record companies. Again, that didn't happen. Though, like most things, it was a little easier on the white artists than on the black folk.

Some black artists made decent livings off their art, and some others (a few) got rich. Many got ripped off, though: stole from by other "artists" or record companies. Dolly Parton stands out as an example of a country artist who grew up poor but was able to turn her skills into a new and rich life. But far too few companies and industry stalwarts that were built on the talent of the blacks and poor whites were owned by the folks makin' the art. And oftentimes the owners weren't very interested in payin' the artists fairly for the contributions, neither.

There's an ongoing issue of individuals stealing the culture of a group for profit without giving any credit. Elvis himself was accused of this for years, though recently some of this criticism has waned as more examples have emerged of him giving credit and helping the black musicians who influenced him. However you feel about it, Elvis unquestionably did the music he saw the black musicians doing and got superrich and famous from it. That happened a lot. A whole lot. Still does.

In country music, we feel it's happening right now with our own Southern culture. You can't turn on the television or radio without hearing someone singing "heartfelt" tunes about workin' hard in their truck and going down to the river. A quick Google search (or, hell, just listening to 'em talk) will alert you to the fact that a lot these current country stars ain't worked a day outside in their life. They wouldn't go to the river to save their life unless it was in a fuckin' limo to some exclusive riverboat party where they would perform by singing the words "beer, truck, America" on repeat.

GIVE US OUR COUNTRY BACK

Does anyone actually from the country have any clue what the *fuck* is going on in Nashville? Taylor Swift a country music singer? Do what now? Look, we ain't gonna shit on the girl. She's clearly got a talent and can do her own thing, and we're terrified of her PR people. But how is that country? How'd that happen? Her idea of oppression is getting broken up with via text.[30]

---

30. And the Grammy for the saddest country song goes to . . . "Drinkin' Since He Ghosted Me" (if she really ever sang country).

Porch Talk with Trae

Music is important to us. Particularly country music. Actual country. Nashville is also important to us. It's one of the coolest cities in the country and a crown jewel of the South. Which is why it hurts so much that the bullshit pop music with a twang that they call "country" is headquartered right there in Music City. There's so much objectively awesome stuff about Nashville that it shouldn't have to be known primarily for the worst music known to man.

My boy Thompson has been my best friend since we were ten or so. He's also unique because he is a red-ass country boy from Celina, Tennessee, but he was raised by hippies. I love the hell out of Thompson's parents, so I don't mean that as a pejorative *at all*—they were of the hippie *persuasion*. So Thompson is like a redneck flower child. Part of this identity is that he is not one to start shit; he ain't much for confrontation. He just wants to have a good time, not cause any trouble. *Most* of the time.

One night we were in Nashville with a couple other friends of ours, just dickin' around, hittin'. In Nashville, live music plays pretty much everywhere. In the theaters, in the bars, in the damn streets. Sidenote: one time in Nashville I paid a black feller $5 to freestyle rap about me and my wife on the side of Second Avenue. And he fuckin' destroyed it. But where there's a ton of music, there's also a ton of *shitty* music, and nowhere on earth embodies that fact like Nashville does. Now, *here's* something you need to know about Thompson: music moves the man. It gets in his veins and makes him do things. If the music is hittin', the boy hollers, he dances, he fuckin' *feels it*. If the music *ain't* hittin' . . . well, the boy feels that too. This will be important.

So we're just goin' from bar to bar, honky-tonkin', just livin' that Nashville life, bayba. Toward the end of the night, once we're all good and drunked up, we land at this fairly well-known bar called the Stage on Broadway. The coolest thing about the Stage is that it has this supremely awesome mural on the wall depicting all of the legends of country music. *Real* country: Hank Williams, Merle Haggard, Loretta Lynn, the Highwaymen. All the greats. It's a sweet-ass painting.

So we're standing by the bar, and there's some pretty-boy cover band playing, and, I mean, they're . . . fine. They have chops and all that, and they're playing other people's songs, so whatever. I don't remember what it was, but probably some Brad Paisley or something relatively innocuous like that. But then that song ends, and they light into a striking rendition of . . . "Drops of Jupiter." By the rock group Train.

I hear the opening chords and think nothing of it, but I almost immediately notice Thompson's face change. A pall comes over the man. He is *aghast*. Plumb, smooth aghast. His eyes fill with rage. Now, at this point, I'm still not understanding what in the hell he is even mad about, but the source of his wrath will soon be revealed to me—and to all of us. He turns from me and the bar, faces the stage, and proceeds to Lose. His. Shit.

"*Train!?!* Fucking *Train?! Are you fuckin' shittin' me??!* You got Waylon and Willie on the wall, and these pussies are playing *Traaaaaaaaain?!? Fuck you! Fuck these motherfuckers! Fuck this shit!* Hey, boys, you know anything by *the Fray*?! How 'bout a little *Snow Patrol!?* Fuck this bar! *Fuck this fucking town!*"

We were escorted out. Hopefully this illustrates how strongly we feel about this music, about the whole culture surrounding it. It means something to us, goddamn it! Give it back.

And at least she's better than some Hollywood halfwit in thousand-dollar boots singing about apple pie and making pop music with an accent. Like whatever you like. But that ain't our culture. We take issue with that being a representation of what it's like to be Southern. Hell the shit no it ain't.

Commercial country has such a hold on the South (and the rest of the country) right now that it's almost unfathomable. How'd it happen? Well, our opinion is that it all started with Garth Brooks.[31] Now we ain't hatin on Chris Gaines.[32] Garth Brooks is a country music god and made amazing records. But folks forget that Nashville kinda didn't know what to do with the arena country master at first. See, his mix of rock and pop into country was not just a cultural shift[33] but also a risk for the industry to get behind at that time.

That, of course, is a laughable notion now. Garth moved the needle to the tune of a career, selling more records than Elvis Presley. Before then, country music was for Southerners and Midwesterners and people elsewhere who were a little more adventurous. Then industry bigwigs realized collectively that these hybrid pop and rock elements were fuckin' cash cows all over the world. So they started mass producing it and makin' copycats. They expanded on the idea as well— which is how Canadian-born would-be pop star Shania Twain came to dominate Nashville and become the queen of pop country.

None of this is intended to shit on Garth. We've fought people over much less. He was an original. And, hell, we kinda like Shania. (At

31. And his amazing, unbelievable backing band.

32. Okay, well, we are hatin' on his alter ego Chris Gaines, but not Garth himself.

33. Look, of course people came before Garth, and this history is a bit paraphrased, but he changed everything.

least she ain't *French* Canadian.)[34] But when Nashville realized it would make more money off rock and pop with an accent than it would off real country music, a lot got lost. The powers that be realized they could keep a financial hold on the South—and the rest of the world— by focusing on feel-good rhythms and shallow lyrics about how much fun partyin' is.

There's still good country music left. Anyone who says otherwise is stupid. Brad Paisley, for example, hits on the guitar better than powdered sugar hits on funnel cakes. But country's not *just* about good tunes. The culture's been lost. If someone wrote "Sunday Morning Comin' Down" today, would it even get on CMT? This former number-one country music hit is about doing drugs, and the protagonist don't find Jesus at the end, so probably not. Liberal Redneck favorite Sturgill Simpson can't get on CMT. He is a Kentuckian: a descendant of coal miners, bluegrass pickers, and preachers. His second album was called *Metamodern Sounds in Country Music*. It has country *in the title*.[35] But when it was nominated for a Grammy, it was for an "Americana" album. And as far as we know, it still ain't been played on *Country* Music Television. Shit.

Is there anything to be done about this? Well, yes and no. Good music is gonna get made and listened to no matter what, and in a lot

34. And she did grow up poor, and also our ladies tell us we can't disparage her, or we will face immediate death.

35. Yes, we're aware that this is a nod to an album that isn't at all country: Ray Charles's landmark 1962 LP *Modern Sounds in Country and Western Music*, on which he covered country songs but in an R&B way. We think Sturgill alluded to this album on purpose (we know he did, but we think we know the purpose) as a dig at the country establishment who ignored him. Maybe it was another reason. Who cares. Just listen to the damn thing.

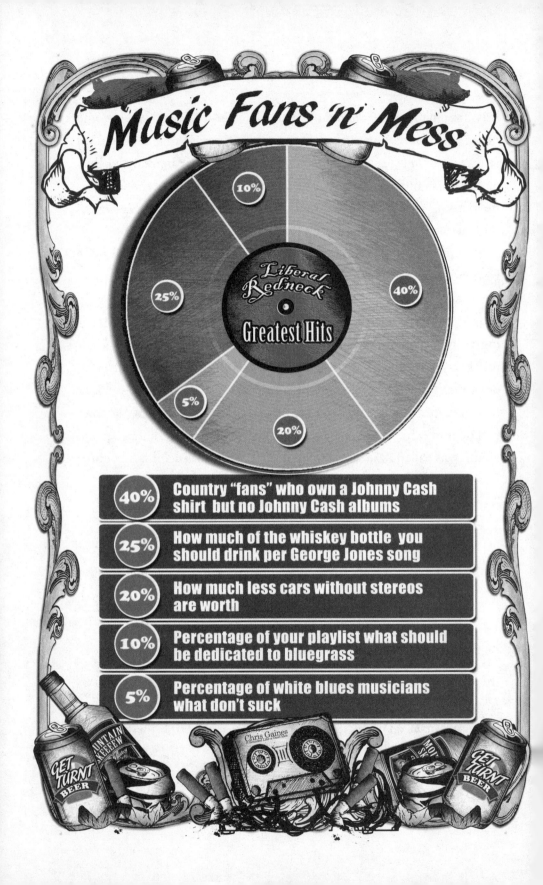

of ways, we can't control what the world thinks of us. If someone in California hears some song about how every ride down a dirt road involves swervin', purdy girls in jean shorts, an old farm, and a bonfire, and thinks that's just all there is to life in the South, well then, so be it. Dirt-road parties hit,[36] and that certainly has a place in our lives. But the culture of country music has become hayride-themed frat parties. Death to bro country.

Authentic artists and music are out there. In country, rap, and everything in between, you don't have to just accept whatever is being sold as representing the South if it don't resonate with you. It's a *great* time to be into good music and be Southern. Atlanta is still makin' great hip hop, and other parts of the South are joining in. Legendary rocker Jack White has moved to Nashville and has a great studio there. Mainstream country is, in our opposite-of-humble opinion, mostly a bunch of painted-up shit, but lots of artists are out there makin' the kind of tunes that hit your soul.

The South's problems seem to have made for some great music. So if nothing else, fuckin' go celebrate that. And support those folks. Buy albums. See shows. For God's sake y'all, dance!

36. **Especially if you don't play shitty music.**

7

Not Racist But . . .

One of the first and most unfortunate things most outsiders think of when they think of the South is our *less than stellar* reputation regarding race relations. Nonwhite people elsewhere in this country speak of being afraid to go to the South, fearful (we assume) that they'll be berated, assaulted, or worse. Apparently even some white people feel the same. Which is stupid, by the way. Stop being so dramatic. This is America. You're white. You'll be fine.

But if you're black, you'll (almost definitely) be fine too. You know how we know?

Because black people already live here. A lot. Of all the black people in this country, 55 percent live in the South. Every state in Dixie has a double-digit percentage of black people in its population. The vast majority of American blacks who live outside the South reside in a few major cities: New York, Detroit, Chicago, DC, etc. Black culture is as deeply ingrained in what makes the South the South as anything. Now, granted, there's an overtly ugly and shameful truth behind *why* most American blacks live in the South, and trust us, we're going to get to that, but the point is this: the South is not the dystopian racial wasteland many apparently think it is.

We're not *more* racist in the South, we're just perhaps *better* at it. See, in bigger cities they have a large amount of cultural diversity. We mainly have three races down here: whites, blacks, and Latinos. So we can really focus our racism in greater detail. We're like the ear, nose, and throat doctors of racism.

Of the ten states with the highest incidence of hate crimes, seven of them are outside the South.[1] There hasn't been a race riot in Dixie Proper[2] in thirty years (there have been eleven total in the rest of the country). When the worst racially motivated domestic terrorist attack in recent American history took place in Charleston, South Carolina, in June 2015, the city did not erupt in racial turmoil; its people of all races mourned together.

We know what you're thinking: "Oh, here we go. More white people talking about how racism is over in America and black people need to just get over it. Spare us, please." Nope. *We're not saying that.* Racism, particularly institutional racism, is a colossal problem in America, the South very much included. We still have a long way to go as a society. All of us. But we *are* saying that Dixie does not at all have a monopoly on racial fucked-up-ness. This is a national problem. To deflect responsibility onto the South alone in the typical "Oh, well it's the South, what do you expect?" fashion is counterproductive to progress.

Still, racism does have a long, tumultuous history in the South and continues to be a major concern for our future as a region, but (a) while we have a very long way to go, we have also *come* a very long

---

1. Way to go Alabama, Tennessee, and Kentucky. Way to go.

2. So not including technically-Southern-but-not-really places like Baltimore and Saint Louis.

Long-ass note: This book is written by three white Southern comedians. Our goal in these pages is to make the South better, and, in our opinion, most of the burden for improvement falls on our fellow red-asses. And so our book is directed largely *at* our people, in hopes of improving the South as a whole. It's also written entirely *from* our perspective. While the last thing we want to do is fail to give our Southern black brothers and sisters' story anything less than the respect it deserves, we also feel very strongly that it's not our place to speak for them. We assure you that any points in this chapter— and indeed throughout the entire book—that seem like crimes of omission or sugarcoating the truth as it relates to Southern black culture were treated that way only in an effort to not be presumptuous or disrespectful. Oh, and lastly, we use the word *black*, not *African American*, for the most part. Hope that ain't a problem. It's just simpler, and also, hell, technically Charlize Theron is African American and Rihanna ain't, so we just ain't fans. Anyway. Let's see how many people we can piss off.

way down here, and (b) most outsiders don't have a *clue* what they're talking about when they talk about racism in the South.

So, uh [*takin' a deep breath*], let's see about addressin' it.

A LEGACY OF SHAME

The South fought a war for slavery. Period. We will never be able to truly move forward, and we will never be taken seriously, if we cannot come to terms with that. Forget what you were taught in your history classes about "The War Between the States" or, our personal favorite, "The War of Northern Aggression." We were taught those same things. Our teachers were misguided at best and willfully regressive at worst. The Civil War was not about "states' rights." Well, actually, yes, it *was* about states' rights: the Southern states' *right to own slaves*. That was the right we were so torn up about, y'all. An important distinction.

Look, we get it: you were told stories about your great-great-great-great-uncle, Captain Beauregard Buford Buttdix, what never owned the first slave and fought valiantly for the Gray at Shiloh. Well, you can still be proud of Uncle Captain Buttdix, y'all. Maybe his reasons for fighting for the Confederates genuinely didn't have anything to do with slavery. Hell, maybe *most* rank-and-file Johnny Rebs didn't care about slavery one way or another. Maybe that's all true. But y'all: *it doesn't matter.* Soldiers have been fighting for misguided causes since General Ugg convinced the Okks to fight for "fire magic" in The Great Spear War of 22874 BC.[3] Just because some Confederate soldiers may have been misguided in their motivations for suiting up, that doesn't change the war's *real cause*: the by then wholly Southern institution of slavery.

Some of you from outside the South may be wondering why we're emphasizing this *irrefutable historical fact that everyone should know* so strongly *already*. Well, it's because there has been an unfortunate tendency down here to deflect as much attention as possible away from the atrocities that the South was responsible for before, during, and after the war, and to focus on the *glory*, the *courage*, and all that kind of shit instead. We name roads, schools, and parks after Confederate leaders. We erect statues in their honor. We revere them and honor them, all while ignoring the gigantic racist elephant in the room.[4] Look, it ain't nothin' wrong with glory and courage, and it's completely legitimate to acknowledge the military greatness of some of the Confederacy's

3. Ain't a word of that real, but y'all get the point.

4. Imagine an elephant with a dip in and a rebel flag tattoo. That's (a) funny, and (b) every University of Alabama fan's dream pet.

leaders, but what's *not* okay is to do so without *also* acknowledging their complicity in and tacit acceptance of one of the single most reprehensible and inhumane practices in human history.[5] It's disingenuous. It's cheap. It's cowardly. We gotta cut that shit out.

So, yes, we fought a war for slavery, and because sometimes the universe gets some shit right (waterfalls, potatoes, Scarlett Johansson), we *lost*. Which is *another* thing we apparently need to remind some of our fellow Southerners of. Not only did we fight a war for slavery, but *we got our asses whupped*. Until we can all agree to accept this and act accordingly, we're never going to be able to move on. It's nothing to be proud of, y'all—it really ain't. We fought and we lost. But our defeat *was* a great victory for morality and for the country as a whole. Southerners tend to act as if the Civil War isn't history but a scientific theory whose results can be disproven if discussed enough. It's not. We lost. Get over it.

So the war ended, and the good guys won. Slavery was abolished, and America was finally truly the Land of the Free. But (and we know this is going to be surprising) many in the postwar South were not thrilled with these developments. Many of those in power saw the black man's freedom as a personal insult—a constant reminder of their failure. And so began a long tradition of powerful Southern whites trying to figure out the best way to hold down black people now that chains were no longer an option.

OL' JIM CROW

So slavery ended, and so did racism, and everyone lived happily ever after in the South and elsewhere, right? Well, no. Obviously that's hilariously retarded to even suggest, but that's essentially the narrative

---

5. **Outside of that time Nelly and Tim McGraw made a song together.**

THE KKK: SHITTIEST "WHITE KNIGHTS" OF ALL TIME

★

This chapter wouldn't be complete without talking about the Klan, even though "talking about the Klan" is right up there with "that test where the doctor shoves his finger up your butt for some reason" on the list of our absolute least favorite pastimes. Off top: fuck the Klan. We know that's a truly incisive stance we're taking there, but seriously, there are very few organizations who have done more damage to the South (or looked more stupid doin' it). Except for maybe the cast of *Country Strong*.

Most everyone is familiar with the Klan. They're racists who dress like ghosts and talk like racist ghosts. They're idiots, and today they seem to exist primarily to reappear from time to time, at some rally or somethin', to remind everyone of the fact that they're idiots. Then one of 'em lapses into a diabetic coma, and they all go home. It's sad, really. But all things considered, we definitely prefer "sad" to "sad but in an overtly terrifying way," which is what the Klan of yesteryear was. Fuck those guys even harder.

On that note: a lot of people may not realize that the Klan has existed in three pretty distinct iterations. The first came about right after the Civil War and was founded in Pulaski, Tennessee (which Trae drives through on his way to visit his in-laws and which is, contrary to popular belief, *not* a cosmopolitan oasis), by some Confederate veterans, the most prominent of which was Nathan Bedford Forrest, who gets credit/blame for founding the Klan. Multiple statues of Forrest still stand in parts of the South to this day. *Sigh*. This first version of the Klan was violent and shitty but flamed out in the 1870s. The Klan was then resurrected for a few years in the 1910s and then again (in its current form) in the 1950s as a response to the civil rights movement.

They seem a little disorganized? That's because they are. The Klan is a shoddy organization—at least these days. In all honesty, the Klan is and really kind of always has been little more than a handful of different loosely connected groups of dipshits in sheets. In the past, some factions were larger and more dangerous, obviously, but most "chapters" of the present-day Klan can pretty much be summarily dismissed as little more than mouth-breathing annoyances.[6]

Like many things and ideas associated with the South, the Klan is much less prominent than people may imagine it to be. We the authors have, among the three of us, lived about ninety years in the *Deep* South and have never once encountered an actual Klansman. They're not taken seriously down here; please do us a favor and keep not taking them seriously as a political group. Fuck the Klan.

6. Obviously we ain't tryin' to dismiss the past and the *awful* and *murderous* actions of the KKK. We're simply saying that the current machination don't deserve much thought in terms of having a real effect on society.

of many native Southerners to this day. "Well, hell, we gave 'em their freedom—*what more do they want?!*" is their attitude, in a nutshell. "Slavery ended a hundred and fifty years ago—*get over it!*" That's another good one. People actually feel this way. The problem with this, of course, is that it completely ignores the *decades* of abuse that the South put black people through in the intervening years since the war ended. And buddy, there's been *a lot*.

Beginning almost immediately after the end of the war, Southern whites used every shifty and backhanded method they could think of

NEW JIM CROW

★

The goddamn "War on Drugs" is an American problem—not an exclusively Southern one. But it needs to be addressed.

First of all, you can't fight a war on drugs. It ain't possible. Wars is fought against humans. Humans is the only things what's ever died in the drug war (and a few dogs, prolly), but no one has ever killed a vial of heroin in the line of duty. Some rock bands have probably decimated a vial of heroin, and then later the vial killed 'em back, and that *might* be a drug war, but the actual drug war is just a fucking bullshit euphemism for a well-thought-out plan to extract wealth under the lie of "keeping us safe." Under the auspices of a "war," police departments are able to purchase expensive-ass equipment, and for-profit prisons make a killing off our tax dollars, while in the meantime our neighborhoods are being destroyed.

And cops are dying too. Because that's what a fucking war is: a thing where people die. This "war" affects poor people almost exclusively, and in the South it's absolutely destroying black people's lives. The "new Jim Crow" is the school-to-prison pipeline that exists in a country that has the highest incarceration rate in the world. It was a phrase coined by civil rights attorney and advocate Michelle Alexander, who wrote a book by the same name, and you ort read it.

The drug war is one of the most sophisticated and expensive forms of social control and repression ever to exist on this earth. However you feel about drugs (they hit) being legal, the way we "punish" drug abusers and sellers while allowing Big Pharma and unethical doctors off the hook is objectively disgusting. The drug war is a bunch of fuckin' horseshit the government hides behind to excuse the disparate treatment of blacks and whites, poor folk and not-poor folk, and those well connected and those not. Just say no to the drug war.

to keep blacks from exercising any rights or influence. Literacy tests, poll taxes, residency requirements, and other bullshit served to keep blacks from voting (and also many poor whites, for the record, but that's what you call "collateral damage"). Then, beginning in the 1880s, searching for its next great dick move, the South began to codify what became known as Jim Crow laws. Basically segregation laws. Separate but equal, whites-only drinking fountains—all that shit. And then Dixie spent the next eighty years fighting tooth and nail to keep these arcane practices in place, which went a *long way* toward solidifying our reputation as "just the worst."

It took many years and the actions of some *supremely* badass motherfuckers (Martin Luther King Jr., Malcolm X, Rosa Parks[7]), but Jim Crow laws finally ended with the Civil Rights Act of 1964. Southern whites, for their part, largely continued the Southern white tradition of "being real dicks about the whole thing," spraying black people with fire hoses, burning crosses, and bombing churches. *Churches*, y'all. And once again, the rest of the country was witness to our asshattery, and the Stigma of Southern Shittiness got embedded even deeper into the American consciousness.

THE MORE THINGS CHANGE

So now slavery has been over for years, and *hey*! We just ended Jim Crow laws! Surely that's that, then. No more racism in the South. We did it, everybody! Who wants barbecue?

Yeah, well . . . naw. Racism is a deep-seated, widespread, and systemic issue, still, in the South. It's not going to just end. But that's how many of our fellow white Southerners want to act. You can catch 'em

---

7. **Doubly badass due to the hittin' Outkast song she inspired.**

on Facebook or Instagram (but never in person unless they *know* there are no black people around), spouting some shit like this:

"Ugh, I'm so over it, y'all. Everyone's always complaining about how racist we are. It's terrible, and, really, that's kinda *reverse racist*, when you think about it. We've swung too far in the opposite direction. It's white people that are being oppressed nowadays! It's true! I can't even state my opinion, which is that black people are lazy and need to take responsibility for themselves, without some *liberal* calling me a racist! It's ridiculous! Look, so we had slaves! First of all, that was, like, a hundred years ago. Secondly, it's not like the slaves were better off in *Africa*! I mean, we kinda did them a *favor*, if you think about it. A lot of slaves were happy and got treated great. There were black Confederate soldiers! And segregation has been over for fifty years! And that one tangentially related and also dubious fact proves that I'm right about everything else I say! I mean, when are they going to *get over it*?! Can't we all just *move on*?! I'm just so sick of hearing about it. Where do they even get that we're still racist anyway?!"

It's 2016. Why *do* people continue to assume the South is racist? Hmm . . .

Well, if you'll allow it, we have some thoughts we'd like to offer. Starting with:

THE GODDAMN FLAG

And here we are. The Stars and Bars. The symbol of the South we have known and loved (and also hated). To many, the flag is a racist icon, pure and simple. It represents nothing more than backward and regressive beliefs and actions. Flying the flag is at best insensitive and at worst openly hateful. How could it not be? After all, it's the flag of the short-lived nation of traitors who saw fit to tear this country apart in pursuit of the freedom to enslave. To many (hell, to most), the Confederate flag is on par with a swastika.

Yet, to many white Southerners of a certain age (those between twenty- and forty-something), the flag elicits a lot of very conflicting memories. Papaw's extensive pocketknife collection. Daddy's even more extensive Skynyrd collection. That asshole in school everybody hated who used to pick fights with the black kids. *His* daddy's also-extensive shitty tattoo collection. Seeing people on the news standing in front of the flag and saying some really shitty things. An objectively badass belt buckle that you could "win" at the county fair.[8] The way people looked at you when you wore that belt buckle to class freshman year of college. The way Papaw looked at you when you told him that it bothered you, and you thought you might be done with it. The way you never really missed it anyway.

The rebel flag's supporters talk about "heritage, not hate." It's not for racist reasons, they say, it's just about being from the South and proud of it, and that's it. People from outside the South hear that and roll their eyes. "Yeah, right. Just say what you really mean. You're a racist." And we *totally get that*. We also get that this is going to sound counterintuitive to the tone of the rest of this chapter, but it's just the honest truth: it really isn't that simple.

The flag issue (unlike the flag's defenders) is a little more nuanced than you might think at first, but, regardless, the flag is done. There's no getting it back. There's no repairing its image. It's irredeemable. Any possibility of the flag ever being seen as a benign symbol of regional pride vanished forever on June 17, 2015, the day of the hate-fueled massacre at Emanuel African Methodist Episcopal Church in downtown Charleston, South Carolina. The minute the pictures of

8. Shit was rigged, and everybody knew it.

Porch Talk with Corey

My first cousins are black. To hear folks from my old church tell it, that was because my aunt "made a mistake." Well, I'll let you in on a little secret: the folks from my old church think Facebook is for sharing that some prince in Nigeria has left them a fortune through email. They're dumber than fuck.

One day sometime in, like, November 2002, me and my family were sitting in a church service. Front row. Me and Dad were a bit fidgety the whole time on account of this was NFL season, and we both had heard enough about the Bible and not enough about what kind of shape Steve McNair's[9] thumb was in, and—

Come on, preacher man, hurry up!

Preacher decided that we needed to watch a video on the new big-screen projector that we had just bought instead of helping a starving family. The video was discussing the aftermath of 9/11. It had been only a year, and the wound was still very fresh.

The video featured several prominent professors, scientists, and politicians discussing the aftermath of the terror attacks and predicting what lay ahead for the country. I was in eighth grade, so I'm a little fuzzy on exactly what the last person to speak said, but she was a college professor. A black woman. She pointed out that history repeated itself and that we should prepare for the worst and hope for the best. After she was done talking, the preacher cut the tape off, and this is what he said—verbatim: "Now, that woman—even though she was black—I agree with everything she said."

9. RIP Tennessee Titans QB Air McNair—forever in our hearts, number 9.

No one in the church batted an eye or even thought different—except my family. We were sitting on the aisle with our black relatives. Thank God my young cousins weren't paying attention on account of kids don't listen in church. And after my family heard that, we all got up and left.

I never went back to that church again in my life—'cept one time on account of I had gotten a hand job from the girl who ran the day care—but other than that, I'm basically a freedom rider.

the murderer—who we will refer to as Stupid Fuckhead Jr.[10]—were released, the flag was forever erased from the hearts of any Southerner with an ounce of compassion. There was Fuckhead Jr., looking like every other piece-of-shit white-boy mass shooter ever: terrible haircut, dead eyes, skinny physique ensuring that he could never harm anyone without a gun in his hand—and the Confederate flag. Where once a fair number of Southerners might have seen that as a symbol of their home, their family, their people, now it had become an unequivocal symbol of hatred. From that day forward, the flag was well and truly dead.

Or, at least, it *should have been*. We certainly hoped it would be. "Surely good ol' boys won't continue to associate with the flag after somethin' like this," we thought. But nothin' makes a redneck want to do something quite like other people implying that he shouldn't. And so the flag lives on. You can't drive to the dollar store in any rural Southern town without passing five flags on the way (and six

10. With someone that terrible, you just got to assume that the parents weren't peaches themselves.

Porch Talk with Trae

SCARS AND BARS

The flag has been a complicated subject for me for a really long time. I'm very progressive, especially in redneck terms. I have always prided myself and still pride myself on being open-minded and accepting, and anyone who knows me well would back me up when I say: I'm not a racist and never have been.

Yet I grew up with the Confederate flag. My dad passed away in 2013, but to this day a rebel flag hangs in his bedroom in the house I grew up in. (My mema lives there currently.) I attribute a lot of my liberal attitudes to how my dad raised me; I genuinely never heard him say a racist word in my life. He loved rock 'n' roll, and he especially loved Lynyrd Skynyrd. Their unofficial logo for years was the rebel flag. (*They* weren't racist either, by the way—I'll fight anybody what says different.) I'm not saying that's why my dad rocked the flag, but I am saying I know for a fact that it didn't hurt.

And I had this damn poster, y'all. It wasn't even a regular rebel flag poster. It was a rebel flag, and in the middle of the flag was a *skull wearing a bandanna,* and the bandanna was the American flag! Skeeew! Goddamn! Mama's new boyfriend hit the jackpot at the county fair that night, tell ye what! I loved that poster.

But looking back on it, there were a *few things* regrettable about that poster. Not the least of which was: Why in the hell does anybody ever put the American flag and the Confederate flag on the same thing at the same time? They were not big fans of each other. Yet most of the most hard-core pro-rebel-flag fellers are the same dudes who scream 'bout 'Merica, "You don't like it, you can *leave!* It's my right as an American to fly that flag!" Yeah? Well, buddy, lemme tell ya, screaming about your rights as an *American* while rockin' the *Confederate* flag is like arguing against gay marriage with a dick in your mouth. Makes no sense. But, see, rednecks are immune to irony. Anyway, I digress.

My point is this: I grew up with the flag, and back then it *never* had any racist connotations for me. Race and racism didn't factor into it at all for me or my dad, either. I know that's hard for people to believe, but it's true. So I was a little bit sympathetic to these good ol' boys on TV hollerin' 'bout how they don't mean nothin' by it, it's just their heritage, and all that. I mean, don't get me wrong: a goodly portion of them *are* racists, I'm certain, but I'm willing to give them the benefit of the doubt based on my own experience.

I haven't worn the stars and bars for goin' on fifteen years, probably. And I don't intend to. But I still think, and will always think, that the whole thing is a little more complicated than the popular interpretation of "If you like the flag, you're a racist."

But here's the thing: it really doesn't matter what it meant to me or what it means to its current defenders. What matters is what means to *other people*. What it says about you to those people. Really, that alone should be enough. For me, it was. It was more than enough.

churches). People continue to fly it from trailer porches and plaster it on hilariously awful bumper stickers (shockingly, never on, like, a Mercedes or anything). There's nothing like seeing a rebel flag sticker that says "If You Think the Civil War Was About Slavery, Then You Need a *History Lesson*" plastered on the back of an '02 Chevy being driven by a guy who *absolutely* failed every history class he ever took.[11]

11. Unless his history class was taught by his football coach, in which case he prolly did fine.

Y'all, seriously: take 'em down. It's way past time. Look, we understand. That design *is* pretty kick-ass, after all. Don't nothin' set off a bandanna in quite the same way. And it means somethin' to you. Your daddy flew it, and his daddy flew it, and his daddy flew it, and his daddy flew it in a war to own slaves, and *that's sorta the whole goddamn point here*, fellers. It's just a flag. Hell, we'll get us a new one. Would that help?

At any rate, it's time to give the Stars and Bars the Indiana Jones treatment: it belongs in a museum, y'all. And speaking of museums, there are a few other reasons besides the flag as to why the image persists of the South as a reserve for revisionist racists, and these reasons could also use some attention.

LET IT GO

In our humble[12] opinion, the South in general's attitude regarding the war and everything that came after needs a major paradigm shift. Put simply: we need to be more like Germany. Ya see, after World War II, Germany as a nation took responsibility for its crimes, owned up to them, and has refused to make excuses for the atrocities that occurred. Germans own it. That's just the way it is. (Or at least the perception of the way it is, and as we keep reiterating, the perception can be just as important as the reality.) How many people in the South could stomach the idea of Nazi statues existing in Germany in order to "honor the past" but "not meant to offend the Jews, of course?" Because y'all do realize that's what most of these Civil War monuments are, right?

The narrative among some of our unenlightened compatriots essentially boils down to this: "Look, slavery and Jim Crow—that's in

---

12. In this case, by "humble" we mean "absolutely correct."

the past! Why can't black people *just get over it*?!" They say this shit to their friend who nods in agreement as they drive past a statue of Confederate general Stonewall Jackson on their way to their kids' football practice at Nathan Bedford Forrest High School. These people are immune to irony. If you're one who complains about Southern blacks' inability to move on while also campaigning *against* renaming Jefferson Davis Boulevard, then frankly, fuck you. It ain't the black people that need to move on, y'all. It's us.

We're not advocating erasing every memory of the Civil War and pretending it never happened. But we need to stop *celebrating it*, for God's sake. How are your black neighbors—or anyone else—supposed to take you seriously when you say you aren't racist while dressed in a historically accurate full-bird Confederate colonel uniform? It's time to stop. Let's stop the reenactments, let's stop the parades and the statues and the ribbon cuttings and the "remembrance dinners" and all that bullshit, and let's leave the war where it belongs: in the history books.

CHANGE GONE COME

The South is our home. It's home to all of us, white and black. Black people easily have had as much of an influence on the culture of the South as white people have, and maybe more. Many classically Southern things are loved by both. Fried chicken, sweet tea, football, barbecue, wife beaters, shitty tattoos, pants that don't fit right, weed, not givin' a fuck—these are a few of our favorite things, y'all. And yet many of us hate one another? Sorry, but that shit just don't check out. *Every* Southerner should be upset when he or she hears people disparage our home. Because yes, they're wrong, and they don't understand, but we have to acknowledge the reasons for these perceptions and do what we can to move past them.

Rebel Flag Replacements

We humbly offer up the following suggestions for a new Rebel Flag, one that captures all of the heritage but none of the hate.

The Intimidator

3

The easiest and most logical solution; 95% of all rednecks already proudly sport some version of this flag on a day-to-day basis, making transition painless and efficient. Also it's badass as hell, son.

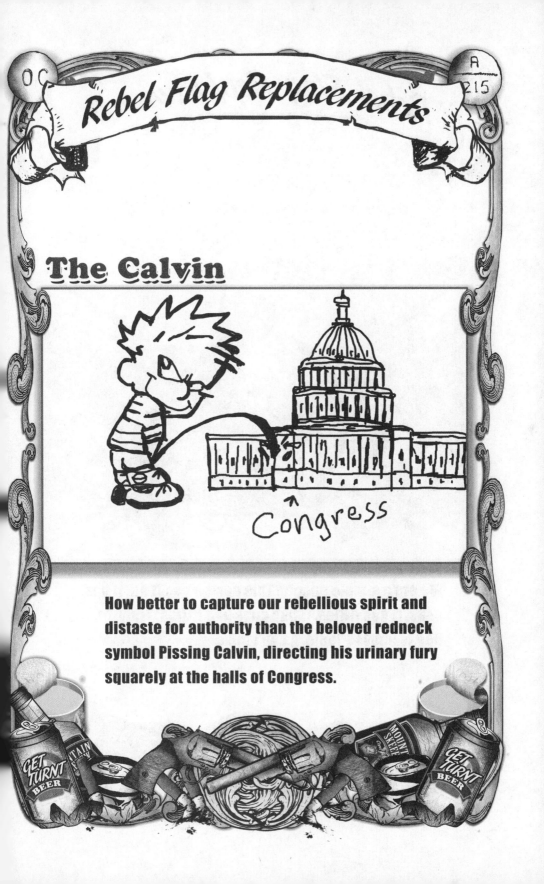

Rebel Flag Replacements

The Calvin

Congress

How better to capture our rebellious spirit and distaste for authority than the beloved redneck symbol Pissing Calvin, directing his urinary fury squarely at the halls of Congress.

Rebel Flag Replacements

Guns & Titties

We are a simple people. This design has it all. It has
guns. It has titties. It has guns and titties. Truly, this
flag is unassailable. A can't miss.

Porch Talk with Drew
COME TO EASTER DINNER

I played football in college. Sports mean a lot of things to people, and they certainly have their fair share of bad traits about 'em. (Athletes committing and/or getting away with rape all the time, for one.) But, of course, sports also do a lot of good in the world. One thing they help with immensely is helping kids from different backgrounds, including different races, understand one another and, as a result, understand more about the world.

A friend of mine from the team came home with me for a few days one Easter break. I lived close to the college, and he couldn't afford to go home to Florida. Like me, he was there on scholarship and didn't have a lot of extra money for traveling. Now, we weren't rich ourselves, but we had plenty of extra food and room for him at our house so that he wouldn't be alone on Easter.

So Calvin came to Sunbright, Tennessee, population six hundred and 100 percent white. Hell, everywhere out in the country in my part of Tennessee is pretty much 100 percent white. So this was something that was gonna be noticed. Now, look, let me go ahead and tell you that Calvin is a six-foot-six defensive end with giant muscles and a proclivity for wearing sleeveless shirts, so, I mean, even if someone wanted to start trouble or whatever, they woulda prolly thought better of it. But I really don't think anyone would have.

What did happen was that a very large black man came to a very small town full of people who had rarely interacted with black people. They were curious, and, being comfortable, I guess, in their own town, they had no qualms about asking him whatever came to their minds. Some questions were less offensive than others. "Do you know Trick Daddy? I think he's from your town," one of my idiot friends asked. Others were pretty blatantly ignorant: "Can I touch your hair?"

For his part, Calvin took it all in stride. He handled every question with grace and the sly smile he usually had when he was playing jokes with all of us on the team. These passive prejudices were not necessarily from a place of ugly, but they certainly weren't from a place of respect. I realized that not only would they make anyone feel uncomfortable and out of place but also that Calvin had clearly experienced these kinds of prejudice before.

When I would apologize profusely, for example, for *my own grandfather* telling him, "I served in 'Nam with black folk. Was proud to do it," Calvin would say, "It's okay, Drew. At least he's proud, and his ignorance isn't the hateful kind. I appreciate that." He was twenty years old. He'd dealt with it before, and he'd dealt with much worse, too. I asked him about it, and I learned so much about his life and how he *really* felt in our tiny college town and about our all-white coaching staff. Obviously I don't know what any of that *actually* felt like for him, but to be frank, before I talked to him about it, I wasn't even aware of it.

DM

To our fellow white Southerners:

Look, y'all, we understand. Believe us, we do. You never owned a slave. Your daddy never did, and his daddy never did, and that may be true all the way back to fuckin' Adam for you. But if your reaction to the dissatisfaction of Southern blacks with the current state of much of our region is bitterness and defiance without a shred of empathy and understanding, then you're absolutely part of the problem. The gripes of black people are legitimate; their concerns are real. Just because *you* don't see it that way doesn't change that fact.

A few stats to make this shit real: in Tennessee and Mississippi, the poverty rate for blacks is about double the rate for whites. The difference is a little higher in South Carolina and Alabama. But Louisiana gets the grand prize, with Georgia and Arkansas as pitiful runners-up. In Georgia, 10 percent of whites live in poverty, while 26 percent of blacks do. In Arkansas, 13 percent of whites live in poverty, as opposed to 36 percent of blacks. And in good ol' Louisiana, 14 percent of whites live in poverty, while *40 percent* of blacks do. Nationwide, only 58 percent of black people graduate from high school compared with more than 75 percent of whites and Asians. And even college-educated black people earn significantly less than white people, get less help paying for college from their families, and are less likely to inherit any wealth. (Hard to imagine, huh, Chad?)

A black driver is about 30 percent more likely to be pulled over by police than a white driver is and more likely to have his vehicle searched. Even United States senator Tim Scott, a black *Republican* from South Carolina, reports being stopped by capital police who did not believe he was a senator—even though he was wearing his senate pin and is purdy recognizable considering he is one of only (shock!) two black senators. Y'all, we got lots of work to do.

And we have a lot of healing to do, and it's never going to be possible until we grow the fuck up and admit that no matter what we personally have or have not done regarding racism down here, we need to atone for the sins of our fathers. We have to.

And to our Southern black friends:

You're right. You're right that you didn't ask for any of this, and you didn't deserve any of it, either. You're right that it isn't fair and isn't right. You're right that the deck is stacked against you and that your home has done you wrong. You're right that the system treats you like second-class citizens unless you can sing, dance, or do something with a ball. You're right about the cops and Congress and this country. You're right about it all. You're right, and they're wrong.

We're truly sorry. You were forcefully removed from your home-land and brought to this continent as human chattel. You were beaten, made to work under horrendous conditions, forbidden to read, to worship, to form families. You were disrespected, dehumanized, disenfranchised, and murdered. We're sorry for our denial and what you went through to achieve the rights the rest of us took for granted. We're sorry about George Wallace, Nathan Bedford Forrest, and all the present-day assholes who still don't get it. We're sorry for their picket signs and their Facebook posts and their sound bites. They don't speak for us all.

We need you. We need your resilience and your faith and your strength—your voice and your heart and your passion. We need your help rebuilding this home we share so it can be a place we all feel proud of.

8

Women in the South

Women in the South (WITS) are the best. Many of the issues they struggle with every day include all the challenges of life in the South that we discuss in this book: poverty, lack of education, addiction, the ever-present watchful eyes of Jesus, and, when it comes to gun control, the use of firearms in domestic abuse.[1] While Southern men are certainly in the shit themselves, the women are more typically on the front lines—and *shew-whee*, son, our gals know how to do battle.

Like their dumbass male counterparts, they come in different personalities and flavors, but they also possess some core traits that unite them as a subspecies of humans we depend on, love, worship, admire— and that we're scared as shit of. Southern women don't fuck around. We got business women, those who skew a little trashy, hippies, belles,

---

[1]. **South Carolina, for example, is the deadliest state for women—with guns responsible for almost seven out of ten domestic violence deaths over the last decade. Hard to make a joke about that.**

~~soccer~~ football moms, weirdos, academics, and all things in between. A common denominator is just how damn tough they all are.

WHAT IS IT LIKE TO BE A WOMAN IN THE SOUTH?

As three straight men, we clearly know the answer to this and all questions. We're God's chosen "all-knowing" people.[2] Let's just let Uncle JR answer:

"It's easy as hell being a woman anywhere, especially the South, by God. Down here we open up doors, do the manual labor, pay most the bills, and *apparently* just because *God made it* to where women are better with kids, that means almost half my fuckin' paycheck goes to child support. I wish I was a woman so I could sit around doing my nails and *complaining*, because that's *all* they do!" Oh, right.

Because of people like Uncle JR, it can be really hard to be a woman here. 'Course, it's also awesome to be a woman here because this is the South. And, as we have established, being *in* the South plain hits, and being *from* the South is even better. Being Southern is so dang important that our Southern hero (and woman) Pat Summitt insisted her flight back home to Tennessee take off on time when she was *going into labor* so that she could make sure her son was born in Tennessee.[3] But the South also has its own special issues related to the female sex. So ladies, please don't think we're tryin' to speak for you,[4] but we gonna have to speak on this stuff.

2. It's *in* the Bible, so it's true.

3. Lord, what an awesome story. No man could ever top that.

4. Problem number one: men speakin' *for* women.

PAT SUMMITT

★

It's not happenstance that we've put Pat Summitt, coach of the University of Tennessee Lady Vols basketball team, first when it comes to this topic. She is the first thing in our minds and first in our hearts when we think of Southern women.

Number one, off top, she was the most mentally strong Southern human—man or woman—we can think of from our lifetime. She did as much for gender equality and women's rights as anyone else from the region ever has. And she did so not through politics or rousing speeches (not that we're saying there's anything wrong with them), but through grit, spirit, domination, and basketball.

How big was she in East Tennessee? Well, they named the gym after her at UT (the Summitt)—the gym where both the women *and the men* play. Might seem like an obvious thing to do for the winningest coach in the history of the college game, but remember: she was a woman, who coached women. This was such a big deal that rumor has it the coach of the UT men's team complained once that he had a hard time with recruits from other areas who didn't wanna play at a school where the women's team was so important. Our response as a fan base: "Who gives a shit?"

Summitt was a hero to little girls *and* little boys all across the South, and, really, the whole country. In big-time sports, where women have all too often been expected to accept secondary roles, she was not only a vocal and powerful leader, but also she was *asked* to be more vocal and assume more roles of power by speaking at all types of engagements and sitting on all types of boards. That's what excellence does: it makes you *undeniable*. And that's what Pat was.

She taught her players how to lead and succeed in a world dominated by men. She taught them their true worth and demanded they give her everything they had. She taught everyone how to look classy in a pantsuit.

She never said, "You *can* be" as good as a man, or good in general; she simply *demanded* the best. Not "the best *for a girl*." She. Demanded. The. Best. What was the result? Not just all those wins and championships,[5] but true and universal support from a mixed-sex fan base and respect nationally in a male-dominated sport. No honest basketball fan could keep her out of the top five college coaches of all time. (*We* know she's number one, but we get that homerism will drop her in some folks' minds.)

Even after her tragic passing in 2016 at the age of only sixty-four, the result of early-onset Alzheimer's, Pat remains a very present hero of ours. We would never compare the plight of three white males with accents to that of a woman in sports with the same damn accent. But you probably won't be surprised to learn that sometimes being super-Southern has led to comedy bookers doubting us, shitting on us, or simply ignoring us because we're just "hick comics." Should we complain in these situations? Should we feel sorry for ourselves? Or should we keep workin' and become so damn good we can't be denied?

Well, what would Pat Summitt do?

Yeah. Exactly. The answer to that question is always the way you should go. We woulda followed her into battle. She is sorely missed.

---

5. Just to give you an idea: 1,098 wins, thirty-two **SEC** regular season and tournament titles, eighteen **Final Four** appearances, and eight National Championships.

Porch Talk with Drew

I was blessed with ten aunts: seven on Mom's side and three on Dad's. A couple have passed on, RIP, and one moved to Arizona (which is fine, I guess). The rest of them are alive, kickin', and Southern as hell. Among them there are ex-biker chicks, Sunday school teachers, nurses, single mothers, a special ed instructor, one rape survivor (that I'm aware of), former beauty queens, and some of the best cooks I've ever known. One died giving birth; stories of her have filled my family get-togethers for years. Another has had multiple pen-pal love affairs with men in prison. Stories of her get told only when the preacher ain't around.

Four of my aunts were my next-door neighbors. I had long stays in the summers with two others. I can't tell you *what it's like* to be raised by so many women because I don't know what it's like *not* to be raised by so many strong-minded, opinionated, beautiful, country ladies.

They babied me. They whupped me when Momma wasn't around and sometimes when she was. They made me chocolate gravy, and they treated me like I belonged to them—because I do. I learned so much about the world through them and their perspectives. When you make a kid who just ate at his other aunt's house another sandwich just because he asked for one, you may not think you're changing how he sees the world, but you are. At various tables in houses, log cabins, and, yes, a couple of trailers, I sat and listened to all kinds of women have all kinds of opinions and insight on all kinds of problems. I heard about love and life as they complained about their husbands, and I learned about the harder side of it while pretending to "remember" another new boyfriend I had never met.

I am so lucky to have had so many extra-loving, feminine hands shaping who I became.

DM

POVERTY AND WOMEN IN THE SOUTH

The abject poverty of the South often falls on women the hardest. In poorer communities, the lack of money is hard on everyone, but the WITS have all the pain and issues as everyone else—plus some additional strife.

First of all, it's a little harder for women to abandon the kids, whether it be forever or just for a few hours. Working men in poor communities often have jobs that are out of town. ("Ain't no jobs 'round here"—top seven Southern phrase.) This gives them little reprieve from the day-to-day stresses of how batshit crazy it is to try to raise toddlers, for example. WITS take care of the kids before and after school, and usually have to deal with them in the summers in between. (Feed 'em Hot Pockets and tell 'em to "shut the hell up or go outside.") There are deadbeat and absent moms 'round here, but usually it's the men who cut and run rather than steeling themselves day after day to fight the good fight and raise decent human beings.[6]

The person most frequently tellin' the kids "No" when they ask for toys or, hell, even food sometimes,[7] is Mom. And that can be heartbreaking after a while. Kids don't have a choice or a way of gettin' out of poverty,[8] and being the one witnessing the toll of that on them is rough. But WITS do it, and they hug 'em tighter, skip meals to afford more for the kids, forgo nonessentials to buy them

---

6. Shout-out to the single dads defying statistics.

7. Not that poor Southern moms ain't feedin' their babies. *Hell,* no. We just all remember growing up being told, "Honey, I'll just make ya somethin' when we get home. That's too expensive."

8. "Yes they do!"—Republicans.

ODE TO SOUTHERN WOMEN: THE BAREFOOT ASS WHUPPER

★

The barefoot ass whupper is what happens when a tomboy becomes a momma but turnt all the way up to eleven. This is your cutoff-denim or Earnhardt shirt as a dress–wearing, Pall Mall hanging from her lip while cussin' at the neighborhood kids for doing burnouts in front of her house gal.

You can find her at the local gas station (the mom-and-pop one, not one of them that fucked the ocean to death) standing barefoot next to the beer cooler bearing down on a Lotto ticket that she got with the twenty she just won on the five-dollar scratcher. Let it ride, bayba!

She can sit at that assembly line cussin' that little shit floor manager whose daddy owns the company for twelve hours without blinking or stopping for water. She can open a tallboy of cheap piss-water beer with her teeth while driving with her knees and roll one on her thigh to burn once she gets to the farm party where she will start a fire by yelling at a log and then roast a weenie with her bare hands.

THE BAREFOOT ASS WHUPPER'S TO-DO LIST

★ Work the concessions at the high school basketball game.
★ Sell raffle tickets for the 4-H Club.[9]
★ Cuss out the chief of police without getting arrested on behalf of some dumbass kid just trying to have a good time.
★ Buy underage kids beer if they water her plants while she's losing her ass at a casino in Tunica.

---

9. A fraternity of rednecks who like hay and horses.

Porch Talk with Drew

I'm a spoiled momma's boy—100 percent. And like most momma's boys, I think my momma is the best in the whole world. The difference between me and other people who say that, though, is that I'm absolutely right.

Nancy Morgan is a saint. There, it's in print, so it's true. Everyone who knows her (even those who aren't her kids) agrees with me. She is a retired schoolteacher: she was the one who hugged and loved all the Goth kids and weird kids and angry kids till they bubbled with the love she radiates. When you ask her how she is so loving, she says, "because God is love, and He's in me." She's a Sunday school teacher: she's the one who makes sure every kid at church gets to open a present at the Christmas service. She's a dedicated wife and mother and grandma.

Even her mistakes are adorable. Growing up, she never got pictures of herself made, on account of that not being a humble thing to do, I guess. Well, one year, she finally decided to get 'em, and she got . . . the Glamour Shots. The wild thing about those big-hair, big-rouge head shots from a movie Burt Reynolds turned down is that they were *crazy* expensive. I don't know why anyone would pay four hundred dollars to look like a backup dancer for Whitesnake, but it was embarrassing. I didn't make fun of her then. Now it's part of my job description, so it's cool.

People talk a lot about toughness, and it's often related to fighting or sports or physical prowess. Well, Mom got her history degree while working during the day and balancing family. I never missed a meal during this time, as she took care of me when Dad was working away. She got her PhD at night (and during the summer), while she was working as a teacher. She was the best teacher I ever had; many classmates felt the same. She's the toughest person I know. She insisted I go to a good college. She insisted I study abroad because even though I'm a small-town ignorant kid from the middle of absolutely nowhere, she wanted me to be so much more. She insisted I get As.

She cheered when I scored touchdowns, and she was there when I got my heart broke. She came to see me sworn in to the Tennessee Bar. (Yes, I'm a lawyer.) She cheers now when I tell religious jokes—even though she disagrees with them. She has kept our family together through sadness and tragedy that I couldn't fathom before they happened. She has made sure we were fed, made sure we were focused, made sure we were sane. She's picked up the slack at every point. She never complains, and through it all, she exudes genuine love.

When I think about what she's made of, it makes me feel kinda weak. A true hillbilly Southern mountain woman, she is the toughest *and* kindest person I know. I don't think that's a coincidence; you have to be tough to be kind. To be honest, that's sort of a lot to live up to, and she should stop being so great. She is making me and everyone else look bad. Thanks for nothing, Mom. I love you.

DM

nicer clothes—they sacrifice. That's why they love their romance novels and bubble baths so damn much, because they're cheap and guilt free.[10]

Women also pick up the slack financially. Southern women work their asses off, make sure the bills are paid and the food is in the fridge, often-times before going home and cleanin' and cookin' for those kids. And, yeah, that means every once in a while a "You'll eat what we goddamn

---

10. You *never* interrupt Momma's bubble bath.

ODE TO SOUTHERN WOMEN:
THE SOUTHERN MOMMA

★

A momma loves you in spite of yourself. A momma holds you when you're hurting, even if it's your fault. Hell, *especially* when it's your fault. A momma sees your faults, but she has a special skill: the ability to see you for who you are at your best rather than at your worst. Mommas don't care about your politics, fame, fortune, or praise. They just care if you're warm, fed, and happy.

Momma tends to put up with the most bullshit. She forgives her boy in prison. She cosigns for her sorry-ass daughter's car behind the husband's back. She fixes your supper every night even when you're married because times are tough. Her work is truly never done. You think it's over when you're eighteen? Shit no, buddy. As long as you're on this earth with a pulse, ya momma is gonna be downright worried about you every night. You're gonna be the last thing she talks to Jesus about, whether you think he's real or not.

THE SOUTHERN MOMMA'S TO-DO LIST

★ Make cupcakes for Vacation Bible School—even after her own children are grown.
★ Have oatmeal creme pies. Always.
★ Let her husband get drunk in the garage every night without complaining.
★ Wear sweater vests with pictures of the sun on them.
★ Make sure children have clean, pressed clothes for church so that they seem to magically appear all ready to wear Sunday morning.

★ Teach her children to say "Yes, ma'am," "No, ma'am,"
 and look people in the eye.
★ Be quicker on the draw than any Wild West sharpshooter
 with a hairbrush, wooden spoon, or spatula when
 someone's fanny is asking for it.
★ Never give up on those she loves.

got!" slips out, hurled at a twelve-year-old who really didn't deserve it,[11] but we let it slide.

Another Southern tradition for women (men figured out early on to pretend they ain't good at this themselves so they wouldn't have to do it) is takin' care of the family members who get sick or old. Or addicted. Or kids caught in the wake of illness or addiction. Southern women take care of their parents, their husband's parents, and often-times other people's kids. They take in their siblings' kids, their cousin's kids, the one who finally got off meth but is on pills now. Show me a person who has worked a shift at the plant, beat her own kid's ass for smokin' weed out back, beat her sister's kid for being there while he did, changed her eighty-year-old demented father's diaper, reheated leftovers from the dinner made the night before, and dyed her roots so they'd look good this weekend—all running on one meal and three glasses of box wine—and I'll show you a Southern woman.

Across races, economic groups, faiths, and all parts of the South, WITS pick up the damn slack. And that really is what's so damn special about them. The good ones, the kind that ya fall in love with and the kind men write country songs about, the type that always has your

---

11. Yes, he did.

back and has been in only four fights her whole life (and three was over her kids)—they do whatever is necessary for their family.

YOUNG MARRIAGE AND MOTHERHOOD

The institution of marriage and the religion behind it is a special thing in the South. Marriage in the South often comes at a very young age. For whatever reason (it's sex), we get married young. And almost as often, we start havin' babies young. This has life-changing implications for WITS.

And it ain't easy. Hell no, it ain't. Especially when these young women grow up faster than their partners. The schism between a twenty-five-year-old mother of two and her husband in the South is all too often *decades* of maturity. Dealin' with his antics—comin' home drunk, spending the extra money at the end of the month (all $15 of it) on a new rifle scope, playin' Call of Duty for four hours instead of *mowing the goddamn lawn, Daryl!*—is a rite of passage that men don't have to endure. Even for young married women who aren't poor, tryin' to overcome their partner's immaturity is often an issue. When you see a man with a little too much money spending it on a ridiculous boat or a four-by-four that costs more than a community college degree, you can just go ahead and assume that some dedicated missus was there when he brought it home, shakin' her head and saying, "Well, Bill, where the hell we gonna put it?"

Having two kids at age twenty-two and needing to feed 'em and be there for them when you'd rather be at the club makes girls grow up quicker than boys. Those responsibilities often prevent young women from attending school because they have to pick up a part-time job while the kids are at school. Part-time jobs mean *careers* are out of the question. Nighttime classes sound nice, but dinner is

Porch Talk with Corey

When I was nine years old, my daddy took me to Hooters for my birthday. This was after we went and test-drove a Dodge Viper. Now, we certainly couldn't afford that Viper, but it was my favorite model car as a kid, and Dad was the shit and knew I'd love it.

First time I remember being confused at how much I loved women's legs was in that Hooters. Without understanding how or why, I knew that's what I wanted. (It was not a choice. You get it.) We got home, and Dad told Momma what we'd done. I thought she was gonna choke him out with an extension cord on the spot. She weren't happy nary bit.

The next year, she wouldn't let us go anywhere and instead insisted on her cooking chicken casserole, mashed potatoes, creamed spinach, crescent rolls, and coconut cake. That became a tradition that still remains to this day. I even flew home one year on my birthday specifically to have that meal. And, buddy, trust me: nearly twenty years later, she will be expecting me this year. That's a momma.

burnin' and "Damn it, we forgot to pay the Internet bill anyway, so it ain't easy to research right now. Also, tomorrow little Bella has to start a new day care because the old one upped their prices, and we just can't afford it this year. The new place ain't as good, but it'll be fine, and her little friend from church goes there. It'll be fine. Besides, Daryl done promised to try to ask for a raise as soon as he goes six months without being late to work, and, Lord, I wish he'd grow up."

And all the while, some of the fathers of these very children believe, like Uncle JR, that it's easier to be a woman in the South on account of "Hell, all they have to do is take care of the kids." Are you fucking serious? Have you ever *met* Southern children? Goddamn, y'all! Between your boy throwing bottle rockets at his sister's head and you worrying that your little girl is gonna get pregnant down by the creek (cause Daddy thinks birth control is for the devil and people from Manhattan), being a parent is a never-ending, never-relaxing, 24/7/365 job.

Being a mother to a bunch of shitty-ass river rats on a constant IV of Mountain Dew would be hard enough if that's all you had to do. But truth is, the majority of women down here also have to work at least part-time to help their sorry-ass husband pay the bills because he can't seem to decipher the spread on a goddamn college football game. Men justify the women taking care of the kids and the house *and* holding down a job because, after all, men are the primary breadwinners in the family. But that's because *we fucking pay women less*! Men claiming superiority over women because men make more money than they do is like claiming you're stronger than a lion that you tranquilized and put in a cage. Sure, you're in a better spot now—but how 'bout you unchain the beast and see what happens?

THE CHURCH AND SEXISM

I do not permit a woman to teach or to exercise authority over a man; rather, she is to remain quiet.

1 TIMOTHY 2:12

For the husband is the head of the wife even as Christ is the head of the church, his body, and is himself its Savior.

EPHESIANS 5:23

These are from the Bible. And while that's not technically a Southern book (you guys might not believe this, but it wasn't even written *in America*!), the South has definitely adopted it as its official manual on how to justify very terrible things that men like to do.

While other places see these verses as outdated (hell, it's called the *Old* Testament), many Southerners still refer to this as the go-to on why gender roles are the way they are and why they should remain that way, lest ye burn in an eternal lake of fire forever. (God sounds like a real peach.)

It's got to be hard for a woman to live under, overcome, or even grudgingly accept a patriarchy no matter where she lives, but to do so in a land where all those rules and ways of the world are supported (according to the population) by the damn *ruler of the universe* has got to be a special type of hell.[12]

Church is important to most folks in the South. So the most important thing going is basically ruled by men as decreed by the Big Man himself. Not only that, but the church puts pressures on women that it does not put on men. Young women are expected to be chaste, moral, and pure, whereas young men are given *way* more leeway, 'cause, ya know, boys will be boys. Girls are expected to marry young and have kids, be a helpmate to their husbands (who are basically like having another child), and, of course, raise perfect little Christian babies to make this world a better place.

So while it's the preacher man who controls the church, it's the women—those helpmates—who keep that shit going. They keep the pews tidy and wash the windows; type up the bulletins; volunteer for Sunday school, the nursery, youth group, and Vacation Bible School; fry the chicken for the postchurch dinners; organize the monthly

12. See what we did there?

potluck dinners, the spaghetti supper to raise money for a new roof, and the church fund drive; plant flowers in the front of the church, make food for sick parishioners, serve food after funerals, put together the Christmas pageant, get Easter lilies for Easter, wash the choir robes, organize the church trip, bake cookies for the bake sale to fund the church trip, pray unceasingly for their husband and their pastor and their kids and never complain, and then make sure their skirts are ironed for Sunday mornin' service. All this while in most churches not being allowed to speak with any authority on the direction or doctrine of the church.

No, no, ladies, the heavy lifting—thinkin' up shit to say, standing up at the lectern telling people what to do, counting the money—that ain't for yuns. So sorry.

NO TEARS IN THAT BEER

Women in the South taking care of everything and everybody with none of the glory and nary a complaint—makes them sound like angels, don't it? Well, we wouldn't argue with that (for definition of angel, see Dolly Parton, below), but don't think our women just keep all their stress bottled up all the time. Instead of complaining and begrudging, they keep working to make their own position in society better through their Pat Summitt grit—but they still throw down.

WITS blow off steam by having a good time, lettin' loose. Now, for some, "lettin' loose" means singin' the last verse of "Shall We Gather at the River" twice on Sunday just to piss off the preacher, but for a lot of women in the South, they got no problem showin' up to church late and hungover and not singin' at all. Southern women bring it. They can sing with abandon, dance barefoot in the kitchen or at a bar with peanut shells all over the floor, and most of them can handle their

Porch Talk with Drew

CHURCH LADIES

 My wife told me a story that continues to shape her to this day. As a little girl, she went to church with a friend. This practice is a common one in the South: you invite your friends to church as a way of extending the weekend hangout sessions because not going to church is not an option.

On this particular day, she was in the congregation playing with her friend and not listening—because she was a kid, and church is boring. "Since I came to your church, tonight you should come to mine," she said to her buddy. "We're having a special event for Halloween called the Pumpkin Patch—" Before she could say another word, an adult turned around from the pew in front of them.

"He will *not* be going with you tonight. *He* is not allowed to go to your church. Your church has a female pastor, and that's a sin."

The person who said this to my at-the-time eight-year-old wife was her friend's mother. This woman told a little girl that her son was forbidden to attend church where a woman preached because it was a sin for a woman to hold a place of authority in the Church.

DM

liquor better than the men. Or maybe they're just better at knowin' when to stop—again, smarter.

Saturday morning, she might be making layered Mexican dip, buffalo chicken dip, spinach dip, pimento cheese dip, pigs in a blanket, BBQ sliders, ham biscuits, cookies, lemon squares, brownies, and a veggie tray (just *in case* someone wants something healthy[13]); packing up the team-colored tablecloth (Tennessee orange) and napkins, folding table, folding chairs, and little football helmet centerpiece; and making sure the beers and magnum of white wine are on ice in the cooler.

But once she gets to the parking lot or wherever they're setting up, that girl has a whole two hours before the game starts, the three hours the game takes, and then the hour after the game avoiding the traffic to get completely and utterly fucked up. And since her husband did at least pack up the TV and satellite to put up in the parking lot, she doesn't even have to go inside the stadium to watch the Vols win.

This is just one example of how WITS fit cuttin' loose into daily Southern life the way Pastor Bill fits in trips to the men's room to admire his hair that he swears looks like it was brushed by the wings of angels. They've also been known to put a little mimosy in a Roo Cup[14] for the kids' softball and football games, knock back some wine at Tuesday night book club, and take a tiny shot of whiskey before the PTA meeting—because who could get through it otherwise? And sitting on the porch enjoying a cold, cold beer while just watching the world go by works any time of the day she can swing it. Chances are, she's earned it.

So, men, don't go out there askin' her what's for supper or if she's seen the channel changer. It's time to get more progressive in our attitudes and policies toward women in the South (and everywhere). The

13. **They won't.**

14. **A reusable cup you get from Circle K convenience stores that you can refill with fountain drinks anytime for twenty-nine cents. Hits.**

ODE TO SOUTHERN WOMEN: THE FREE SPIRIT

★

This is the gal with a heart of gold who lives to bring everybody together in the name of a good time. She is friends with *everyone* and doesn't discriminate against *anybody*. If there's a band playing, whether it be a Johnny Cash cover band at a hole-in-the-wall bar, 38 Special playing at the fairgrounds, or the high school marching band, she's the one hollering louder than anybody else. The next morning's rough, but she still smiles (and looks great) because hangovers are for pussies.

Look for her in the front row or out back sitting on top of a picnic table taking a smoke break. She'll be wearing a tank top because sleeves are hot and restrictive, and she's got to be able to move, bayba! A tattoo gives a feminine touch to her flip-flops, but she's just as apt to be barefoot no matter what condition the floor or the ground. She feels life from her head to her toes. She might get into a few scrapes here and there—bumping into some snobby-ass bitch after she just got a full beer (don't stand in the crowd if you don't want to get bumped—this ain't a sorority formal), but she just turns the experience into a good story to reenact the next morning.

THE FREE SPIRIT TO-DO LIST

★ Take up a collection at work for a coworker who's in the hospital with bills piling up—even if it's the grumpy guy nobody's been missing.
★ Stock up on whiskey (and a purse that hides whiskey) so there's plenty for sharing.
★ Organize a memorial get-together for a buddy who passed away—with kegs and a band.

★ Buy a new pair of 7-Eleven sunglasses cause your other ones must have fallen off your head while you were dancing on the pontoon boat, and you didn't notice.

★ Treat people you just met like they're your best friends and invite them to your momma's for supper because they probably need a friend or at least some home cookin'.

★ Dance like nobody's watchin'. Because they're not. No one cares, and if they are, then bless their hearts, they need a life. Dance. Whenever. Wherever.

WITS ain't waitin' around. They're gonna keep doin' what they're doin' and figure maybe one day the rest of the world will catch up. In the meantime, they will kick their feet up when they can and celebrate all the things and people they work so hard to take care of. Life in the South ain't always easy for a woman, but we believe if you took a poll, most of 'em wouldn't want to live anywhere else. (What does a Yankee woman even *do* on a fall Saturday?) Like someone very special to us (Dolly) once said, "The way I see it, if you want the rainbow, you gotta put up with the rain."

DOLLY PARTON

As if we need to explain why she hits . . .

My God, do we love Dolly Parton. We love her so fuckin' much. Our wives and girlfriends love her. Gay men really love her. The preacher loves her. Grannies, papaws, exchange students, poets, accountants—they *all* love her. A hero and idol to little girls and boys all over the world, she's transcendent. She's an icon. She's a titan. A businesswoman. A humanitarian. But she is also East Tennessean, and it's hard to put into words what that means to folks around here.

ODE TO SOUTHERN WOMEN: THE SOUTHERN BELLE

★

Aside from the gentle and porcelain looks of her outward appearance (sunscreen, dummies. Use it), no good Southern belle is a stranger to rolling up her sleeves and going all the way in on some yard work. In big, wavy straw hat, pink rubber gloves, denim button-up, and tan capris, she tirelessly plants hydrangeas[15] and hangs ferns in just the right places. She lays stones as a walkway to her front door, which she repaints every spring. (Well, she makes her sorry-ass son do it.) The water fountain in her yard is always crystal clear. (It also no longer has that statue of a little black boy with a fishing rod in it—she learned her lesson from Paula Deen.)

If she can't go to the Kentucky Derby[16] herself, dagnabbit, then she will just host her own mint julep–themed party in her living room. That will be more fun anyway. She'll serve pimento cheese and chicken salad sandwiches cut into quarters with toothpicks in them. (Pretty sure they do this so they can eat twelve of something and not feel bad.) Then they will sit, highballs in hand, and discuss why their kids are better at whatever it is they're braggin' about and then catch up on all the gossip they missed this week. (Someone's a floozy. Guaranteed.)

---

15. Most Southern flower there is. Hell, the name sounds like someone saying hello to an eighty-year-old Pentecostal lady.

16. A place for racists to yell at horses.

THE SOUTHERN BELLE'S TO-DO LIST

★ Have a Pinterest board for every possible occasion.
★ Organize her stacks of every magazine that has ever had a pie on the cover of it. Ever.
★ Look purdy. (Look, we ain't sayin' it *ort* be a duty, but it seems to be.)
★ Never complain.
★ That's it—they're often rich and got less they have to do.

Dolly grew up dirt poor. One of her early homes had *dirt* floors. She was a farmer's daughter. That accent, which she never lost or even turned down, was as ingrained in her as her love for her home county (where she has invested and created an industry—seriously, look it up). Coming from that to where she is while maintaining her sense of self is stunning. There's so much to say about her, but one thing that we cannot quite put into words is how inspiring it is that she has been so authentically Dolly, and therefore authentically Southern, through all her accomplishments.

By the time we were in our teens, Dolly was already a superstar, and it was striking how the media treated her so differently than most Southern or country stars. In interviews, no one called her one of the best "Southern" or "country" singers of all time—they simply called her one of the best. No one commented on her accent and called it "cute" or told her how they "love it so-oooo much."

There are many Southern celebrities *in the South*. But very few reach a level of international fame and accolades the way Dolly has. The ones that do either shy away from that Southern aspect or become *defined* by that Southern *otherness*.

Dolly somehow did neither. She is that rare example of a famous

Porch Talk with Trae

Because my momma was a pillhead and dealer for most of my childhood, my mema filled the role of Southern momma.

Mema got married to Pa when she was sixteen, and she stood by him for fifty years—right up until he died of a heart attack/stubbornness at the age of sixty-nine. She will almost kill you with cornbread if you don't force her to stop feeding it to you, and when you do that, she will *not* appreciate it. She loves her family unconditionally. Now, every momma would make that claim, but Mema's case is utterly unassailable. Because Mema, who was born and lived her entire life in one of the most rural regions of Tennessee, had two sons, and only two sons. And one of those sons happened to be gay.

In the rural South, during that time period (and hell, even today), gay people were disowned by their families for being what they are. It's horrific and shameful that this is the case, but it simply is. As a Southern father today, that shit astonishes me and makes my blood boil. I genuinely can't fathom how parents could allow something like sexual orientation to affect the way they feel about their child.

Far as I'm concerned, if you're one of those "No son o' mine" types, then you ain't no goddamn daddy, and you should be ashamed of yourself. But here's the thing: that's comparatively easy for me to say nowadays. While I don't think I would have felt a single bit differently about it if I had been born fifty years earlier, the fact remains that it was a much more difficult stand for parents of that generation to take.

But not for Mema. That was her baby boy. So I grew up with my uncle *and* his partner coming to every family dinner, every holiday. To be honest, I never thought anything of it because that's just how it was. And we had Mema to thank for that.

A *lot of people* do not appreciate my pro-gay statements. Because assholes never die. (For the record: didn't care then, still don't care now. Bring it on, dipshits.) But one day Mema called me and said a package had arrived for me at the house I grew up in (where she now lives), and it was addressed to "The Liberal Redneck." I haven't lived at that address for fifteen years. So I was a little freaked out at first. Now, it ended up being a sweet present, a really beautiful gesture from a fan, so all was well, but at first I was worried. It could just as likely have been something *terrible,* and I didn't want Mema to see anything like that.

This was the conversation:

"Mema, *don't open that.*"

"Well, Trae, honey, I ain't gonna just open your mail. Honey, you know me. I don't do nothin' like that. Do you really think I would jus—"

"No, Mema, I don't care about that. I'm just worried it'll be something really bad. Because, look, a lot of people really do not appreciate these videos I've been making."

"I know that."

"Well, I just don't want you to see anything like that."

"Well, honey, nothing anybody could say is gonna make me love you any less. They can kiss my ass."

Damn. I'm gonna go call Mema. See y'all.

person who for so long has so consistently been herself—big hair, thick accent, bubbly smile, and tacky clothes—that the world finally just accepted her. Not just in an "Entertain us, funny songbird!" kind of way, but truly and wholly without ridicule. Y'all, have you *seen* how she dresses? But everyone just allows it. Because she's that good.

For kids like us growing up, who sound like her and think like her and have parents who act like hers prolly did, that acceptance of her was unreal. We suppose that's why we get so defensive of her. I've seen a Southern white man nearly come to blows with another because that man said it was bullshit that UT awarded her that PhD. For all the little girls in the South who had Dolly to look up to as a Southerner and a woman who made her own damn music, movies, business decisions—well, we don't even know how much that means. Probably the whole world.

IS IT JUST US?

Sexism isn't exclusively a Southern thing—but we do seem to be pretty good at it. Just like going fast and blowing up shit. Sure, people from the North *can* do that, but there's a reason they gave us NASA.

In northern metropolitan cities, women are catcalled and sexually assaulted on public transportation at an alarming rate. Lotsa date-raping male athletes are of the northern Ivy League persuasion. Nationwide, women are paid seventy-nine cents to the dollar that men are paid. Only 4.4 percent of Fortune 500 CEOs are women. One in five women are raped. So sexism is not just in the South, but son of a bitch, we ain't doing anyone no favors by acting like that makes it okay.

There aren't any easy solutions to most of these problems, but we have a suggestion as a place to start here at home (and fuckin' everywhere, really): accountability. That's it.

It's a difficult concept for entitled men to grasp. But we have got to take a step back and own up to what we've done here—maybe not necessarily what we've personally done, but certainly what we have allowed to continue. As powerful and smart as the women are, they need our help in moving forward because we have set into place laws and rituals that constantly set them two steps back for every one forward, and it's bullshit.

Going forward, we have to swallow our (misplaced) pride and accept the fact that women are our equals (betters). We have to understand that sometimes they're gonna be our boss and we have to listen to what they say because (a) that's how jobs work, and (b) she deserves to be there—and in today's society, probably more so than you. Because she had to achieve a hell of a lot more to get there than you did. We need to move forward and always be progressing. Or one day our women might finally decide to get up, take off, and never come back. And then this whole place would just fall apart. It really would.

Corn from a Jar

If you're anything like us, then you like three things: twenty-four-hour sports channels, buffalo-flavored anything, and a good excuse to get turnt. Getting drunk is fun no matter who or where you are, but getting drunk in the South is more than just something to do, it's a rite[1] of passage.

We spend our childhoods absolutely enamored by whatever that is in Papaw's glass. We see the beer cans our dads keep crushing in the boat and just *know* that since we aren't allowed to have it yet, it must be magical. We long for the day that we can share a beer with our old man, knowing that when that day comes, we will finally be as cool as him. (We won't be: we will puke in a hot tub next to the girl whose titties we will now not be touching. Won't hit.)

We get to high school (some of us middle school), and we finally

1. Upon first sip of that lukewarm Natty Ice that got shook up when tossed our way from the back of a beat-up truck . . . Lord, we was wrong. So very wrong.

get a chance to experiment with the mythical liquid. It always starts out with domestic light beer (piss water) and we are just *so goddamn excited*! "Wooo-hooo! Ain't nothing here on out 'cept pussy, touch-downs, and bonfires, baby! We ain't ever gonna die!"

That's when it hits our lips and—oh, dear God! What the hell is this? Did they boil hot dogs in old Sprite? This is what we couldn't have? This is what's supposed to be so goddamn delightful? No thanks—this shit is nasty. That's when the more experienced guy at the party (a sophomore) comes up and gives you the advice that will change your life forever: "You just gotta acquire the taste, man. You'll get used to it." (He then goes and bangs your girlfriend.) Get *used* to it? That ain't how it went with macaroni and cheese—no siree Bob. First bite and you're hooked. Hits immediately. Can't fathom how something so shitty could get better over time. Fortunately for us, though, beer is not like *True Blood*, and that actually is the case. After a while, you not only learn to tolerate the skunky taste, but hell, you start to crave it. It makes food taste better, sports more fun to watch, and women easier to put up with.[2]

Soon you've got to move on to something stronger: whiskey, moon-shine, drugs . . . and the next thing you know, you're in college and are introduced to the fact that there are types of beer out there that *weren't* in the seafoam-green fridge by the dartboard in your daddy's garage. Holy shit! Craft beer is awesome! And, boy howdy, do we have some hittin' ones south of the Mason-Dixon!

Alcohol is so great, you guys! What could possibly go wrong? Yeah, that's the problem for everything that's great in this world. We certainly manage to find a way to fuck up alcohol for everyone else. You have teen pregnancy, DUIs, alcohol poisoning, a staggering

---

2. **Compared to men who just suck no matter how drunk you are.**

increase in domestic violence—all the result of a common theme we have going down here in the South: rules are for pussies!

While alcohol certainly helps ease the tension when meeting your future in-laws for the first time, it has also destroyed countless families both physically and financially. Does the good outweigh the bad? Is this a problem of substance or self-control? We will throw our white male opinion into the hat and see if we can't figure out this thing. Before that, though, let's take a look at how we got here.

SOUTHERN BOOZE: A HISTORY

Whiskey and Bourbon

Jasper Newton "Jack" Daniel was born sometime in 1850. The exact date of his birth is unknown (I assume booze was involved), but most people celebrate his birthday on September 5. He was one of Calaway and Lucinda Daniel's ten kids (some sources say it was thirteen), so if you know anything about how *that* is, dude was gonna hit the bottle sooner or later.[3] Well, he grew up and in 1875 decided to take the world by storm with his hittin'-ass whiskey. He never married or had children, so who knows how he was able to revolutionize alcohol. All the extra time on his hands? No one crushing his dreams and shitting themselves every four hours? Truly a mystery. I think, however, if he knew how many basic-ass-shitty-as-fuck country songs[4] he would inspire over the years, he probably would've just said to hell with it.

3. Siblings suck.

4. There are some extremely fine ones too, though. We ain't about to disparage the classics; you know which ones they are. (And if you don't, you suck.)

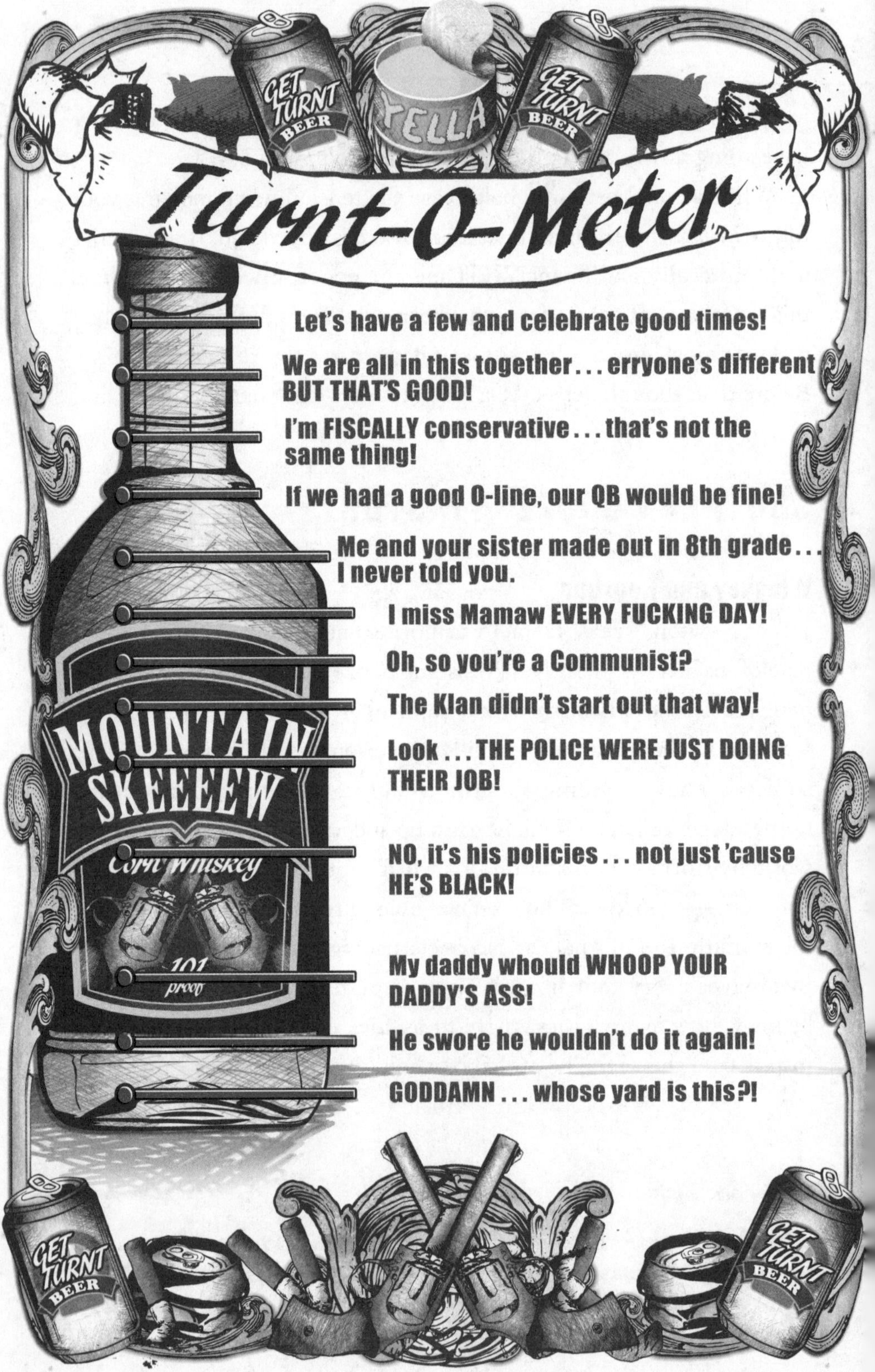

GET TURNT BEER
YELLA
GET TURNT BEER
Turnt-O-Meter
Let's have a few and celebrate good times!
We are all in this together . . . erryone's different BUT THAT'S GOOD!
I'm FISCALLY conservative . . . that's not the same thing!
If we had a good O-line, our QB would be fine!
Me and your sister made out in 8th grade . . . I never told you.
I miss Mamaw EVERY FUCKING DAY!
Oh, so you're a Communist?
The Klan didn't start out that way!
Look . . . THE POLICE WERE JUST DOING THEIR JOB!
NO, it's his policies . . . not just 'cause HE'S BLACK!
My daddy whould WHOOP YOUR DADDY'S ASS!
He swore he wouldn't do it again!
GODDAMN . . . whose yard is this?!
MOUNTAIN SKEEEW
Corn Whiskey
101 proof
GET TURNT BEER
GET TURNT BEER

Now, jokes about free time aside, we have to point out that right as we were researching (drinking a lot) for this book, a story came out that one of the slaves on Jasper Newton Daniel's land named Nearis Green is *actually* responsible for making the recipe taste so unique, and so good. Imagine *that*: not having any kids or other bothersome things *and* literally owning a man who knows how to make whiskey. My God, slavery is sad as hell, ain't it? The company has recently (perhaps for good reasons or perhaps for PR purposes) embraced this story and confirmed that Nearis had a "role" in the makin' of the mash. Whether he is truly the distiller and originator of one of the most popular spirits on the planet, or was more of an overseer who learned from Jasper, as others say, doesn't matter. What matters is that we acknowledge that yet again, an empire that has made numerous white people rich was built around the work and skill of slaves. Here's to you, Nearis Green—we're so sorry your life was not your own, and we're so thankful you shared your skills with the world anyway.

As with a lot of things in the South ('cause aside from racism and not giving a fuck about books and oral hygiene, we do a shit ton right), Old No. 7 quickly became a national phenomenon: Frank Sinatra, Dean Martin, Lemmy Kilmister (a Brit, you say?)—hell, even the GD dog on *Family Guy*—all enjoyed Lynchburg, Tennessee's, finest. Bluto chugs it in *Animal House*, and Clark Griswold cites the whiskey as his method for getting through the holidays in *Christmas Vacation*. It's easily one of the most recognized brands and bottles in the entire world.

For many young folk in the South, it's the first thing they ever puked up aside from too many of them cheap-ass ice pops that you can buy by the thousand in them red nets. Taking a shot of JD without making a face is how young boys figured they could get a piece of ass. (Being honest, it worked every now and then.) And it remains a favorite for

Porch Talk with Trae
QUITTIN' THE BOOZE

I like drinkin', and I like cheese. Verily, yes I do. As many men of such predilections are prone to do, I have struggled with my weight over the years. I was a fat kid growing up—a big ol' stupid, fat, dork-ass kid. I was still funny, though. Fat kids are hilarious. But nothing else about it was very cool. So I decided when I was about twelve or thirteen that I was gonna leave the Cheetos life behind me once and for all.

I tried basically starving myself (fat redneck kids are dumb), and it was working but not like I felt it *should h*ave been working. And one day I had an epiphany: I came home from school and, as I did every day, pulled out a bottle of that sweet, sweet orange drank. Talkin' bout Sunny D, y'all. Nectar of the Trailer gods. I used to drink—I shit you not—about a bottle of Sunny D *a day.* And it had never occurred to me that that might be a little of a problem. But on this particular afternoon, I happened to notice the calories on the side of the bottle and realized that I was getting an extra *two thousand* calories a day from just that liquid sugar. That probably seems hilarious to some of y'all that I didn't already know that's how it worked, but again, fat, poor redneck kids—they's a lot we don't know. So anyway, I put two and two together and cut every drink but water out of my diet immediately. No sodas, no Sunny D, no sweet tea. None of that. And I lost thirty-five pounds. Just like that.

You probably wonderin' what the hell that has to do with booze. Well, fast-forward about twenty years. After being relatively slim throughout the latter part of high school and most of college, I had gotten married and lazy and ballooned up to 225 pounds, heaviest I've ever been. Corey had also been talkin' about being a fat piece of trash at that time, so we decided we were going to have a weight-loss competition.

And we were going to blog about it. Because we're pretentious fat fucks. This was also during the last season of one of our number one TV jams, *Downton Abbey.* (We know. We know.) So we made it a combination *Downton*/weight-loss blog and called it *Downton Flabbey.* It hit. But that ain't the point. The point is that I decided if I was going to whip CoFo's ass like I wanted to, I was going to *have* to stop drinking. I kept thinking back to when I was a kid and how much of a difference quitting the demon D had made for me, and I knew that there was just no good way to go about this shit while still gettin' turnt. It was just too many empty calories. No way around it.

So I stopped. Completely. Other than some whiskey during the Super Bowl—because this is still America, goddamn it—I didn't have a drop of alcohol for the entire length of the contest. First of all, it worked like a charm: I dropped twenty pounds in ten weeks. But also, I genuinely could not *believe* how much better I felt. Clearer headed, slept better—just generally didn't wake up feeling like I had been beaten with socks filled with shit soap.

The first weekend after I stopped drinking, I slept in until like ten thirty, and I swear I woke up feeling like Tom Cruise. Or, ya know, what I imagine that alien-ass motherfucker feels like every day. I was goin' for runs and shit. It was awesome. And it really wasn't hard, either, to be honest. Because, look, booze hits, to be sure. But feeling like a soccer player every day hits too. I'd recommend quittin' the sauce to anybody.

But then the weight-loss challenge ended, and me and Corey celebrated that occasion by gettin' just plum tore-down drunk and hittin' for bout eighteen solid hours. I barrel-rolled off that wagon at breakneck speed and ain't looked back. Look, I never said I recommended quittin' boozin' *forever*—I just said you should try it out. And you should. The bottle will be waitin' on you when you need it. It always is.

your average veteran detective to sip straight from the bottle while saying something like, "Shoulda got out while I was young . . ."

Wanna know something crazy, though? Lynchburg, Tennessee, the town where Jack Daniel's is distilled? It's in a dry county, baby! That's right. Moore County, Tennessee. The folks who *work* in the Jack Daniel's distillery can't even buy it in the same goddamn town. Ain't that *dumb* as hell? Keep reading for more on blue laws and how stupid they are.

Jack Daniel's is technically a "Tennessee whiskey." We bein' Tennessee boys, we also call it nectar of the gods and signature drink of those that hits, but we ort say a little thing or two about its northern cousin, Kentucky bourbon. It, too, is a corn-based whiskey and also aged in charred oak barrels. In fact, they got more barrels of that sweet, sweet liquor aging in Kentucky than they've got people. The formerly humble bourbon has become very popular in the ranks of fancy restaurants with "bar programs" and bartenders in suspenders with tattoos and hittin' handlebar moustaches. This is fine with us—if you ain't got no connection to the South other than enjoying a $40 swalla of ol' Pappy Van Winkle's over a hand-carved piece of ice, then you're gettin' a pretty sweet taste of what we've got to offer.

But you ain't wrong either if you try one of the hundred or so other Kentucky bourbons available. And while that artfully carved piece of ice is pretty cool, most bourbon tastes just as good right outta the bottle. Wild Turkey, for example: it don't mess around with cut crystal. It's more of a cut-to-the-chase type of creature, but each bourbon has its own personality and most have cool-as-shit names, too: Old Crow, Old Blowhard, Old Grand Dad, Old Fitz, Old Tub, Old Forrester (personal fave of CoFo), Fighting Cock, Four Roses, Heaven Hill; old pards like Ezra Brooks, Elijah Craig, and Basil Hayden; and Jack Daniel's wannabes Jim Beam and Evan Williams. I'm telling ya, if we're talking strictly beverages, the South wins every fuckin' time.

Moonshine

Moonshine isn't just a drink, it's a response. Its entire popularity was brought about by Prohibition.[5] Know what else Prohibition made popular? *The goddamn mob.* ('Preciate ya, ya dumb-fuck teetotalers.) If we were to describe moonshine without getting super scientific (which, even though our papaws know how to do it, it totally is), we'd probably just stick to two things:

1. **Taste.**
2. **How fucked up it gets you.**

Pretty simple. The answers are "awful," and "a whole goddamn lot."

Moonshine tastes like gasoline that got filtered through one of your mamaw's hair nets. And then after that, someone poured the juice from a can of corn in it. And then they shook it over a fire that Satan made with his penis and a piece of flint. It don't hit. Never met a sumbitch that *actually* liked the taste of it. If someone says he does, he is either lying or he doesn't actually have an inside to his mouth. When Prohibition started in 1920, people didn't just throw in the towel and say, "Well, gee golly, I guess if they say we ort not drink, that must be what's best for us, a skeet da deet." Shit, naw, buddy—au contraire. They proceeded to get *more* fucked up by cooking up themselves a batch of hybrid poison that was one part whiskey and one part dragon semen.

Shit works, though! Hot damn, buddy! One shot of that white lightnin', and you will straight-up barefoot kick a tree off its goddamn root while high-fiving a fucking bear. Shit is *fierrrrreeeeeeey*! Unlike other forms of alcohol that actually taste decent or can be fancied up to taste decent, moonshine's sole purpose is to get you totally commode-huggin' drunk.

<hr>

5. A dismal and shitty fucking time to be a person.

Porch Talk with Drew

The only time I've ever driven drunk, the devil moonshine was to blame. It's not something I'm proud of, and obviously *I* am the one to blame, but, man, that stuff will change your outlook quick if you ain't careful.

I was partying with friends at a lake house, and some good ol' boy brought some white lightning by. I had already got my red up earlier that night over a girl—y'all know how it is. And, well, I figured I'd fix my issues with some of Pappy's medicine. It was a good idea and was working—until the damn girl came by the party. I was far too deep down the demon well in that homemade liquor drink to get on top of my emotions, and, well, I told her what was on my heart.

She ain't respond in a way I liked, so I left. One of my friends, in an effort to stop me, grabbed my guitar out of my truck and said, "You can't leave your guitar here." "Fuck that stupid guitar," were my exact words, I believe. I drove about an hour (we was deep in the woods), realized how stupid I was being, and pulled into a Save a Lot parking space. I woke up three hours later, puked in a McDonald's bathroom, and drove home. I ain't had more than one drink of moonshine in a given night since.

DM

Moonshiners get their name on account of they worked primarily at night so they wouldn't get caught by the fuzz for running that sweet drunk nectar. Most stills were out in the woods, and the shiners would work under the light of the moon. It's just a coincidence that it happens to be the best time (and place) to get shit faced. In order to ensure that they could get away quickly if they *were* caught up in a scuff with the law, moonshiners would rig their cars up sweet so they could outrun the coppers. So even though we just gave Prohibition shit for helping perpetuate the mob, I guess we've also got to give it credit for something awesome it created: NASCAR.

That's right, baby. All them boys in souped-up cars running from the county mounties got together one day and thought, "Hell, wouldn't it be fun if we did this, but, like, without the cops and in, like, a field or some shit?" So they did. The early days of NASCAR were made up almost exclusively of bootleggers, and they put on one hell of a show. If it wasn't for Prohibition, we wouldn't have NASCAR, and if it wasn't for NASCAR we wouldn't have Dale Earnhardt,[6] and if we didn't have Dale Earnhardt, then our mamaws wouldn't have any plates on their walls.

Any party worth its salt in the South will have a jar of moonshine floating around. Usually a few different flavors. Apple-pie moonshine is a fairly big deal 'round here because the only thing more American than apple pie is getting piss drunk and trying to finger your buddy's sister on a pontoon boat—so when you can combine the two, you've really got a time on your hands.

White Lightning, Mountain Dew, Skull Cracker, Bush Whiskey, Stumphole—no matter what you call it, if you're from the South, you've drank it—and probably still do to this day among certain friends because you don't wanna get called a pussy in front of your old lady. Perfectly solid logic.

Piss-Water Beer

Ain't much looks more inherently Southern than a red-and-white can of tasteless, watered-down, skunky-ass domestic "beer." While the word *beer* does have quotes around it to show sarcasm and allude to the fact

6. **Jesus's cousin.**

RIP NUMBER THREE

★

On April 29, 1951, in Kannapolis, North Carolina, a child was born. It's never been proven, but it *is* speculated that three wise ol' boys followed the light from a Waffle House to find the boy swaddled in homemade quilts and offer him gifts of chrome, fried chicken, and Skoal Bandits (easier for babies to dip). A Christlike figure in the South, this child would grow up to be the greatest NASCAR driver of all time: Dale Earnhardt. The Intimidator.

With seventy-six wins and 428 top tens in the Sprint Cup Series alone, the man had to turn down more pussy than a feral cat at a rescue center. He had three wives, four kids, and five-feet worth of wiener. The man is a larger-than-life legend in NASCAR, and since NASCAR is a redneck thing, he's a larger-than-life legend in the South.

From T-shirts, jackets, license plates, bumper stickers, commemorative plates, and jelly jars, the number three was plastered on everything in the South throughout the 1990s and early 2000s. Really, the only difference today is that when you see it displayed, there are angel wings on both sides of it. Only reason he got into heaven was 'cause Jesus was a fan— 'cause Dale sure drove like a man going to hell.

Tragically, he died in a wreck on February 18, 2001, at the Daytona 500. His death completely revolutionized the way safety restraints in stock cars were designed and mandated, and dozens of lives have been saved since. Earnhardt himself rejected seat-belt precautions that could have saved his life, but when you're a product of the fifties and have done nothing but hit at an extremely high level (in both racing and ass smashing) your entire life, precautions are for pussies.

Dale's extra-large T-shirts have been used as day dresses for a specific breed of Southern women for years, and his name is invoked posthumously as an example of greatness:

"How great was that chicken?" "Earnhardt."

"Skeeeeww! You see that firework show? Earnhardt, baby!"

"God, baby, that was amazing! Was is it good for you?" ". . . Kyle Petty." Ouch.

Earnhardt is chiseled upon the Southern Mount Rushmore[7] alongside Skynyrd, Mark Twain, Outkast, and Martin Luther King Jr. (Now, there's not a lot of overlap among people who are fans of all four, but the list checks out.) NASCAR has not been the same since he left, and it's likely that a character of his magnitude will never surface in the sport again.

Hope you're going left on streets of gold, number three.

7. Believe ours is called Mount Keith.

that it's very much *barely* beer, please believe that we still fucks with it. Look, if you're gonna be on a boat all goddamn day in the Georgia heat, you can't be sippin' on hoppy-ass IPAs the whole time—naw, naw. You gotta stay hydrated, baby. Everyone in the South knows that it's much better to have thirty light beers over the course of six hours than it is to have six of them good beers. It just makes sense. Them light beers is watered down, ergo they got water in 'em. That's what the doctors say we ort drink. Skeew—loophole!

Tailgates, farm parties, above-ground-pool bashes—everyone will have their own cooler filled to the brim with their choice of the soda of the South, and there's an unspoken "no beer left behind" policy. No

Porch Talk with Corey

Back in 2008, the Georgia Bulldogs had an outside shot of getting to the National Championship. All that had to happen was, like: Mizzou had to beat someone, West Virginia had to do something or another, Oklahoma was involved somehow (y'all, I'm sorry, I was drunk—ain't gonna remember it all correctly). And the moon had to be aligned with Pluto, and Pat Robertson had to vote Democrat. Well, I'll be goddamned if all of that didn't happen! (Except the Pat Robertson thing—we'd have better luck explaining climate change to a trump supporter.[8])

This was our year, baby! It was finally gonna happen in my lifetime. After years of going 9-3 only to crap out at the end of the season or have our running back snap his goddamn leg on a pointless sweep in the first quarter, we were actually going to have a chance to play for the BCS (Bowl Championship Series)[9] National Championship.

Well, wouldn't ya know? That's exactly what *didn't* happen. The powers that be decided once again that the Big Ten deserved a hand job and get to go to the big game, while a great team in the literal greatest conference on earth needed to play a team that—while good—plays in a conference that means nothing in a state that's basically closer to Japan than it is to America.

None of that matters, however, as far as the story goes. Point is, the night all that insane-scenario bullshit went down, me and my buddy William decided that if UGA was going to the National Championship, we should do our part for the team and die before that happened. So we hollered at

---

8. Not a proper noun. Shouldn't be capitalized.

9. A system designed to let **Ohio State** do whatever the fuck it wants regardless of its weak-ass schedule.

his daddy's moonshine that was in the freezer. (That's where you put alcohol that won't freeze on account of it's made out of gasoline.) In the midst of this shit-faced buffet was a thirty rack of beer and some cherries that had been soaking in moonshine for a few months. We made up a new game: ScheBeers. It wasn't so much a game as it was us making up a name that incorporated, in some variation, the names of all three beverages. (A liquor-soaked cherry *is too* a drink.)

What you'd do is eat one of the soaked cherries, take a shot of moonshine, and then chug a beer. Sounds great, huh? Yeah, well we did that about thirteen times. The night progressed, and we got redder and redder—howling at the moon because "This is our year, *baby*!!!! *Skeeeeeeewwwwww!*" At about three in the morning, I decided it would be a good idea to walk to my momma's house and go to sleep. It ain't a far walk at all, but when you're drunker than three Navy SEALs on shore leave, it's a whole thing. I staggered my (at the time) happy Georgia Bulldawg–fan ass up the street and walked up the driveway. The door to Momma's house looked like it was ten miles away, but I was bound and determined to get there—tumbler full of beer in hand. I approached the front steps and started getting the leans. I took two hard steps to the left and caught some stupid bush Momma had planted right at my ankles. I tripped, fell, and hit my head on a birdbath.

That's where Momma found me—just laid out for dead. I somehow still had all the beer in my tumbler and my tumbler in my hand. (I hit.) Momma cussed me out and drug my ass into bed, where I would sleep for the better part of what felt like a decade.

Upon waking the next day, I was informed that regardless of the circumstances, Georgia would still not be going to the National Championship. We would go on to play Hawaii in the Sugar Bowl and absolutely embarrass their pineapple-eating asses, but that doesn't matter . . . this was our year.

That's the shitty part about alcohol. When you wake up, your problems are still there—only worse. Go Dawgs.

matter how much you buy, it will somehow not be enough to get you through to that inevitable three-in-the-morning Krystal burger run. "Oh, that's fine, guys. Just go buy more." Yeah, well, here's the thing about that:

BLUE LAWS, BIBLE, BOREDOM

See, a multitude of small Southern towns, if not dry altogether, have some very weird alcohol laws on the books. They're too concerned with what the bearded Lord thinks to give a fuck about revenue— revenue that would probably help a town that ain't had a pot to piss in since goddamn NAFTA.[10] In many places, you can't buy it on Sunday (as if going to church didn't already ruin football enough), meaning that you've gotta get your shit together by 11:59 on Saturday night— hell, that's early for a damn farm party! Several towns will *have* beer but cannot legally have it cold. (We know what you're doing: trying to keep rednecks from chugging them in the parking lot. Well, *fuck* y'all. We know how ice works.) Many places will not serve until the polls close on Election Day. (Folks might get drunk and realize they're voting against their own interest literally always.) And more often than not, you can't sell alcohol within a certain distance from a church—the place that makes you want to drink the most.

Religion is the common thread here in the way that alcohol has gotten such a devilish stigma. See, there ain't a lot of Catholics down here, which is a bummer because them SOBs know how to throw down. The smaller towns are chock full of Southern Baptists, Independent Baptists, Church of Christs, and Church of Gods, and those

---

10. **The North American Free Trade Agreement, or "Why Uncle Ernest smells bad and rides a bicycle to the gas station."**

people tend to think that drinking turns you into a devil-worshiping bass player that's into butt stuff. Which is unfair—Uncle Dwayne is into all that, especially butt stuff, and he ain't never had a drop to drink. And hell, they's plenty of religious drunks down here—it's just that when it comes time to pass laws and shit, they vote with their Bible, not their brain.

Deeply religious folk are always trying to take away the hittinest shit from us: rock 'n' roll, booze, *titties*! Seriously, all the time—can't let us have fun worth a damn. But let us tell them that maybe—just maybe—it's not cool that they discriminate against people for their sexual orientation and then all of a sudden it's "I have religious freedom! You're persecuting me! This is exactly what it probably says in the Bible I've never read!" *Well, then quit trying to ruin our good time!*

Jesus drank wine *in the Bibl*e, y'all. Yun's make up a bunch of shit he *never* said about gay people but then just ignore the fact that one time a party started sucking and he abracadabraed some well water into Pinot and got that bitch turnt!

CELEBRATE!

You ever been to a wedding without alcohol? They exist, and they're absolutely the worst thing you can imagine. A wedding is full of things that don't hit without alcohol:

1. Doing the electric slide.
2. Talking to your relatives.
3. Existing.

Here's a list of things that *do* hit with alcohol:

1. Literally everything.

Alcohol is so prominently used in celebration because, simply, it makes you feel good. It loosens you up so that you can be the best version of yourself—for the first few tugs at least. Having a baby? Champagne! Getting married? Champagne! Going through a divorce? Jager![11] How the hell are you supposed to celebrate something without catching a buzz? Are there people out there who just clink some chicken wings together and say "Cheers!"? I mean, not that we ain't celebrated with some chicken wings—sure as shit have—but we was also drunk. Bet money.

Theme parties are getting more common as we get older. You know what I mean: these fake proms that thirty-five-year-old gals throw for their friend who's had a rough year and just needs to "get back out there, girl; fuck him and his whore momma!" or that pretentious dude from high school who wore a scarf in the summer and who always wanted to have a *Great Gatsby* party for his birthday because "the twenties were the last great era; intelligence has taken a backseat to vanity ever since. This world is full of buffoons who don't deserve my brilliance." (No one goes, and he dies alone in his tub.) Remember the theme of the parties when you were younger? *Gettin' drunk as shit!*

Them parties never don't hit.

DROWNING YOUR SORROWS

Alcohol is a weird beast, though. Not only do we require it upon receiving good news, we pine for it when things turn sour. Alcohol is certainly not a permanent solution to sadness and depression, but it damn sure masks it for a while.

---

11. **Pancake syrup that gets you as fucked up as bone cancer.**

Smart people like to get drunk—like, statistically and shit. Smart people also get depressed all the time, y'all. Their brains is taking in so much information, and if you've been out in the world lately (or the GD Internet), a lot of that information is just as sad as it can be (which is why dumb people[12] are so GD happy). A lot of people think alcohol temporarily makes you happy—it doesn't. It temporarily makes you dumb, and happiness is a side effect of dumb. Why do you think alcohol and drug abuse are so prevalent among the smarter members of society? Cause that shit is liquid stupidity, and we're all just chasing that retard dragon, baby! Every time someone dies, you've got the obligatory crazy aunt showing up with a flask of cheap whiskey and a fistful of benzos to medicate everyone into a coma. Hits.

When life kicks your ass and everything sucks, being drunk still feels good. No matter how the economy is doing, you will still find the bar stools filled with people and the jukebox filled with quarters. People will get drunk on the very last ten dollars they've got to their name. *Especially* then. What the hell good is ten dollars? Think you can slap that in a CD and get a high rate of interest and a quick return? Shit, no, buddy. You got three options:

1. **Buy a lottery ticket.**
2. **Get drunk.**
3. **Buy a slightly cheaper lottery ticket and get slightly less drunk.**

THE DARK SIDE

A lot of people get drunk because they lost their job; a lot of people lost their job because they got drunk. Alcoholism is rampant down

12. **People who did not buy this book.**

here in Dixie. It makes sense if you think about it: a lot of us work outside. Working outside is hot. Beer is cold. Working outside is shitty. Beer is not. Now, it ain't a damn thing wrong with someone enjoying a cold beer (or several) after a long, hard day. Ain't a thing wrong with having one on your day off. Hell, it ain't nothing wrong with having one at eight in the sumbitching morning if'n you want to. This is America, baby. You're free, Carol. Be free.

Problem is, though, and please believe this really sucks, not everyone can handle that shit. Some people can get drunk one day and then be sober a month. Some people can have a regulated two beers per night and never go any further. But there are some folks for which this is not the case. We tend to overlook or even make fun of this very shitty disease, but in truth, it's very sad. Okay, look, your uncle's pants falling down at your sister's wedding to reveal his Molly Hatchet tattoo to the world: that's funny. Once. But when it becomes a pattern, these people need help. Remember Otis from *The Andy Griffith Show*? Lovable town drunk who had the keys to the jail so he could let himself in once he'd finished his bender? Hilarious premise, but God dern, y'all, Otis needed help.

A lot of us in the South use our religion to judge the shit out of someone. That ort be the opposite. Lotsa Bible-thumpers ain't got compassion one for a drunkard cause "being a drunkard is a sin— they don't need rehab, they need Jesus." Well, unless the good Lord is gonna show back up here on earth to hold a man down in his bed when he's shaking with the delirium tremens and use some of that old wine magic he's got to turn some saltines into Xanaxes, naw, them folk need to see a professional.

It ain't just the physical harm they can cause themselves. Good ol' boys love to get drunk and burn rubber on the way to the lake. South Carolina is home to the highest percentage of traffic fatalities caused by alcohol in the United States—stop doing that mess. Alcohol can be cited as a reason *for* and a justification *of* domestic violence. Alcohol makes you lose your sense of judgment, so you pop your girlfriend for "talking back to me." She then turns around and says, "It was only cause he's drunk—he's normally not like this. It won't happen again." Until it does. And this ain't Hollywood. Everyone ain't gonna get the *Fried Green Tomatoes* treatment. It'd be great if the Deep South wasn't viewed as a bunch of drunk, redneck wife beaters, but that's the stereotype. Hell, they named the goddamn shirt after it!

We can do better.

LAST CALL

Alcohol is a truly amazing substance. Sure, it's been responsible for many deaths, but you've also gotta give it credit for all the births. Southerners are gonna drink beer. It's what we do. Ask any good ol' boy at any time of the day if he'd like a cold one, and guarantee you if he says no, it's cause he's already got one. From tailgating at schools in the greatest conference in college football to getting drunk and sunburnt in Panama City, Florida,[13] booze and Southerners go together like pork and beans. Our culture is so rich in alcohol history that it flows through just about everything we do: beer-battering catfish, shoving a beer can up a chicken's ass before you throw it on the grill, reconstituting a pot of turkey chili, or decorating your house with vintage Budweiser cans and Jim Beam bottles. We do more than just drink it, we live it.

Every boy has a PBR hat, every girl has a monogrammed koozie for holding drinks, and every old man has his sippin' whiskey. Without alcohol, you might not have had the courage to ask your wife out

---

13. **The farthest south you can be in Florida before it becomes the North again, and official underage drinking capital of the world.**

when you first met her. You might not have felt comfortable enough crying at your daughter's wedding. Hell, you might not have foolishly spent your last dime on them Skynyrd tickets on October 20, 1977, in Greenville, South Carolina. If that were the case, you wouldn't have your soulmate, your daughter wouldn't know how much she means to you, and you would have missed Ronnie Van Zant's final performance here on earth. Wouldn't that have sucked?

To all you religious buttholes who try to block liquor sales from getting passed in your town: if you don't like it, don't drink it. Ever since the plant went to Mexico, we sure could use a little bit more cash flow through these parts, and, God knows, the boiled peanut stand isn't carrying us the way we thought it would.

To all yuns who lay drunk all the time, hit ya women, mistreat your kids, and fail them financially because of your disease: get help. You're giving people the fuel they need to justify their backward-ass voting. You're perpetuating decades-long stereotypes about the South that some of us are working to get past. And you're hurting the next generation of Southerners. And you should want them to be the greatest one yet. They can be. Hell, they *will* be.

Have a few, but don't be a dick. The world is watching.

10

Cold, Dead Hands

Have you ever stared down a buck through a scope so technologically advanced you could see the deer blink before you squeezed the trigger? Used a shotgun on skeet? Taken a few shots at the range with a 9 millimeter? No? Well, you ort get out there and try it.

The simple fact of guns is that they're fun as shit. The simple fact of gun violence, however, is that it's a real and awful problem, and as a country we're doing almost nothing to address it. Whatever you think ort be done, it's kinda undeniable at this point that we ain't doing much. Why? Well, you can say, "Look no further than the lobbyists who have hijacked the National Rifle Association (NRA) and bankrolled a campaign to distort the Second Amendment and people's view of gun regulation," and you wouldn't be *wrong*. But that'd be incomplete. To write it all off as that simple would be a mistake. Gun culture, specifically in the South, has much deeper roots than that.

When politicians and lobbyists stoke the fears of pro-gun citizens, they're not *just* tapping into a childish paranoia. Often we hear the tired mockery, in an awful, fake Southern accent, "They'll take *mah guns!*" but that phrase is not coming just from some idiot being para-noid. Someone who fears gun control is not afraid of losing just his[1] weapons but also his culture and a part of his identity.

HUNTING

Hunting has been a part of the human story since before the written word. We don't, as a species, need to read,[2] but we *have* to eat. And while farming is nice, and gathering seems like a fun activity you can pay a white woman named Vinju to teach you in a class in Portland, hunting is the meat of how we've gotten by. And meat has to be killed. In spite of how stupid cows are, most animals ain't tryin' to *be killed*, so hunting was the way to get meat till recently. Now, of course, we can just go to the butcher[3] and order up a filet to cut and size, go home, scream at the Braves for an hour while it marinates in a blend we didn't make ourselves, cook it on an electric stove, and then eat it, digest it, and shit it out in a running toilet we don't know how to fix. It's a really, really great time to be alive.

But used to be, you had to hunt to eat. Some people like to honor this. Most all of us in the South hunted growing up. Whether our fa-thers or uncles or friends' families took us, we spent at least one morn-ing walkin' into the woods before daylight, sitting as quietly as possible

---

1. And some hers too, but mostly it's dudes. Dudes like guns.

2. You need to read this book.

3. Support local butchers, y'all.

against a tree, [4] and falling asleep immediately until an adult woke us and said, "Time to go." And most of us, even from a young age, would go on these excursions with a loaded weapon in our tiny, young hands. It's just tradition. It's how we do it.

This will never change in the South, and we ain't sayin' it should. Hunting is a wonderful culture mostly full of responsible and decent humans who love the outdoors, enjoy bonding with others, and play a role in protecting the environment. It requires skill, dedication, patience, and commitment. [5]

Learning about rifles and shotguns as part of the hunting culture is also a wonderful tradition. The truth is, for some men and boys, hunting provides their main—if not only—form of bonding and time spent together. Lots of Southern men have a hard time with "feelings," on account of feelings being "for pussies," yet they make real connections on huntin' trips. Time spent in the woods, with no distractions or outside temptations, becomes sacred for a lot of folk. And even for people who go alone, hunting provides a much-needed break from everything. This is why you hear some hunters describe it as a "pure" or almost religious experience—because being out in the woods can be a tiny three-to-four-hour spiritual revitalization.

You may think that sounds silly. Well, keep that in mind the next time you put on $60 yoga britches and pay $20 to stretch for forty-five minutes with strangers. Or go to church, or book club, or whatever it is

---

4. Others of us recall fondly that first memory of "hunting" from a vehicle. At night or in the day, this is highly illegal and highly fun: there's a heater, the radio, and beer. As with many things, we do not condone this behavior but concede its hittery.

5. This is why we authors don't hunt anymore. We ain't into most of them things at six a.m. You want us to get up in winter before dawn and dress like a Navy SEAL? Naw. No thanks.

you do for yourself. Hunting is that kind of self-indulgent activity for a lot of rednecks, and making fun of rednecks for havin' an introspective ritual is about as full of shit as you can get, Tristan.

> Tristan: Rednecks are dumb and never self-reflect.
> Tristan [*next breath*]: Time spent alone in the woods
> with your thoughts while contemplating the movements
> of wild animals is stupid.

Your prejudice is showing.

Now, you may fairly point out that hunting does not *require* guns. Well, love don't require sex, but *shoo-wee*, it sure do make it a lot better. Besides, guns are actually pretty integral to certain types of hunting. Killing a turkey with a bow is harder than convincing your Aunt Tammy that Dolly Parton isn't a literal angel—sure, it's *possible*, but why even argue? Most hunters are responsible gun owners who keep their weapons hidden away safely. And most hunting guns are rifles (the nonautomatic, nonassault type), which, while certainly danger-ous, aren't exactly at the forefront of crime and mass shootings.

Hunting is passed on as a family tradition. Fathers take sons and daughters. They then take their kids. It continues. Guns are a huge part of that. They're passed down in the South from one generation to the next as well. Some folks have land, others pass on heirlooms like jewelry. Family Bibles are another big thing. But Papaw's gun is as important an inheritance as any to many families.

HOME PROTECTION AND THE SECOND AMENDMENT

But, of course, a big part of the Southern culture surrounding guns re-lates to another tradition we've passed down: protecting ourselves, our families, and our way of life. A man protecting his home[6] goes as far back in our culture as the Hatfields and the McCoys and their standing feud. We don't wanna be bothered, we don't wanna change, and we sure as hell ain't gonna let no one rob or hurt us.

This probably goes back to a time when, in a lot of the South, there was no one else to rely on for help in dangerous situations. To be honest, this is still the case in most rural areas. Local police forces may be great, but four officers serving hundreds of square miles just can't control everything. That's why every Halloween, redneck teens are able to run amok *The Purge*–style egging houses and causin' havoc.[7] If the small-town police can't prevent four sixteen-year-olds from trickin' ol' Mr. Jones's drunk ass into steppin' on a flamin' bag of poop, again, they ain't gonna be able to protect a family. So for a family living in a holler[8] twenty miles from a town with one cop car, a shotgun is a reasonable step for security.

And there is nothing wrong with that attitude. A big part of being a redneck is not needin' or wantin' anything from anyone, by God. Self-reliance may not require a gun, but it sure does help.[9] Besides, we ain't about to tell any of these proud holler folk that they ort give up anything, much less their gun. That would not end well.

6. This has just traditionally been the stereotype, and we're referencing it. Please, no women with guns shoot us for reporting that news. But send us pictures with your guns, as we find that sexy.

7. And never be arrested or *shot*.

8. This means "hollow," like a hollow bottom at the foot of a small mountain. We assume most of yuns knew that, but we wanna point out that sometimes "holler" means "to yell at," and other times it means "partake of," as in "I do want cheesecake, but first I'm a *holler* at this sammich."

9. With hunting, snakes, intruders, shit to do when ya drinkin', etc.

Porch Talk with Drew

A LITTLE BOY'S GUN

When I was eight, I got my hunting license after takin' a hunter's safety course at the elementary school one town over. Funnest lessons I'd ever had.

That same year, my father gave me the gun he'd promised me for as long as I'd been asking for it—which is to say for as long as I could talk. The gun was a .22 caliber rifle, or as everyone I've ever known calls them, simply "a twenty-two." It was short, maybe two feet long from stock to barrel, and, as I recall, had a very basic scope on it. My father had always explained that it was my brother's gun, and it would be mine when I was ready. It was a proud day for me when Dad told me Dustin was ready for a bigger gun and I would get the little one. It wasn't the first gun I actually hunted with, nor was it the oldest gun in my family, but it was the one I was most attracted to as a kid, because of its size.

Dad called my twenty-two a "little boy's gun," probably because that was what he'd heard it called when he was a boy, as if it were a type of gun you could ask for at the store: "Yes, can we see what you have in little boys' guns and also grab a pistol?" There is so much to ponder in those three words. *Little* stands out not just to tell how small the weapon was compared with other rifles, but also how small I was compared with what most people would imagine a gun owner looking like. *Boy* certainly reveals something of gender norms and hunting culture in the South. My father takes his only granddaughter hunting whenever she will go and has made no bones about how much he enjoys it. She wears pink camouflage and looks adorable. She makes him wear pink as well—he's less adorable. However, there's no doubt that a rifle like that is known colloquially as a little boy's gun for a reason tied up in sexism. Then, of course, there is *gun*. One could be easily fooled by the first two innocent words—"little boy's"—that this is some different kind of gun or even a toy. It's not. It's a real-life, bullet-firing, very effective, and very dangerous weapon. My father imparted this fact upon us gravely. But I now wonder if all gun-loving fathers are so responsible.

The twenty-two now belongs to one of my nephews and no doubt will be passed on to my niece if she continues to show any interest in learning how to shoot. It has been in my family for thirty years. It always will be. I haven't decided if I will change the "name." I highly doubt it.

DM

This admirable attitude of self-reliance and defending your hearth and home has morphed into something else, it seems, though. As proud defenders of the Second Amendment will inform you—whether you want to hear it or not—everyone is coming for our guns. And soon. The president, Congress, ISIS, all of them: they want Daryl's shotgun he got from his grandad!

From gun shows, where they openly promote their product by imploring customers to buy "while you still can," to homegrown militias who apparently believe in their blessed little hearts that they, a group of overweight forty- and fifty-year-old men who have never even had Boy Scout–level training and can't jog a mile, are the protectors of America, the Second Amendment has by far got to be the most countercultured of all the amendments. Obviously, there are groups that take the First Amendment very seriously, but it's tough to imagine a group of soccer moms getting together on the weekends to discuss "tactics" on how to keep free speech alive and comparing notes on their sweet new semiautomatic megaphones they use to proudly shout about their rights at "free speech shows."

Second Amendment counterculture[10] is alive and well, *especially* in the South. It's passed down from generation to generation as proudly and seemingly almost as frequently as Papaw's muzzle loader.[11] The results of this are mixed, to say the least.

GUN SHOWS

Gun shows are one of the strangest and most surreal traditions of the American West, parts of the Midwest, and, of course, home sweet home: the South.

At gun shows, you can trade, buy, and sometimes shoot new and exciting weapons such as pistols, rifles, assault rifles, and nuclear warheads. You can shop for new guns and in some states take classes for open-carry permits and other little technical hurdles between you and that sweet, sweet metal death machine. Gun shows are very popular among gun enthusiasts because they're temporary "pop-up" shops where traveling salesmen can bring their caches of weapons through everyone's region.

Used weapons are a huge market in the US, and gun shows feature rare weapons, antiques, discontinued models, many knowledgeable salesmen, and a general feeling that we're all gonna fuckin' die soon, and, hell, why not load up and prepare for the End Times? Are they a little ridiculous in scale and scope? Who gives a shit, you pussy? Hold this beer while we blow up something beautiful.

10. **The mere fact that this is a thing that can be referenced is pretty stellar, really.**

11. **The guns you load from the end of the barrel like in old war movies, you fake redneck.**

So, yeah, they are a bit much. Gun shows also have the distinction of being at the center of a *very* intense political hotbed that gets regurgitated by the lizards in Congress every couple of years: the "gun show loophole." The gun show loophole is either the biggest skirting of federal licensing requirements known to the United States—*or* something liberals made up to take away guns.

The argument goes that because of our rich national tradition of passing down guns, as well as buying and trading guns to our buddies and neighbors,[12] anyone who sells just a few guns here and there really ort not have to register as an official licensed gun seller because, I mean, hell, Daryl sells only to people he knows and loves, and why them federal assholes tryin' to *get in my business anyway*?! The argument against this loophole is that some of these traveling gun show salesmen sell lots and lots of guns, and they do so across state lines, with little to no record of their transactions. Because unlike with cars, motorcycles, boats, houses, land, a shed, sometimes cattle, explosives, chemicals you could get high off of, your own life if you're male in case the government reinstates the draft, and your wedding wish list at nineteen different g-damn stores, in many states you don't have to register guns and/or you don't have to register who sold you the gun. Isn't that lovely?

So, gun-control proponents argue, there are entities who do business across state lines, dodging registration, avoiding fees as a gun seller, and even skipping some taxes. (Cash is king.) Now, to accomplish much of this, these alleged sellers would have to break many other laws, which is why Second Amendment defenders claim there is no loophole. And, they say, this type of business is impossible to maintain.

---

12. **Presumably trading them for horses over whiskey at the local saloon.**

WELCOME TO THE GUN SHOW

★

And now a tour of the gun show from our Uncle JR:

"Step right this way, ladies and gentleman and also kids![13] Step right up, step right up! We have what you're looking for!

"Welcome to the Lee County[14] Gun Show and Car Expo! I am your tour guide, JR, the most knowledgeable gun toter, firearms expert, knife fighter, and nunchuk aficionado in the whole wide world.[15] I shall be the *best* tour guide you ever had as we wander around the expo center. We'll weave through warheads, bounce off bullets, gallop about the guns, and peruse the pistols! This will be a *day to remember*!

"First, let's begin with the handguns. Now, handguns are a key section of the gun show because they provide the best and most advanced in home- and self-protection. Handguns are great because they're easy to hide, easy to get to, easy to maintain, and so easy to use that a child could do it. For now, a child can't own one—but give us a few years! And, guess what? You don't have to register it in forty states![16] So

---

13. In thirty states, it's legal for a child to own a rifle or shotgun but *not* a handgun or assault rifle.

14. There are eight Lee Counties in the South. All of them are named for the Confederate Civil War general Robert E. Lee.

15. Copyrighted only in America, though.

16. In California, Washington, DC, Hawaii, Illinois, Maryland, Michigan, New Jersey, New York, and Oregon you do. In Massachusetts, you kinda do, and in a few others, you sorta do. But mostly, nah.

come on, pick one out, and then we'll go get you an open-carry permit today![17] Isn't this fun?

"Now let's go over to the knives section. We have lots of nice knives!

"Just kidding, *hahahahahahahahaha*! Fuck knives—they're for huge pussies. *Hahahahahahahahahahaha*! Except for my papaw's knives what have the rebel flag on them. Anyway!

"Time to move on to the shotguns.[18] These guns fire a spread of pellets instead of a single bullet, so as to do much more damage at a close range—they're perfect for women and children. They're generally regulated less than rifles and handguns in large part because they're seen to be bulky and less dangerous on account of how long it takes to reload them. Of course, that was decades ago, and now we have all types of death-machine ones![19] We can have a look at a few of them and find the perfect fit for you or any mentally ill person you know, or even those you don't know about. All of you can legally buy a gun for them and then give it to them and it would be totally legal! *Hahaha!* What a country. And, again, after we buy 'em, we can get the carry permit today!

"Just kidding! You don't even need a carry permit for one of these.[20]

---

17. In many states, you can just do it at the damn show.

18. Shotguns are guns fired from the shoulder like rifles, but they have spread bullets that fire multiple pellets so as to hit a larger target area with less damage done from a distance (and holy shit, so much more damage done at a close distance).

19. To be fair, semiautomatic and automatic weapons are very regulated.

20. As best we can tell, this is true in all states, though there are states where getting them in the first place is tough.

"Finally, let's get on over here to the sporting rifles. These used to be called assault rifles but America doesn't like assault rifles, so the NSSF[21] spent massive amounts of money on a PR push to change the name so we could keep selling them![22] Man, those guys sure are swell. They spend so-oooo much money each year making sure we can keep havin' our gun shows and buying military-grade weapons, and they do it out of the goodness of their freedom-loving hearts.[23] I just love them and the Constitution and America and the flag and bullets and grenades, and my great-grandfather [*Uncle JR starts crying*] was in the Revolutionary War against the evil tyrants the British [*music starts playing*], who are our greatest allies in the war on terror, and we're all brave, and I need these weapons, and someone should carve the Second Amendment into Mount Rushmore [*eagles fly overhead*], and we should all have guns and . . .

"What was I saying? I blacked out—where are we? Holy shit, look at all these AR-15s. My God, isn't this one beautiful? Let's shoot it! I love assault ri—I mean, *sporting* rifles. Almost as much as I do America and about the same as I do my wife! *Freedom!*"

21. **National Shooting Sports Foundation.**

22. **Yes. Really.**

23. **They do it for money.**

Well, shit. Let's just follow this down the ol' American-way logic of capitalism . . .

Would one make more money skirting the law by avoiding taxes, skipping the fees as a licensed dealer, and being able to avoid most of the regulations and practices you have to follow as a registered federal firearms dealer? Why, yes, one would! Then someone is doing it. Come on. That's the only thing more American than guns and pie: makin' money.

The other downside of that, of course, is that many of the regulations and practices governing federally registered gun dealers are designed to make sure guns are not being sold to the wrong type of folk and that we're keeping track of who owns what. And while the dealers themselves may be after the almighty dollar, what much of the culture protecting them is after is protecting what they see as their right not to be kept track of. They don't want the government keeping tabs on who owns guns. If they're tracking the "bad guys," the logic goes, they're tracking the good guys too. This is simply unacceptable in these circles. These are the same people who will not get a smartphone because "the government tracks those" and who think *all* banks are a front for the Illuminati's secret war on the white man. So are these the "good guys"?

MILITIAS

A well-regulated militia, being necessary to the security of a free state, the right of the people to keep and bear arms, shall not be infringed.

—SECOND AMENDMENT

Militias are a whole next-level thing. For the uninitiated, militias are nonmilitary (as in citizens; as in anyone can join) "forces" of—*by God*—*American* citizens who arm themselves and organize for some common goal or purpose. Generally speaking, these are legal, and the people behind them are allowed to execute their plans.[24] Those plans and purposes range from antitax initiatives and survivalism (most proponents of which don't necessarily engage in or encourage violence) to *eradicating the Jews*.[25] There are groups founded in the South or that have a very strong presence in the South whose stated goal is some version of simply living free of a tyrannical government—and then there are groups who simply claim to want to *eradicate the Jews*. One group of organized citizens was originally founded under the common goal/mission statement of "protecting ourselves" and has now grown to be an international presence. Oh wait, no. That's a gang called MS-13.[26] Our bad.

How could we tell? Honestly, a lot of those people are insane. Sorry—there's nothing else to say about it. Loving guns and being a bit paranoid that the government is out to get you is a healthy, normal activity; but grown men organizing their friends, buying matching outfits, and unironically calling themselves the "Sons

---

24. Generally speaking, because, obviously, some of these people are outright criminals.

25. Eradicating Jews is a common theme. This is laughable in most places where militias are en vogue (the South, Idaho, Montana, etc.) because there are so few Jews there it's downright doubtful that most of their members have ever even met a Jew. That's the way of militias.

26. MS-13 was started by Salvadorans to protect themselves from other, already active gangs. Every gang seemingly starts out this way. Most militias do too. "We're protecting ourselves from the tyrannical government." Then the gang members end up becoming criminals. But being white, it's apparently (in the eyes of the media) somehow different for militia members.

of" *anything* is ridiculous unless they're being cheeky or are a group of bikers.[27]

Of course, many of those involved in this culture just *love* to focus on the fourth word of the Second Amendment and gleefully skip right the fuck over the descriptive first three. "A well-regulated militia," it reads, which seems pretty clear to us. "Naw, the militia ort be regulated, *not the guns*, you idiot!" Oh, okay, so the guns should be free, just not the people. We agree, set all those assault rifles free, Daryl. Let 'em go. And then we'll relegate you and your militia to the background. No?

THEY *ARE* COMING FOR ME

But as we said, there are many seemingly healthy and normal folk also worried about losing their guns. Regular hardworking Americans in the South are a little itchy, to say the least, about the government infringing on their rights. It's to the point where you'd almost swear that mistrusting the government was also a family tradition in the South. *Well*, you wouldn't be far off.

Harking back to that blasted fucking war[28] we all need to let go of (meaning the anger and pride, not the shame), we have a deep mistrust of the government and all of its dealings in the South. Some of this is ridiculous: what the Union "did to us" was more than 150 years ago and ain't have shit to do with your life, Daryl. Also, we "did it" to ourselves. On the other hand, the South does have a more recent history of being the doormat of certain bureaucratic and federal institutions.

27. Biker gangs, call yourselves whatever you want—please don't hurt us!—you're awesome.

28. Come on, we all know which one. *The* War. Damn it.

Porch Talk with Corey

One time at a farm party, an ol' boy from our hometown showed up in a black Lincoln Continental with a jar of moonshine, a pistol, and a girl he'd just married the day before. No one knew it, 'cause they just went to the courthouse. He said a farm party was as good as any honeymoon he could go on (true), so here they were.

At some point in the evening, after very much of the moonshine had up and disappeared, someone decided it'd be a good idea to start making fun of ol' boy for getting married. Someone called him a queer. (To this stupid guy, a man marrying a woman somehow qualified as queer.) Well, even jokingly questioning a redneck's sexual orientation whilst hammered is grounds for trouble. That's not logical, nor is it okay, but it's something everyone knows.

The groom staggered over to his car and then staggered back waving his gun in the air and pointed it right at our buddy who had "insulted" him. He was so drunk that buddy was able to knock the gun out of his hands. Then me and everyone there started to beat the ever-loving shit out of him. This turned into an all-out brawl: fists and feet were flying, and at one point my girl cousin smashed a beer bottle over another girl's head because, "That bitch was talking shit about my brother—I heard her!"

Luckily for us, no one was killed. I ended up getting a hand job for my bravery, and the night basically continued as a normal farm party would.

I don't know if ol' boy would've actually shot anyone. I don't know if he would have shot *everyone*. But I do know you shouldn't mix booze and guns—and maybe have your honeymoon somewhere other than a bonfire.

They're divorced now. :)

For example, in 1933—the depths of the Great Depression—the Tennessee Valley Authority (TVA) brought electricity to the South. It provided jobs to many Southerners and "caught us up" to the rest of the country. It also displaced many farmers and families in the name of progress by taking their land. This practice *continued* well into the 1970s, long after President Franklin D. Roosevelt's New Deal was fulfilled. For example, the Tellico Dam in Tennessee was built in the 1960s and early 1970s. Construction was halted over a legal case that the farmers won (on an environmental technicality) in the US Supreme Court. Then Congress simply passed a new bill changing the laws to get around the ruling. Farmers had to give up all of their land for a dam that was proven to be unnecessary. After the river was dammed, a large portion of the farms was not under water. The TVA gave those portions back to the farmers. *Hahahaha*, just kidding. They fucking broke it into lots and sold it to rich people for upward of six times what they'd forced the farmers to take for their plots.

There are many, many beautiful state and federal parks and land management areas all over the South. The Great Smoky Mountains National Park is the second most visited national park in the United States and, for our money, the most beautiful. It's a shining example of how great a national park can be—but also of how the government often has to take someone's land to make such places. Many Southerners lost their farms and cabins to make room for the park. For Southerners, the idea of the government coming in and taking land for the "good of the whole" is neither foreign nor uncommon.

What does this have to do with guns? Well, number one, it provides a little context for all these folks screaming about how scared they are the government will take their guns. Guns are property. Land is property. The connection isn't hard to make. Secondly, when you develop such a deep and cultural fear of the boogeyman government, guns are the only real and visceral thing you have to hang on to in the event that boogeyman comes for you. And finally, when other people from outside your culture tell you that you're crazy for fearing this boogeyman, *they* sound insane.

So we have deep and long-held traditions related to guns for hunting and protection. We have a long-standing mistrust of the government and outsiders in general. We have certain people who are afraid that their weapons are the only piece of security they have left. This provides the perfect situation for a large lobby of connected corporations and perverted special-interest groups to come take advantage of these traditions and fears and people who just want to live their lives the way they always have. Enter the NRA, stage right.[29]

THE GUN LOBBY

Pro-gun interest groups spent nearly $4 million on elections and more than $27 million on lobbying efforts in 2014 alone.[30] Compare that with less than $500,000 and $4 million, respectively, for gun-control lobbying efforts, and it's not hard to see why they seem to keep winning at nearly every voting turn.[31] The difference in the amount of money spent is staggering (much like a man with a gunshot wound in his leg), and was even greater in 2012.

At the forefront of this is the National Rifle Association. One of the biggest spenders, and the perceived if not literal figurehead of gun rights groups, the NRA serves as a good measuring stick for where the

29. **Extreme, far right.**

30. **According to OpenSecrets.org, the online wing of the bipartisan nonprofit Center for Responsive Politics.**

31. **Well, that and guns. Not a coincidence that the folks *with* the guns keep winning gun debates.**

gun rights "movement" stands in America. Seemingly, the gun rights movement is a wannabe Rambo, standing in a field, holding an assault rifle, and juggling three handguns while riding a horse. He's strapped to the teeth with ammo and other weapons, draped in an American flag, shouting obscenities about militias, and drinking a Mountain Dew spiked with whiskey.[32] He has the whole Bible tattooed on his face and smells like Brut aftershave.

But isn't that what the NRA *wants* anyone who dares question it to think that's what the gun rights groups are? A bunch of loud, paranoid, ignorant, wannabe GI Joes? Because the truth is much more sinister. As terrifying as that image may be, the real, deep, awfulness of the NRA is that it has perverted its own cause (and, along the way, its own people) in the name of winning at all costs.

The NRA was founded in 1875 to advance and teach rifle marksmanship. Aww, don't that sound quaint: a group of no doubt white men (no one else was allowed to own guns) sitting around debating the newest and most advanced ways that a "looking glass might be mounted on top of a rifle in order to more accurately aim at targets further away" in between drinking moonshine and laughing about all the minorities wanting to vote or be considered people. The NRA existed for more than *a hundred years* as a civic group celebrating gun culture without ever lobbying directly for anything. Then in 1975 it began to throw its blaze-orange hat into the political ring, and it hasn't looked back.[33]

And we aren't gonna convince anyone on the other side of the aisle that this was anything but necessary. Frankly, being into guns

---

32. **Not for nothing, but if Ted Nugent ever decides to make music again, this would be a hittin'-ass album cover.**

33. **Or anywhere, really, other than right down the damn barrel.**

ourselves and understanding the history of the culture, we think it's fine and dandy that a group got together collectively and began to exert some political will. We do wish they'd have the same fervor and monetary backing for, say, a group of black legal gun carriers in Ferguson, Missouri, as they do white folks.[34] But our point is, a group attempting to promote the safe recreational use of guns and honor the Second Amendment might be good for America. We'll never know, because that is absolutely *not* what the NRA has become.

The NRA and the gun lobby as a whole have done nothing but stoke paranoia, treat facts like insurance (hey, only when we need 'em), buy votes, and refuse under any circumstances to ever compromise for the sake of safety, the greater good, or out of respect for anyone in the electorate who feels differently than they do. Take, for example, last year when the federal government changed a procedure for taking guns abroad for hunting. The law had been that you filled out paperwork in advance, by hand, presumably at home, or you would not be permitted to take a hunting rifle overseas. The change was to make this form electronic, and now you had to complete it at the airport before leaving.

Not only was this seen as affront to the Second Amendment and a tyrannical move by the Obama administration, but it was also apparently so important that the NRA spent gobs of money and time *campaigning* to make sure all its members knew of the atrocity and the unfairness that ol' awful president Barack Obama had committed. The organization spent thousands of dollars and a lot of time claiming that a change from a paper system to an in-person computer one proved how tyrannical and unrepentantly anti-gun Obama is.

---

34. The NRA has been astoundingly silent when black Americans take up the banner for the Second Amendment in large numbers.

This is not the action of a group concerned with makin' sure its members enjoy their guns in a reasonable and "well-regulated"[35] manner. This is a group trying desperately to keep its members scared and paranoid that something awful is going to happen if they don't continue to donate money and vehemently oppose all measures that suggest any minor change in the way we regulate guns. This is the action of a group trying to maintain not the status quo of "freedom from (imagined) oppression," but trying to maintain *power*.

That's really what this group is after. Power. Maintaining it. Gathering more of it. And eventually abusing it. Why? Because that's what lobby groups do. No matter how they start out, no matter what issues are important to them and their members in the beginning, by their very nature, in order to survive, lobbying groups, super PACs, and, really, any political group, have to grow to survive. In order to grow, they have to keep accumulating power, no matter what. So power is the driving force. Oh, and money. Let's talk about money.

THE OTHER GUN LOBBY

In 2014 the National Shooting Sports Foundation spent just over $3 million on lobbying efforts for pro-gun causes. The NRA spent $3.3 million. Therefore, the NSSF is just barely the second most active gun lobbying organization in the United States. It often works hand in hand with the NRA and even defers to it much of the time.

Of course, all this is fine, right? I mean, if *another* group of American citizens came together to exert political will and throw money at gun issues, then it would just mean that even more Americans were

---

35. **We're quoting the actual Constitution. You can't fuck with that, gun folks.**

Porch Talk with Trae

DOUBLE STANDARDS, DOUBLE BARRELS

So in my old job, I worked with this older black feller: we'll call him Barrett. Barrett is awesome. He routinely referred to himself as an OG, and then, if you were white, would proceed to explain what an OG was (original gangster), no matter how many times that exchange had taken place. He was old-school as hell. His ringtone was the theme song to *Sanford and Son*, hand to God. Barrett hits, is what I'm saying. He was one of my favorite people at that job.

Barrett was ex-military and damned proud of it. (Rightfully so.) Like many vets, he was *extremely* pro-gun. He was at one gun show or another every other weekend. His house had a damn *vault* where he kept his *arsenal*. I think he told me once he owned upward of two hundred guns. When I left for another job, he was looking into buying a *tank*. I really cannot emphasize enough how hard this man hit. Anyway. One day Barrett told me the following, and I swear this is verbatim: "Trae, let me tell you somethin' right now. The damn NRA is hands down one of the single most racist organizations in this entire country. No doubt about it. [*Pause.*] And I been a card-carryin' member for thirty-five years. Sometimes you gotta compartmentalize."

That conversation has stuck with me for years. First of all, that shit is objectively hilarious. Secondly, I think it really illustrates just how deeply rooted gun culture is in this country. I'm not a huge anti-gun guy myself, but for the record: *fuck* the NRA. With a prickly pear.

passionate about this issue. A lot of people are pro-gun, and that's how democracy works. Right, NSSF?[36]

But the NSSF is not an organization of citizens[37] founded to advance the sport of rifle shooting. It's the lobbying arm of the gun-manufacturing industry. Major American gun and ammunition makers (and some foreign ones) pay the bills, organize the structure, and run the NSSF.

And while we think that any corporations exerting so much political will are a reality uglier than corporate art,[38] we have to acknowledge that law is law,[39] and they can, of course, spend money to support any causes that they see fit. We all can. Us, you, our neighbor the accountant, Apple (the company, but also Gwyneth Paltrow's daughter), Jimmy your local butcher, Nike, that guy who picked on you in grad school, Boeing—we're all equal![40] So things being equal,[41] the NSSF can propose and advocate for less strict gun laws and protect the Second Amendment however it wants to. That's what they're doing right? Well . . .

One way this brave collection of "citizens" that only exists on paper has protected the Second Amendment is to recently propose legislation

36. **Super far right.**

37. **Okay, technically it is, thanks to _Citizens United_, since organizations are now people, too.**

38. **Cannot stress enough that _Citizens United v. FEC_ is a psychotic ruling and hurts.**

39. **It's a horrible law.**

40. **We're not equal. This law is a travesty.**

41. **They aren't, though.**

that would prevent the EPA[42] from banning harmful chemicals in ammunition. You can see how our Founding Fathers would have wanted this: an organization spending millions of dollars to fight environmental regulations on behalf of a corporation so as to protect that corporation's right to bear arms.[43] What a country we live in.

The National Shooting Sports Foundation's whole plan is to make more money. That's it. And that's a fine plan, we suppose (hell, who don't want more money? Only creepy religious people, like them dudes in robes). But pretending to care about the rights of American citizens any further than its right to spend gobs of money on their weapons is a travesty. We all have to live in this country. Some of us love guns, and some of us hate guns, but any of us who support the groups that make money off our fears and our tragedies having such a large say in the conversation is pathetic. That'd be like—well, how seemingly every other goddamn industry and politics in general works, but, guys, come on, let's stop!

When the NSSF fights against legislation designed to prevent mass shootings[44] because it "won't work and is a violation of rights," we understand that many people agree with that argument. But that's not, at all, even a little bit why the organization lobbies so hard. It

---

42. Environmental Protection Agency.

43. Sometimes the truth is so absurd your heart won't make a joke.

44. The NSSF is located in Newtown, Connecticut. Yes, that one. Where, in December 2012, an extremely disturbed kid walked into an elementary school and shot to death twenty little kids between six and seven years old and six staffers—after killing his own mother. This fact, and presumable coincidence, has been cited by "passionate" folks on both sides of the issue as some sort of proof or indication of shenanigans. We won't stoop so low on either side, but simply say it's time for reform. Rest in peace, all victims.

works hand in hand with the NRA and certain senators, and spends millions of dollars per year for one reason and one reason only: to make more money. And every time a shooting happens, it makes even more money.

Yes. For real. When a mass shooting makes national headlines, the gun lobby *purposefully* stokes up fear and paranoia over proposed new gun laws so that scared citizens get out their checkbooks and buy a new AR-15 (or sporting rifle[45]). So why would the NSSF have any interest in stopping mass shootings? Why would it engage politically and invest in compromise, a reform plan that attempts to make all Americans safer, or any sort of reckoning of the role guns play in gun violence?[46] It won't.

However you feel about guns and their place in America—whether we're talking about rifles for hunting or assault rifles, or anything in between—it's undeniable that the gun lobby has refused to acknowledge or entertain *any* sort of regulation or reform aimed[47] at making us a safer and saner nation. The reason why: because that does not make it more money. A customer base kept terrified at all times that this will be "the last chance before the government bans" whatever gun manufacturers are peddling is much more valuable. A customer base absolutely convinced that the just-about-anyone-can-buy culture we have is politically necessary without seeing that it serves those companies is what they're after. They have achieved it. An honest conversation (would never happen) with the NSSF about regulation would go like this:

45. **They're evil.**

46. **That's a stellar sentence. The gun lobby won't recognize the role guns play in gun violence. It's *in the words "gun violence"*!**

47. **That was an accident, but we left it in there on purpose.**

"But surely you don't think people with a history of mental illness and violence should be allowed to have weapons, right?"
NSSF: "Okay, now these people you speak of, do they have money? Like, money they could spend on weapons—specifically the ones we make and would sell them so we can get that money? They do? Okay, then for sure, I think the Second Amendment made it clear that those mentally ill people should have guns."

SO NOW WHAT?

The gun lobby, like every single lobby, lies. It's what lobbies do; part of their job description. They have fostered a paranoid and insular culture. They have created an *us* (anyone who wants to have guns) and a *them* (anyone who even mentions gun control or regulation).

And in their minds, *we*—as in anyone who has mentioned their transgressions—are a part of the *them*. But that just ain't true. Like nearly every single thing in life, making this issue black and white is completely disingenuous and calculated.[48] Hunting is a wonderful and awesome American tradition. A person's right to protect his or her home with a gun may be "ridiculous" to many folk, but if you think someone else doesn't deserve certain rights just because you disagree with them, then you're exactly like the folk against gay marriage. Also, no one gives a fuck what you think, Tristan. Now make me a latte.

But . . . there has to be better regulation and a more intensive/realistic take on mental health in this country. And the campaigns for gun regulation and for more mental health services can work together on

---

48. It's the latter. We cannot stress this enough: the gun lobby, like *all* lobbies, is at its core a lying and conniving institution.

background checks. Doctors need to acknowledge the epidemic of gun violence and diagnose us for what we are: sick. We, as a nation, are ill. And we need to cure ourselves.

Some responsible gun owners are worried about the "slippery slope" of gun laws. This isn't a crazy fear. First we make it harder to get AR-15s, then it's pistols, then it's all types of guns, etc., etc. It happens over time, they say, not all at once.

The problem is, as a country, we're on another, more dangerous and more painful slippery slope. Gun violence is reaching new heights. Two Colorado teenagers got their hands on enough warlike weapons to kill thirteen people at their own high school, Columbine, in 1999, and it did nothing to change our national psyche. In January 2011, Arizona congresswoman Gabby Giffords was shot and permanently disabled by a crazy man in a shooting that also killed six people and injured others. Almost two years later in Newtown, Connecticut, a tragedy so unspeakable happened that we're brought to tears thinking about one six- or seven-year-old, much less twenty. In 2016, in an Orlando, Florida, nightclub, the largest mass shooting in our nation's history was perpetrated by a disturbed guy with a history of domestic violence.[49] This slippery slope, so much more dangerous and so much more prevalent than the regulation feared by gun advocates, is becoming a free fall. Every time we think we've reached the bottom, we sink lower.

This epidemic has to stop. We have to try. Liberal Rednecks love

---

49. **Obviously, and awfully, these tragedies are timeless—they're burned into our national conscience and are unforgettable in every sense of the word. However, we can't tell you how heartbreaking it is to consider that these things will become worse and multiply, and that in the future, we'll have to add others to this section. We hope not. My God, we hope not.**

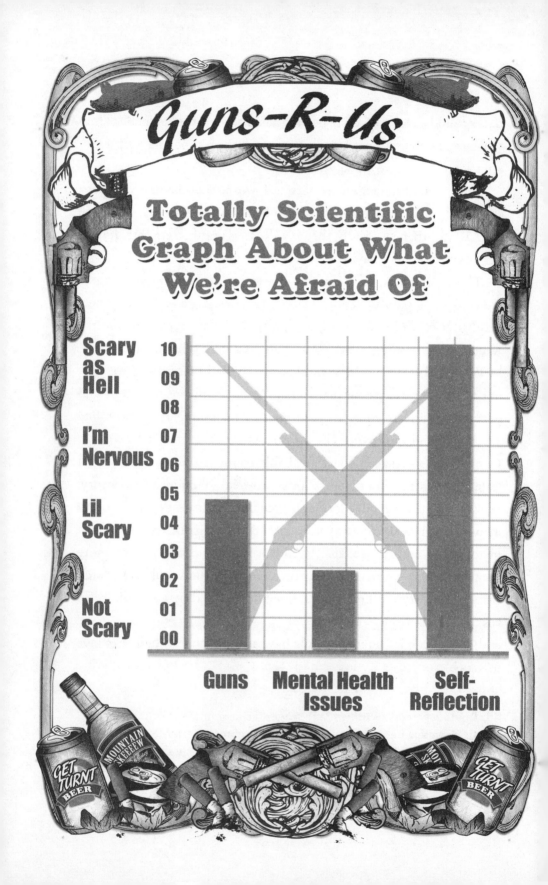

Porch Talk with Trae

 I despise the NRA. I mean, I'm about as soft on guns as any redneck you'll ever meet.

And I own seventeen guns. I can also shoot the dick off a hummingbird, by God. My grandpa gave me a gun when I's knee high to a grasshopper, just like every other son of the South. I inherited Pa's arsenal when he died, and still have it all. I've taken gun classes and routinely participated in impromptu rounds of Hold My Beer Target Shooting with my buddies. Point being: it really is just a part of who we are. But, hell, I do think we could do a background check or two. I mean, Jesus Christ, guys.

guns. Shootin' cans and shit like that hits so hard. Oh! And if you've never been fishing with a gun, then you ain't livin' right. But we as a nation have to take some measure to stop this madness. For one another, for everyone, we have to change. The South, being home to great traditions of responsible hunting and responsible gun ownership, can lead the way. Let's jump in with registration, universal background checks, changing the fearful culture surrounding *any* gun regulations, and getting rid of military-grade war machines. Let's get rid of the us-and-them mentality surrounding guns and start genuinely thinking about *we*. Anyone, on either side of the debate, who simply refuses to allow for a *we*, who won't compromise at all, well, let's just leave them out. It's obviously what they want deep down.

11

Pillbillies

O ne thing about our people is that we like to get fucked up. Now, we ain't sayin' that rednecks occupy any particular higher plane of partydom than any of the world's other renowned degenerates (the Irish, the Catholics, the Irish Catholics, etc.), but by God, we can hang with any of 'em.[1] This is a point of pride.

Now look here, off top: it ain't a damn thing wrong with gettin' plum turnt. Hell, we can't hardly trust a teetotaler anyhow. If you live your life 100 percent sober at all times and are not either (a) a tiny little babychild, (b) a sweet old mamaw,[2] or (c) under a court order after runnin' your truck through the side of another Waffle House, well, they's somethin' just ain't right about that. You some kinda alien or a Mormon[3] or somethin' now, hell.

1. **Except maybe Russians. Them motherfuckers is somethin' else.**

2. **Note:** *Some* **Southern mamaws get as fucked up as apartheid, for the record.**

3. **Same difference.**

Having said all of that, our penchant for self-medication has taken a sinister turn in recent years. A modern-day epidemic is sweeping through the poor rural South, and, though it's no secret, it's rarely given the attention it deserves. While America was waging its all-time most futile war,[4] the "War on Drugs"—with the US Drug Enforcement Administration (DEA) scaring white kids and locking up black men over illegal drugs like crack, heroin, ecstasy, and, for some stupid fucking reason, marijuana—the rural South was getting its shit at the Rite Aid. Before anyone even noticed, small-town Southern America had gotten dangerously, desperately addicted to pills.

So what exactly happened? Well, take this shit with a grain of salt. We are comics, but we happen to be three comics who have seen this epidemic up close and personal. We have all lost people close to us, one way or another, to this mess. Most everyone who grew up in the rural South in the last thirty years has; it's that far-reaching. This is *extremely* complex, but we'll give you the best version we can. So, here we go.[5]

BIRTH OF A PILLBILLY PLAGUE

The opiate epidemic is a relatively recent one, beginning in earnest in the mid- to late 1990s.[6] Around this time, Big Pharma, the

---

4. Which is really saying something, when you think about it.

5. Everything that follows in this chapter is based on either firsthand experience, your standard Google-Fu, or interviews with actual experts like Dr. Robert Pack of East Tennessee State University—a true gentleman and a scholar. Believe that's the first time we ever meant that unironically.

6. Much like the "bro country" phenomenon. Coincidence? Probably, but they're both plagues.

world-renowned satanic lizard cartel, got together at its annual Expo of Evil and, in between *Eyes Wide Shut* parties and goat sacrifices, realized that it had been a little while since it did something awful. Obviously, that could not stand. At the same time, its cloven-hooved, goat-headed cohorts with the Illuminati were trying to decide on a new way to subjugate the poor. So they put together their horned heads and developed a new chemical scourge to unleash upon the huddled masses: OxyContin. (This is not the actual story of the invention of OxyContin.[7])

OxyContin hit the market in 1996. Introduced by Purdue Pharma, the drug was a new formulation of oxycodone (which is similar to the narcotic heroin) and said to provide pain relief for twelve hours at a time. This distinction was crucial: its twelve-hour efficacy was the only thing setting OxyContin apart from the competition. Purdue launched the drug with an aggressive marketing campaign, claiming that OxyContin was safer and more effective than other narcotics on the market. Company sales reps plied doctors with extravagant dinners and weekend resort trips[8] to convince them of the unique advantages of their new miracle drug. And it worked. Doctors prescribed OxyContin in record numbers, and Purdue's revenues soared. There was just one problem: all the claims about the drug being safer and longer lasting? Yeah, weren't hardly none of that shit true.[9]

Patients complained that the drug did not work for twelve hours (or the length of a Garth Brooks boxed set; the '90s hit). Doctors responded initially by prescribing it more frequently. Well, Purdue

---

7. **Bet it's pretty close, though.**

8. **And not, like, Red Lobster and Dollywood, y'all. We talkin' uptown shit.**

9. **A pharmaceutical company lied to make money? Be still our hearts.**

wasn't having that. See, if it became firmly established that Oxy-Contin didn't actually last twelve hours, then it would be no better than any other regular old fiercely addictive and brutally compromising narcotic—and that would be a real shame. So Purdue instructed doctors repeatedly *not* to prescribe the drug more frequently but instead to prescribe *higher doses*. Of heroin.[10] Who could have ever predicted this would lead to problems?[11]

So people were taking higher and higher doses of Oxy, but the drug's effects weren't lasting any longer. And people were gettin' more and more fucked up—and experiencing stronger cravings when the effects wore off early. We don't know how much you know about cravings, but they don't hit. Conversely, you know what does hit? Satisfying your cravings. Especially when your cravings are for a little magic disk in a cabinet three feet away from you that will make your insides not feel like they're melting anymore. Them's hard cravings to ignore, there. People who were prescribed the drug for totally legitimate reasons— like pain from cancer or chronic back problems—started getting very rapidly and powerfully dependent on OxyContin.

This may come as a shock,[12] but *some* people take pills that they don't really need because it feels good. We know, right? The horror. But it happens. And these people figured out very quickly that while OxyContin was formulated to release its effective drugs very slowly in your body, if you just crushed that shit up and took it to straight to the brain, you could fuck that sweet, sweet drug pussy all at once. Talking 'bout snortin' pills, old people. All the cool kids are doin' it. Not really.

---

10. Basically.

11. Anyone. Even stupid little kids, probably.

12. Depending on how white you are.

SOUTHERN SIDE PIECES: METH AND BENZOS

★

If you're from the South (or just know about the South, really), you will probably think to yourself, if you haven't already, "Wait, what about meth? Don't hillbillies love meth? I was told there would be meth." Well, fret not, there's also still plenty of meth down here. It's as terrible as it ever was, and cooks have only gotten better at making it. (Meth cooks are true entrepreneurial spirits.) We are relegating it to the side of this chapter because we feel that (a) the meth problem has been covered extensively, while the pill problem has been comparatively ignored, and (b) as horrific as the meth problem is, the pill epidemic is legitimately worse. Yeah. So while there are still plenty of unsavory skinny-ass Juggalo-lookin' motherfuckers blowing themselves up in trailer parks all across Dixie, we are simply choosing to focus on pills.

And speaking of pills, this chapter would also be incomplete if we didn't address opiates' lazy cousin benzodiazepines, the most commonly used one around here being Xanax. Actually, they're most commonly known in the South as "my nerve pills," but it's all the same. Benzos are antianxiety medications, and they're also *hugely* popular down here. Usually if people are fuckin' with Oxys/Roxys/Percocets/whatever, they're *also* fuckin' with some Xanax bars ("bars" is another name for benzo tablets). But they're not the same thing and don't affect you in the same way, and, *in our opinion*, are, frankly, just an ancillary factor in the larger opioid epidemic. But again, we felt that to leave them out completely wouldn't be appropriate. Now back to your regularly scheduled program.

It's actually mostly the kinda skanky kids. The cool kids do molly these days, don't you know shit? At any rate, people (skanky kids and adults alike) found that snorting Oxys was *pretty rad, dudes*.

Just like that, OxyContin was one of the most in-demand drugs for actual patients and recreational users in the history of the United States. Revenues for Purdue Pharma were in the billions. They couldn't make this shit fast enough. And now that people everywhere had gotten the metaphorical taste of blood in their mouths for prescription narcotics,[13] use and abuse of long-prescribed opiates like Lortabs, Percocets, Roxicodones, etc., all began to skyrocket. Prescriptions of opioids, and in turn the number of opioid-related overdoses, *quadrupled* between 1999 and 2014. Mamaws everywhere started locking up their medicine cabinets. The pain pill epidemic was in full swing.

WHY THE SOUTH?

Why was the origin of the opiate epidemic initially focused on the South? And make no mistake: it absolutely was. The epicenter for this phenomenon was the poor rural South. To be more specific, central Appalachia. To be even *more* specific, coal country. The coal country region of the South is made up of eastern Kentucky, southwestern Virginia, and southern West Virginia, and it was the geographical Patient Zero of the country's opiate problem. One metric that illustrates this is the opiate overdose rate. For our purposes here, let's consider an opiate overdose rate of more than twenty in one hundred thousand to be "Very Shitty."[14] In 2002 there was a cluster of twenty-three contiguous counties in central Appalachia

13. Mmmm, *heroin blood.*

14. Because it ain't not shitty, y'all.

with a Very Shitty overdose rate. In the entire rest of the United States, there was not one single other set of neighboring counties with a Very Shitty overdose rate. Not even in Mississippi, y'all. In central Appalachia? Twenty-three counties, all clustered together. Fast-forward fifteen years, and there are such clusters to be found in every state from Maine to Arizona. And it all started in the coal-black heart of Dixie.

So . . . why? What made Appalachia more susceptible to this phenomenon than any other region? Well, even the most informed experts on the pill problem have not reached a complete consensus, other than to agree that there isn't just one factor at play. A confluence of issues, a perfect poverty storm, led to the Pillbilly Problem.

One of the primary factors is something that experts call "social determinants," which is basically a scientific way of saying "the shitty parts of being poor." And for the extremely poor people in places like central Appalachia, these determinants are varied and numerous.[15] This is the kinda stuff that right-wingers don't want to hear about. You start talking about how the hopelessness and drudgery of poverty can lead people to turn to drugs, and they respond with "Oh, boo hoo! You didn't see *me* shoving a needle in my arm when the Kappas passed me over the first time! These people need to suck it up!" This is because these right-wingers have trouble relating to the struggle of poverty. And by "have trouble relating to," we mean "are short-sighted narcissistic pieces of shit who lack empathy for." Hope that's clear. We don't want to give the impression that we *don't* hate people like that. Because we do. We hate people like that. The reality is that when people have repeatedly and authoritatively had the hope beaten out of them by life and the world around them, not just for their entire lives but for generations, well, they start to make poor decisions. And

---

15. See chapter 2, "The Draw," for more information/transcendent prose.

smoking your grandma's cancer medicine off a piece of tinfoil in a dollar store parking lot is a *fairly* poor decision.[16]

Some of those who turn to pills as a result of poverty and hopelessness genuinely don't intend to. Not to get high, anyway. Many people turn to pills as a *job*. A parallel of this story has become a very familiar narrative in popular culture: a poor black kid from the ghetto with no prospects and no options turns to selling crack because he's hungry, or his baby's hungry, and he has no choice. You'd do the same thing in his shoes. Now, a lot of white people with money still don't give the first bit of a damn about this story, but it's one they're familiar with. Mostly because of Jay Z. But still. See, that's the thing: our people don't have a Jay Z.[17] The only remotely mainstream narratives about our homeland revolve around dirt roads and farmer's tans and shit. But that same exact story plays out every day in the rural South. Poor people who see no reasonable alternative start selling pills to pay the bills,[18] and in many, many cases, they end up addicted themselves.

So people in Appalachia are poor. They're hopeless. They're looking for something, anything, to make life *just not suck so much*, just for a little while. We totally get that. We normally use liquid cheese for the same purpose. (Seriously, Trae and Corey particularly[19] would mainline liquid cheese if that was the only way to get their "yella fix." As an aside, food scientists have recently suggested

---

16. Depending on what else you had goin' on that day.

17. Until now, amirite?!

18. If mainstream country was worth a damn, "Sellin' Pills to Pay the Bills" would be a hittin' single.

19. Drew isn't fat, but Trae and Corey would like it noted he's terrible in plenty of other ways.

that cheese actually activates some of the same parts of your brain that opiates do. No, for real.)

So yes, we understand the escapism factor (in using cheese, of course). Life is hard for so many in the South, and people just want to escape. People hurt a lot down here. And we don't mean just figuratively. People work down in coal mines and up on hot roofs. People tar roads and "cut 'baccer";[20] they trim trees, haul hay, frame houses, work the river. People work hard, and working hard can lead to a man getting down in his back, or aggravating an old knee injury he got playing ball, or any number of things that just . . . hurt. And when you hurt, you want it to stop.

Well, don't you worry none, darlin'; Big Pharma's got just the thing.

PILL MILLS

One thing that makes the opiate problem different from many of the rest of our country's addiction problems is the fact that, with opiates, you can get your fix and your oil changed at basically the same place. And we mean the oil in your car, not some weird sex thing (though they probably have that too). The point is this: you can get pills in strip malls, Walmarts, etc. You don't have to go through a drug dealer to get what you want. Well, *technically* we suppose they're still "drug dealers," but not in the street sense. Pills are different. They're sold by family doctors. Kindly old white men with degrees. And that matters.

Purdue Pharma, the maker of OxyContin, marketed the drug aggressively toward Appalachia because they're evil, and evil people are smart. They already knew all about the "social determinants" and issues with pain both literal and figurative. They came after

---

20. "Harvest tobacco," for our Yankee friends.

Pills-N-Mess Reference Guide

Part 1

CODEINE:
Ingredients: Uhh . . . codeine
Street Names: Schoolboy, Sizzurp, Pills You Can Drank Bayba!!!, and Lean
Uses: Cough suppressant, pain reliever, bringin' rednecks and rappers together, gettin' plum turnt

LORTAB/VICODIN:
Ingredients: Hydrocodone, acetaminophen, and the stuff that makes you feel the way pizza makes you feel
Street Names: Hydros, Vikes, Freshman Year, Lordy Dordy, Praise the Lort, and Vic-Odin's Raven
Uses: Moderate to severe pain relief, escaping reality, abusing your mamaw's trust

ROXYCODONE:

Ingredients: Oxycodone and the letter *R*
Street Names: Roxies, Blues, Thirties, Roxy Music, Roxy Lady, The Rox and the Hound, Titties in a Pill
Uses: Moderate to severe pain relief, oral analgesic, gettin' fucked up in a barn, jeopardizing a once-promising future

PERCOCET:
Ingredients: Oxycodone, acetaminophen, and the fallacious warmth of a dubious god
Street Names: Percs, Blue Dynamite, Paulas, Trae's Mama, Percocet Yo Ass Down
Uses: Severe pain relief, knockin' over Coke machines and callin' yourself "Percules," Throwing It All Away

Pills-N-Mess Reference Guide

Part 2

OXYCONTIN:

Ingredients: Time-released formulation of oxycodone, and The Arrogance of Man
Street Names: Oxy, OC, Kickers, Hillbilly Heroin, Scourge of the Trailer Park, Brain Blowjob
Uses: Severe or chronic pain relief, just saying Fuck It, chemically subjugating the poor, hangovers

MORPHINE:

Ingredients: Morphine (don't need nothin' else, baby)
Street Names: M, Morph, Auntie Em, If God Was a Drug, Eat Shit Hitler, Liquid Buttfuckin', The Grandaddy of Them All (As In Pills)
Uses: Extreme pain, making cancer not as shitty, embracing the sweet release of death

HEROIN:

Ingredients: Synthesized Morphine and the Opposite of Hope
Street Names: H, Horse, Smack, Junk, Dream Murder, Absence of Love, Mama's Worst Nightmare, Fuck This Shit
Uses: Substituting for pills after the law cracks down, well and truly giving up, submitting yourself forever unto the abyss

Porch Talk with Trae

DEAR MAMA,

So this chapter, like the one on poverty (seriously, the two are irreparably linked), is a deeply personal one for me. I have been talking onstage about my mama being a pillbilly for years now, and I discovered only recently that oftentimes, even though I state *explicitly* "This is true. My mama sold pills and was a pillhead," a lot of people *still* think it's just jokes or something. That I'm making it up. Which is so weird to me. I don't know if it's just so crazy or unrelatable to the vast majority of people that they assume it's not true, or if it's that some people are just convinced that everything comedians say is made up, or what, but at any rate, I get it a lot.

So let me state again, for y'all, the readers: my mother is a recovering drug addict whose only occupation for most of my childhood (and a chunk of my adult life) was selling opiates. And not, like, from a Kroger supermarket. From a trailer. She has been locked up numerous times for her exploits— however, she would like the record to show that "I did it for a long damn time 'fore them sumbitches ever caught me, though." This is a real quote, verbatim. Some of y'all are probably still skeptical. Well, I don't know what to tell ya. But I guess I'll tell ya some more shit anyway.

Like most kids, I didn't understand a lot of shit. It didn't become really clear to me until probably the age of, I dunno, twelve or so, what was going on with her. She had been selling pills for a while leading up to that, and would do so for years afterward, but she herself didn't get hopelessly strung out on them until my teenage years. See, she wasn't the only pillhead in our family. My aunt, her only sibling, was arguably worse off. (I mentioned that my first cousin BJ fatally overdosed on pills at age thirty-four.) I can remember my grandma crying in the bathroom for hours because my aunt had stolen from her again. When I went over to their trailer, I found my littler, seven-year-old cousin eating frozen biscuits because his mama had been unconscious for a while, and he was hungry. Then, when I was sixteen, my aunt fell asleep at the wheel and ran her car off the road and was killed. That's when Mom *really* went off the rails.

We already weren't on the best of terms. She had pawned my electric guitar without telling me, she owed me money outside of that, she just wasn't around—I mean, there were plenty of reasons. But when my aunt died, shit got *bad*.
In fact, I think I'll spare you most of that, as this is still a comedy book (save it for the autobiography, na'msayin?), but suffice to say that I basically cut her out of my life completely before I left high school and had little to no contact with her for years, up until the last time she got out of prison and my first son was about to be born. I told her I would give her one last chance, and so far (five years later as of me writing this), she has done well. But if I'm being honest, in the back of my mind I'm just waiting on that phone call telling me she got arrested again or got found unconscious in another parking lot or worse. I think I probably always will be.

the rural South and the doctors in those areas *hard*. And it worked. Sales exploded.

Look, doctors are just like the rest of us. 'Course, they can bring people back from the dead and routinely shake their dicks at God by reversing nature's will through the application of knowledge so expansive and specialized that it was not all too long ago considered the realm of magic and faith alone. Other than that, though, they're just like the rest

Porch Talk with Trae
SHOP AROUND

Now, don't get it twisted (that's weed, not pills): the so-called pill mills are far from the only source of opiates. Did I mention my mama sold 'em? I try not to talk about it much. (I talk about it all the time.) There is *absolutely* a secondary market for opiates, and beyond that, plenty of people get them from family practices, ob/gyns, you name it. (Probably not optometrists, though. I'm guessing.)

Plenty of your more stereotypical drug dealers now sell opiates too. Why wouldn't they? Supply and demand, baby. But they're also cutting them with other drugs, as drug dealers are wont to do. This adds a whole new level of Scary Not-Hittery to the opiate epidemic. So yeah, this whole thing is a bit of a mess. I mean, just a real pickle, y'all.

of us. Meaning they like money. And when OxyContin started selling like hotcakes,[21] leading to a broader opiate outbreak, many opportunistic doctors jumped on board the hype train.[22] Pain clinics where patients could obtain opiates with little to no serious effort—in some instances, straight from the clinic itself—began popping up all over the South. These clinics quickly became known as pill mills. Some of them would open up in a trailer set up in the middle of a field. Which is honestly kind of poetic in its terribleness.

21. **Hotcakes that *tear your family apart*.**

22. **Next stop: Ethical Bankruptcy Station.**

The establishment of these pill mills slowed down the response to the pill problem to an insane degree. Because the sources of the epidemic seemed legitimate, it took a long time for law enforcement to even take notice, and once they did, they found that crooked doctors made for much harder targets than street dealers with neck tattoos or dreadlocks. Imagine that. For one thing, pain is inherently subjective, making it next to impossible to prove with certainty that a doctor was prescribing a narcotic for illegitimate reasons. Or that he had any way of knowing that the patient was lying to him. Or that he was a piece of shit. (It's the lab coats—they look so professional.) And so it took an inordinately long time for a response to the problem to gain any traction. And by the time it did, it was far, far too late.

PILLBILLY BLUES

So here we are. OxyContin was the match, Appalachia was the kindling, and now the whole damn South is on fire[23] (which of course means there will be weenies roasting on wire coat hangers). The severity of this epidemic really cannot be overstated. Opiate prescription rates have skyrocketed, and overdose rates have risen in direct parallel. The states are trying to implement new legal measures to curtail the problem, but there is still a very long way to go. And in the interim, we have to live with all these *damn pillbillies*.

We're not making fun of people losing themselves to addiction, which is really fuckin' sad. But, having said that, pillbillies do a lot of dumb shit, and we can't not talk about it, so any of our sensitive dearies out there reading this: y'all buckle up.

Pillbillies ain't the most pleasurable to be around. Addiction makes

---

23. **And the smoke will get you *lit*, son.**

Porch Talk with Drew

The first time my brother did pills in front of me, I was fourteen years old. He and a friend of his I'll call Aaron stopped on the side of the road, chopped up a Percocet, and snorted it off the hood. I was trying desperately not to look anything other than totally cool. I was terrified. Aaron is dead now.

My brother's addiction to pills evolved and changed, and so did he and I and our relationship. I rode hours with my mother to see him in rehab for the first time not long after that day on the side of the road. What a sad a place it was, even though it was built and designed to be nice. I thought then that nothing could be as sad as a rehab facility.

Now he's in prison. And prison is, of course, much sadder. My brother seems to be clean. And, honestly, I never thought he would be again. Also, in prison he seems to have come to terms with himself and his demons more than he ever did on the outside.

But when I look at his children, I see the hole left behind by a father in prison for crimes and reasons that, however many there are, all lead back to one thing: pills. It makes me hate pills, and addiction, and the pharmaceutical industry, and our government's lack of fucks given about it because of money. Sometimes I've also hated my brother. But I've seen enough to know he obviously didn't *want* to end up in this situation—it was just that he wanted pills more than he wanted *not* to end up like this. And that is the power of addiction.

So I've seen enough to look anyone in the eye and tell 'em pills will absolutely ruin your life and are not worth whatever amount of joy or release they give you. But I've also seen enough to know that no one can be told that or talked out of trying drugs, addiction, or anything else. I've tried drugs myself (not pills, though—I just can't stomach the idea of it). You will do as you wish. But please be careful.

DM

Porch Talk with Trae

"I NEED THIS OKRA, MAN"

So, when me and my little sister (she's three years younger) were little, our mama and her . . . *clientele* used to try to hide all the pill-slingin', drug-dealin' mess from us. I mean, God bless 'em, I guess. My cousins weren't so lucky. Neither were a *lot* of kids. Lotta pillbillies'll chase that damned Trailer Dragon right in front of their baby. So, yeah, I suppose I appreciate the effort to keep it from us. They would talk in code and shit like that, all to try to trick us. Because people think kids are dumb. And they are. Kids are dumb.

But here's the thing, guys: pillheads are just *so much dumber.* Their code words were always just awful; nothing ever checked out. It was the shittiest cover-up of all time. It was like if Nixon had used cats for Watergate. One day—I'll never forget it—this lady flags down my mama as we're pullin' out of the projects. She runs over and then sees me and my sister at the last minute and starts improvising. There ain't much funnier than a pillhead goin' off the cuff. This is *exactly* what she said:

"Hey, honey, you got a minute?" she says to Mama. "I's just wonde—oh, *oh!* Oh, uh . . . I was just wonderin' if you had any, uh . . . ye know, uh . . . any . . . *vegetables?*"

I shit you not. Vegetables! I was nine years old, and I still weren't havin' none of that bullshit. It's hilarious to me that she thought I would buy that. Hell, we lived with Mama; we hadn't seen a *vegetable* in six damn months. She slept 'til noon; she was *not a farmer.* And honestly, y'all, I think even if I had been enough of a dumbass little kid to just accept that—just totally take it at face value—I think that would have fucked me up even worse. I would have been sitting back there just like, "Goddamn, is *that* what broccoli *does to people?!*"

Trae

people do some weird/funny/awful things, and pillbillies are no exception. Good, salt-of-the-earth people they generally are not. Many of them steal, they're neglectful, they're a danger to themselves and others, they can be embarrassing, they take too fucking long at the counter at the gas station—these are all true, but not of *every* pillbilly. The one thing that *is* true of almost every single pillbilly, however, is that they *lie*. Lawd, do they lie.

Pillbillies lie to their doctors. They lie to their friends. They lie to their family. They lie to themselves.[24] That's how they get in the shape they do. They tell themselves they got it under control, that it ain't that bad, that they can stop whenever they want to. And next thing they know, they're trading their butt for muscle relaxers because they know a guy that will trade those and a Xanax for some Roxys. Which is kind of ironic when you think about it, because they could probably really use those muscle relaxers for the whole butt thing.

(Look, we realize this is getting a little extreme. But that's the nature of the subject. Hell, if anything, we're taking it fairly easy. But if this is all a bit much for you, flip on over to chapter four and read us waxing poetic on biscuits for a little bit. Or watch that video on YouTube where that ol' boy acts like he's his dog. Either way. But once you do that, bring your ass back here. This shit is important. Love y'all.)

People who live in a bubble insulated from addiction would probably be stunned and appalled at the lengths people will go to for their fix. Mothers will trade their WIC vouchers.[25] People will drag their kids from doctor's office to doctor's office, lying to get a damn smorgasbord

---

24. **They also lie to the law, but we pretty much fine with that.**

25. **WIC stands for Women, Infants, and Children, a government supplemental nutrition program. See chapter two on the Draw. You know, if you ain't sad enough.**

of pills, some of which they'll take and others they'll trade for more pills. People will find any way possible to launder their food stamps into cash (see chapter two for a flowchart on how to go about this[26]), and guess what that cash is used for?

More pills. It's always more pills. Because when you're hopelessly addicted, there can never be enough pills. If it were possible to ever have enough pills, then, trust us, America would have enough. Nearly three hundred million scripts are written for opiates in this country every year, which is enough for every man, woman, and child to have a bottle of pills. That's . . . hot damn, that's a lot of pills, y'all. So if you're one of our beloved Yankee readers, and you're making your way through this section feeling grateful that you don't have to deal with all this, then think again. The pill plague may have originated in southern Appalachia, but at this point, it's absolutely a national crisis.[27] Y'all will appropriate the shit out of our culture if it's something that hits. You tried to take Elvis from us, you basically stole Timberlake . . . and now PILLS!

SO WHAT DO WE DO?

Stop taking pills. Next question. No, obviously, buddy, this thing is a bear.

One of the first orders of business was shutting down the pill mills, and many states have cracked down on them heavily. The initial impact was minimal, as addicts simply turned to other legitimate sources, and so across-the-board restrictions related to opiates were passed. However, this has been less than effective as well, evidenced by the fact that

---

26. **We never said we were responsible people.**

27. **Much like Nancy Grace.**

(a) opiate prescription statistics are still sky-high, and (b) many opiate abusers have started turning to good old-fashioned heroin now that their pills have gotten harder to come by. This is . . . less than desirable. The answer remains very far away, and the epidemic rages on. So, what do we do next?

As insightful generational talents with a genuine passion for the subject, we're *almost definitely* right on this. But yeah, this is just our take.[28]

This problem exists on a spectrum (like autism and the color maroon at the paint store), all the way from prevention on the left side to overdose treatment on the right side. Measures are necessary at every step along the way, but we are going to focus on two broad categories: prevention and response. That is, how do we keep people from gettin' hooked on the demon pills in the first place, but, failing that, what do we do with people who *do* get addicted? Not sure if you've heard all the stories about prom pregnancies down here, but rednecks are not huge fans of prevention.

Anyway, let's do it. First, let's cover what we should *not* do.

NOT D.A.R.E.

If you don't know what D.A.R.E. is, welcome to America. It's great to have you. D.A.R.E. is an antidrug program created in the early eighties as part of the War on Drugs. It stands for Drug Abuse Resistance Education, and it's aimed at young schoolchildren, with the intent of keeping them away from drugs by educating them about the dangers of substance abuse. The program was organized, administered, and executed by local police departments across the country, with actual cops leading the sessions. Our fellow Freedom Spreaders will not be

---

28. **It's a hot-ass take, though.**

surprised to hear that this shit don't work, even for a little while. Multiple studies and reports over the years have shown that the program is pretty much an abject bust, having little to no effect on the likelihood of a kid deciding whether or not to get turnt.[29] Anyone who grew up in D.A.R.E. like we did will tell you that all most kids took away from the program was a great T-shirt to get stoned in.

Despite its failure, the program lives on today, though many experts have posited that it exists in its current form more as a type of community outreach for police departments (it's certainly courteous of them to meet the kids they will one day lock up for nonviolent crimes). Which is pretty funny considering that one of the reasons the program failed in the first place is that kids who are at risk for drug use ain't tryin' to listen to no tight-ass cop tell them what to do.[30] The other reason the program failed is the same reason teen pregnancies go up in areas that practice abstinence-only sex ed: telling kids not to do something is a surefire way to make them want to do the absolute shit out of that thing.[31] Especially if that thing feels good. D.A.R.E. was never going to work, and it shouldn't even be a factor in addressing the opiate epidemic. Let's just get that out of the way now.

ALSO NOT PRISON

Seriously, not prison. We have a major problem in this country with incarcerating nonviolent drug offenders. Now, this subject could obviously be its own damn *book*, so we'll try to keep it succinct. Put simply:

29. **Into a shell of his former self by years of drug use.**

30. **This is speculation. But it's also an Objective Universal Fact.**

31. **Absolutely 100 percent true.**

Porch Talk with Drew
I WON AT D.A.R.E.

I won the D.A.R.E. essay contest in sixth grade. The contest, which as I recall was as mandatory as drug tests (and as effective, which is to say not at all), was to see who could write the best essay on why he/she will never try drugs. I was eleven.

Now, of course, I won because I am just the best writer, but, like, guys, you see how ridiculous this whole premise is, right? We were *made* to write an essay in *sixth grade* about why we will *never* try drugs. I think the only way out of it was to drop out of the program, which meant not going to D.A.R.E. but instead sitting silently with your head down in the library. I really, truly cannot for the life of me figure out why no one took a look at this practice and went, "Ya know, actually, we're just teachin' the kids to lie about drugs."

Perhaps it was because the D.A.R.E. officer himself wasn't a true believer. One day he showed us the D.A.R.E. police vehicle, and we could see his chewing tobacco. This dude was super lucky he had sixth graders and not eighth graders callin' him out—we were mostly polite about it.

Years later, that poor, lost man would succumb to pills. The fuckin' D.A.R.E. officer became a pillhead. This stands as proof of (a) how ridiculous the pill epidemic is in the South and (b) how much *horseshit* and how hollow the program is. It's the embodiment of hypocrisy and doing the absolute least you can.

"Hey, let's keep kids off drugs by scaring them and then forcing them to agree not to ever do 'em."

"Okay, has that ever worked?"

"No."

"Okay, let's do it."

D.A.R.E. to keep kids off drugs. Shit. Wish we'd D.A.R.E. to be fuckin' honest.

DM

research, experience, and *common damn sense* all demonstrate that locking away an addict with more hardened and violent criminals *doesn't help him.* Except it does help someone: namely, the executives, shareholders, and everyone else with a stake in the private prisons that profit from stripping these people of their freedom . . . you know, rich white people.

Wake up, Amer—okay, enough of all that shit, but sincerely, it's a pretty fucked-up situation. There is little to no evidence to suggest that a hardline punitive approach to combatting the drug problem has any real efficacy. It's fuckin' dumber'n shit and ort not be a thing.

We've already established that the bleakness and lack of hope inherent in living in poverty are huge factors in the spread of addiction. So we take people who have gotten sucked into that Vortex of Shit, and we separate them from their loved ones and any support system they may have, subject them to an overtly traumatic experience, and leave them standing on the other side of it with even fewer prospects than they had before—and that's supposed to *help? Word?!* It's not even logical. That's like cutting off someone's wiener 'cause they had a headache.

Yet many of our fellow Southerners take this stance. You break the law, you go to the pen. It's your own damn fault; don't come cryin' to us about it. You don't wanna be behind bars, then don't get on drugs. End of story. This is how a lot of those on the Right feel. Yet most of the fellers we know that go on like this will get hammered drunk on the lake and then drive their uninsured truck home, only stopping to shoot at a deer without getting out of the cab. But hey, least they ain't pillheads!

Everybody fucks up. Everybody does things they ort not do. Some of these things are objectively terrible and harmful and cannot be tolerated. Getting hooked on pills, in and of itself, is not one of those things. We have to move beyond this zero-tolerance bullshit. We're not North Korea (*yet*; please vote). Let's help these people.

PREVENTION: IT'S ALL ABOUT OPTIONS, BAYBA

Having stated fairly emphatically that we don't believe D.A.R.E. is worth a damn, we should probably follow that up by saying that we are all about education, generally speaking. But education in and of itself, particularly when it focuses on abstinence, just flat-out doesn't work. Kids still need to be taught about drugs, and about their dangers, and all that good stuff. Nobody is saying that they shouldn't. We just can't *only* do that and expect it to change anything.

So how do we keep people from swallerin' a tablet of Pharmaceutical Feel Better? Well, we can try to make them *actually* feel better, for starters. Feel better about their futures, their prospects, their *lives*. Hell, just giving people something to *do* will go a long way toward keeping them from walking the dope rope. So what are we really saying here? Well, remember those social determinants? The shitty parts of poverty[32] and the effect they have on addiction rates? Let's start there. If you address the poverty problem, you address this problem at the same time; it's just the nature of the relationship between the two. We've covered what we think about addressing poverty in the South in chapter two, so we're not going to rehash it all here, but basically, let's stop voting for wealthy draconian fuckheads; let's stop making people feel like shit for wanting to read. Let's rise up, y'all. If we can make shit just *less awful*, then that alone will go a long way toward getting the South off pills.

What else? Well, it's all about options. When people have options, they're less likely to land on "get lost in an Oxy fog for the next twenty years." Options for employment, options for purpose, options for recreation—options just help. But that all relates to people who turn to pills for reasons that are largely psychological. What about people who

---

32. **Which is all of the parts of poverty.**

first get hooked as a result of legitimate physical pain? Well, they need options too. Surely there are other ways to address pain medicinally that could be developed, but we ain't doctors.[33] Also, we sortly suspect that even if the people what make drugs did know about other ways to go about it, they wouldn't have any interest in doing so. Addiction is good for business. They have no incentive to develop truly viable treatments for pain that *don't* lead to the patient sucking dick for their product. They're just not going to do it anytime soon. And we recognize that. However, there is *this one thing*: another option for pain treatment that has been backed up by science and also proven to be a much safer alternative than prescription narcotics. And what is this miracle drug?

#420BLAZEIT

Look, this was always going to come up. It weren't no damn way we were gonna get through this whole book without pushing for legal weed. But this is the right place to do it. And we're not the only ones who feel this way. Experts on the opiate epidemic are watching the legal-weed states with extreme interest. Marijuana advocates have preached the medicinal properties of jazz cabbage for a while now, including using it for pain management. If the South would get off its ass and legalize marijuana—at the very least, for medicinal uses—then we could actually give it a real shot. It may be too late for people who are already dependent on opiates; switching to pot after that would probably be like going to limp-wristed hand jobs after years of Viagra-fueled porn orgies. *But* it could become a legitimately viable option for people with pain who are seeking treatment for the first time, keeping them from turning to pills in the first place.

33. **We're pretty much the opposite of doctors.**

And, hell, it's not like the South doesn't smoke the hell out of pot anyway. Yeah, for the record, in case some of you are unaware: rednecks get high as eagle dicks . . . giraffe pussy . . . Corey's cholesterol. Weed also *grows* super well down here, like most things do (such as the fresh vegetables we then batter and throw into boiling oil). So it would make sense for the South to be a forerunner in the legalization movement. As with so many things, though, we just don't seem to want to do what makes sense, *for some reason*. (It's Jesus.) But even if you're a Southerner who isn't particularly keen on smoking or growing the devil's lettuce, frankly, you should still be in favor of this. Anyone who has ever met both a pothead and a pillhead knows that while they both dress terribly and smell worse, you'll take a pothead every day of the week. So let's trade pills for pot and see if shit don't get a little better down here, y'all. We bet it will. You know why?

Options. That's what prevention comes down to. Giving people options. The more options you have, the farther down the list "stealing from Memaw to get high" ends up. School, sports, jobs, even joints—all of these are alternatives preferable to pills. But no matter what we do, we'll never keep everyone from gettin' strung out. So what do we do with those who slip through the cracks?

RESPONSE: TREATMENT, Y'ALL

It ain't nothin' wrong with goin' to rehab. Hell, it's just about a redneck rite of passage. Some of the most hittinest red-ass motherfuckers of all time went to rehab. Brett Favre, Johnny Cash, Foghorn Leghorn[34]— the list goes on and on. So let's all agree that rehab is *just fine*. But

---

34. Ol' Fog's crippling **PCP** addiction is one of Hollywood's worst-kept secrets.

the problem is that you can't just say, "All right, rehab for everybody! Whew, glad we took care of that! Now let's knock out systemic racism and take lunch." Treatment for addiction takes a number of different forms, and people respond to them all in different ways. There is no one universal way to go about it.

First of all, there's detox: the process of removing all of the toxins and poisons (read: the sweet, sweet drugs) from your system over the course of days. At the end, there will no longer be any drugs physically present in your body. Not to get overly scientific, but for many, the detox process *does not hit*. At all. By this point, most addicts' bodies are physically dependent on the drug in question, and so does not respond well to the drug's sudden absence. People in detox can have extreme nausea, body aches, fever, even seizures. Like we said: don't hit. And if you're *also* physically dependent on benzodiazepines like Xanax, the detox process can literally kill you if you try to go cold turkey. Isn't that an ironic twist? Dying while trying to quit drugs? That Lord sure is a jokester. Which is what we're getting at: there are a lotta ways to skin a strung-out cat. And detox is only the first step on the road to recovery. After that, there are also numerous approaches to staying clean. Some people need to do replacement therapy (where opioid-replacement drugs like methadone and Suboxone are substituted for the real thing to wean the patient off—which is as crazy as it sounds; not as easy as the transition to lactose-free milk). Others can go fully abstinent. The twelve-step method has worked wonders for a lot of people. Others have no interest in hollerin' at Jesus about all this.[35] There is no one way to treat addicts.

Except that every approach should have one common denominator: we can treat them with empathy and compassion instead of

---

35. **If you ain't know, twelve-step programs are faith based.**

fear, anger, and disgust—which is all we can really say as authors/ voices for the voiceless. We can't institute new policies or implement sweeping reforms. What is important is that we stop writing off these people or locking them away. This plague is spreading rapidly, and it's not just poor hillbillies anymore. It's in the suburbs, in private schools. The country is being ravaged, and it's not going to get better until we face it head-on. And that's going to mean a lot of different things along the way, but as long as we agree to face it with love and not hate, with the promise of redemption (wasn't Christ all about that?) and not the threat of retribution, then we'll figure this out. That's what we do.

Porch Talk with Trae

DEAR MAMA, CONTINUED

 This problem has had a *colossal* impact on me. So it's hard for me to stay objective about it. But one thing I've had to do over the years is evolve in my feelings toward addicts and addiction.

I used to have no sympathy whatsoever for addicts. I was very bitter about addiction. I took it personally. I didn't understand why my mom couldn't *just fucking stop.* It didn't make sense to me. And so I projected that same anger toward other addicts too. Stop being a fucking loser. Get a goddamn job. Be a man. All that shit. And that's the rhetoric that still emanates from the Right on this subject, by and large.

If I'm being honest, there is still a part of me that feels that way. But I've also largely softened on the whole thing over the years. I realize now that my mom has serious mental problems, things that genuinely are not her fault. Now, none of that shit was my fault or my sister's fault *either*, but still. She doesn't want to be the way she is. No addict does. And giving up on addicts and treating them like shit and turning them away or locking them up—none of that changes anything. None of that fixes anything. Look, having said that: another thing I've learned is that you cannot help someone who doesn't want to help themselves. There is a difference between being supportive and being an enabler. But once someone has taken the steps to actually help themselves, then it benefits everyone involved to support them as much as possible. And to me, that's the stance we need to take on the issue as a whole. Yeah, these people have hurt us. Badly. But not as badly as they've hurt themselves. And helping them get their shit together helps us all in the end.

Tw

12

Movin' On

It's been a hell of a ride, ain't it? Fried food, hooch, great music, jokes, Jesus, and a talk about racism—tell us that don't describe most good parties you been to. But now we gotta speak on how we might improve all our lives—everyone.

"You mean, discuss the future?" Yes. Now, look, we ain't got no crystal balls (or anything made of crystal, for that matter). But we also ain't gonna shy away from goin' in. So here is how we feel about what everyone might do to pitch in and make this hellish thing called existence a bit more tolerable.

Trae's Final Porch Talk

SOME THOUGHTS CONCERNING REDNECKS

 I'm-a speak for a moment if I may to the "classic" rednecks out there reading this. (Yes, *we know:* some joke about rednecks not reading. Again.) The ones who are tired and confused and damn sure not gonna change just because some politician or dumb-fuck comedian said something "smart" about them.

Y'all, don't get us wrong, hell. You *should* be proud. You got a lot to be proud of. You work hard, you love your momma, you don't ask for nothin', you feed your babies, you're a hell of a damn good shot, and you're great at blowing shit up. We know that the few of you who might actually read this book are going to at times be pretty infuriated with us for some of this heathen shit talkin' we been doin'. But *please* believe that it's coming from a genuine place. Y'all are our people, and you always will be. We don't want to put you down or trash your lifestyle or anything—we just want the South to do *better*. That's all. And we know that we can. But not without you.

And we get it. You've never done nothin' but the best you could, and you've gotten shit to show for it. The jobs are all gone. The money went with 'em. The needle took your momma; the law took your brother. You're worried about what your kids are going to do. What kind of life will they even be able to have in a country that so clearly long ago gave up on them? Because that's the thing: nobody gives a shit about what you're going through. They can't, hell— ain't got time. Too busy caring *so hard* and *so deeply* about everybody else's problems. The conservatives just talk about the "American Dream" and "pulling yourself up by your bootstraps" like you don't know your way around a pair of boots or like you ain't ever dreamed. Well, fuck them trying to sell everybody on being a rich man like them one day, but hell, you know that ain't gonna happen. You don't even *want* to be rich; you just want to be *okay*. To not have to worry so much . . . and maybe have a hittin'-ass boat.

And the liberals are even worse. They claim to be the party of the common man, but they look at you and all they do is sneer. Look down their noses at you. Call you a bigot, a moron, an inbred hick. Well, fuck them too. They don't know shit about your life, about what it's like.

But we do. We know all about it because it's been our life too. We've lived it, y'all. And to some other Southerners, that makes us traitors—Benedict Cletuses or something like that. They think we've forgotten where we came from. Turned our backs. Well, frankly, if you feel that way, then fuck you very kindly also. We ain't forgot shit. We remember it all. And it's exactly because we remember that we *want this shit to change.* And it isn't ever going to change for the better if we don't start with ourselves. That's how it works.

So stop hating people. Actually don't. Hating people hits. But hate the *right people*. Stop hating the people who are going through the same struggles at the same hands of the same assholes that you are. Poor black people and poor white people, particularly in the South, are in this thing together, y'all. And until both sides realize that, we ain't goin' nowhere. Stop hating poor Hispanic people, too. The ones who *are* in America aren't takin' your damn jobs— they're taking jobs nobody else will do. And the ones down in Mexico that *did* take your old factory job? Don't hate them either. Hate the rich motherfucker that *sent* your job there so he could put a new finish on his yacht or Scotchgard his newest human-flesh suit. Hate him, not the poor ol' boy with mouths to feed just like you.

Stop hating people that have absolutely nothing to do with you, your life, or your problems. Gay people don't want to ruin your marriage (Your momma does, though. She *"never* liked that bitch") or turn your kids gay or force your neighbor to marry a dog ('at would make the Tuesday night dog fights a little more awkward) or whatever the fuck—they just want to be who they are. That's it. Don't hate them. Instead hate the hypocritical preacher on the TV on Sunday mornings who thinks that he has to have a private jet to literally be closer to God. (How else is He gonna hear him?) Don't listen to that asshole. Don't listen when he tells you that God has a plan for you, that He will deliver you from your strife if you simply stay the course. Fuck that. If there's one thing you already know, it's that ain't nobody givin' you *shit*, least of all Jesus's daddy, so go out there and take it yourself. Don't listen when he tells you that people in other places (the Muslims, the gays, the Jews, whatever) are out to get you and your way of life. They would have to give a shit about you first, and we've already established that they absolutely do not. All he's doing is fanning the flames of a bullshit dumpster fire that has kept his sorry ass very warm for a very long time. We're not saying abandon your faith—we're just asking that you place it well.

Stop hating your pillbilly brother. He's not lazy, he's just trying to stop the pain. Instead, hate the pharmaceutical companies and the whore doctors and the lizard politicians who have made themselves extravagantly wealthy by dealing death to people whose lives aren't worth shit to them, all while locking up blacks in record numbers for refusing to play by their rules when it comes to drugs. They put the poor black man in the pen and the poor white man in the ground. Fuck. Them.

And lastly, y'all: stop hating yourself. That's right, we know. We know that under that hyperaggressive and supremely loud exterior, you hide a lot of fear, a lot of anger. That's no secret to anyone, but what we realize that other people don't is that your fear and your anger are *not* toward blacks, gays, Muslims, etc. Not really. It's toward *yourself*. You're afraid of what the future holds. You're angry at the cards you've been dealt. And you know what? You *should be*. It's *not* fair; none of this is. It ain't your fault. But when you refuse to direct your anger toward those who *are* at fault and instead misappropriate it onto everyone else, then all you do is play right into their hands. Well, fuck that. Don't let them do that to you anymore; don't give them the goddamn satisfaction. Stop playing their game; stop being their pawns.

Look around at all the other people who have suffered at the hands of these motherfuckers and see them for the potential allies that they are. Stand together. Fight back. Now that'd be something to be proud of.

Corey's Final Porch Talk

SOME THOUGHTS CONCERNING LIBERALS

Sometimes I'm ashamed of where I come from. Other times I'm ashamed that I'm ashamed of where I come from. It can be a bit of a struggle to decide why I feel bad on any given day (it's the booze). Other days, like any redneck, I'm proud, ornery, and defiant! Who the fuck am I to think that due to my political leanings, slightly above average intelligence, and genuine compassion for all of mankind I'm somehow better than the people around me? I mean, I am—but seriously, who am I to think that?

So I'm-a try not to feel bad or too proud for a minute and think beyond the South. We've done our best to shed light on some of the more regrettable things about the South, so there's no reason to beat a dead horse (unless you're trying to tenderize it for horse chili—I feel that). What I instead would like to do is take a jab back at the rest of you alleged nice people for assuming that we're the only region in the Union responsible for our country's embarrassment.

So let's address the real problem I have here: liberals and progressives. Yeah, I said that shit. And yes, *I am a liberal. And I am a progressive* (on account of having a brain and empathy). Let's face it, though: states are just bordered-off pieces of dirt. The people who inhabit them are how they're represented. This book is written proof that liberals exist even in the South, and let me tell ya somethin': so-called progressives can be just as judgmental and hypocritical as the right-wingers we're trying to stand up against.

Hey, little miss Blogger University Graduate! You wanna talk shit to the redneck for not voting like you think he ort? His candidate is prejudiced? I hear ya. But you just called him a redneck. Now, I'm certainly not going to say that callin' him that as an insult is as bad as say, voting for Trump, but it's certainly derogatory. It's certainly a slur the way *you* meant it. You irresponsibly group a certain type of people together to call them out for irresponsibly grouping certain types of people together—guess rednecks ain't the only ones who have a hard time grasping irony. I'm guilty of it as well—we all are—but we have got to get better, and we have got to notice the hypocrisy in ourselves before we unjustly try to exploit it in others.

Because this whole nation has issues. You don't think people in Idaho like to get fucked up? Sure do. Matter of fact, the number one drug of choice in Idaho is meth. Thought that was just a hillbilly thing? Well, it may be, but apparently they got themselves plenty of hillbillies over there. (I used to only know you for potatoes, Idaho; now I know you for meth and potatoes.) 'Sup, California? With your organic-kale-wrap-eating asses. How's it going? You constantly talk shit about us in your movies, turn your surgically readjusted noses up at us when we visit your state, and feign an unwarranted sense of superiority when discussing where you live. That's cool . . . I'm not gonna give you shit for that; we in the South can certainly respect discrimination based on absolutely no facts—it's our way. But were you aware that you have one of the highest poverty rates in the entire country? That's right, baby: being poor as shit ain't just a Southern thing. (Phew, I knew it!)

New York City! I love ya, baby, I really do. Hell, I used to live up in ya (Forest Hills, Queens—represent) but I gotta tell ya, I see a lot of disrespect toward women in ya streets. It's true that down here in the South we tend to use the Bible as a way to suppress our women, but at least we hide our sexism behind a centuries-old fairy tale—y'all just catcall the shit out of women publicly and show no regard for their bodies, safety, or sense of worth. "Why don't you smile more, sweetheart?" "Ooooh, come here, momma! Bring that ass over!" They have to plaster signs all over the subway begging you not to grope them while they're waiting for their stop. And guys, those antiharassment ads are taking up valuable space; they need more room to promote the play *Hamilton*. Get your shit together.

Chicago: y'all murder a lot. Baltimore: ditto. Nevada: you treat Native Americans like shit. Oklahoma: y'all got some crazy zealots in office. Alaska: Sarah Palin. Detroit? Nah. You've been through enough. All you had was wide receiver Calvin Johnson of the Lions, and now that he's gone, I'm not gonna pour salt in the wound.

Point is, we all are all messed up, somehow. Now, did my calling out your state or city on sexism, drugs, poverty, and government corruption hurt your feelings? Did it make you mad? Well, you know what!? When you talk shit about how racist all our mamaws and papaws are and how uneducated my people are, it gets my red the fuck up too! *We all have problems, and we all hate outsiders snidely pointin' 'em out.*

We claim to be the best country on earth, and maybe we are. I ain't been many other places. People certainly seem to love coming here; I know that because my uncle yells about it often while cleaning his gun. But if we want to keep claiming to be the best country on earth, we're going to have to hold everyone responsible for upholding those standards. It's not one state's fault that we suck, and it's not to one state's credit that we're great. We're all in this together. I know it doesn't really *ever* seem like it due to the fact that the media are the devil and continue their divisive path on the way to stirring up fear and driving up ad revenue, but we can't just continue to put it all on them. At the end of the day, they have to have something to report, and we're providing them with plenty of material.

We're scared of anything different—and far too proud of things that we have assumed to be right.

You know what pride comes before, don't ya?

Drew's Final Porch Talk
SOME THOUGHTS CONCERNING CHIPS

Chips hit. Poker chips are great, if you have a lot of 'em. So are potato chips. I like chips off the old block and Chippendales dancers. (They're all just tryin' to pay their way through mechanic's school, shit.) Chipper Jones is great. I even like the one dude I know named Chip, even though I assumed I'd hate him because that sounds like the name of the date-rapiest dude at the country club I ain't allowed at. But not all chips hit. Chipped teeth usually hurt. Having a chip on your shoulder—well, that could go either way.

Nearly every person I have ever met has or used to have a chip on his shoulder—something that makes him feel like either the whole world is against him or the whole world expects a certain thing out of him, and he, by God, ain't havin' it. Usually these chips are really just a place of insecurity and anger about being judged.

This isn't true of every single person, but this is true of every *type* of person. I know rich kids who want desperately to prove they've earned whatever they have. Pretty women (and men) who just *know* the world is gonna assume all they are is a pretty face, so they overcompensate. I can't tell ya how many times I've seen a Yankee talk a little too much about NASCAR in an attempt to fit in. And, of course, we have 'em in the South. Lord, we got chips on our shoulders down here! (Anyone got a chip company called Southern Shoulder Chips, because that would hit.)

I have a huge chip myself. I have a chip on my shoulder so big I often think I *am* a chip. Just a big ol' delicious chip walkin' around trying to fight everyone.

I can't pretend like it hasn't served me well—there have been times when using that chip as motivation and fuel has won me battles and gotten me things I needed or wanted. I come from a *very* tiny place in the middle of nowhere Appalachia. It's the kind of place British people do documentaries on and "regular" white Americans go, "Wow, can you believe this is here?" That big ol' chip kept me going when law school professors made fun of my accent (true story), and it got me degrees and accolades.

But as I get older, I notice this chip has a very, very dark side. It's gotten me in rows with people I love, respect, or both. Numerous times, a conversation has ended with me going, "Damn, my bad. I just got defensive for no reason, and I can see now that I just attacked you." It can kinda make me a dick, y'all.

And I feel like a lot of our problems in the South— and, really, in the whole damn world—come from all of us clinging too tightly to our chips. We're so hell-bent on either proving that "they" are wrong about us or proving to "them" that we just don't give a damn what "they" think, that we're losing sight of the fact that there is no "they."

Do y'all get that? Do *I*, even? Hell, I don't know. But it's true. I mean, look, I've done a lot of mushrooms in my time (one benefit of living near cows and not near police), so maybe I'm just talkin' out my ass, but I really don't think there's a "they" (other than the government with its lizard politicians and large corporations made up of evil). Pardon me for being all kumbaya, but there is only "we." And, yes, we fight and we fracture, we quibble and we write books about how we ort be better, and we're arrogant and scared and stupid, but *we* are all those things, together. I'm not saying let's all get along and sing Kelly Clarkson songs. (That would hit, though: "Since U Been Gone" is my jam.) Hell, naw, that ain't gonna happen. We humans are a shit show.

But we can be more empathetic. We can listen to each other and let go of these feelings of inadequacies. Do you feel like people different from you judge you (whether they're rich, poor, black, white, redneck, Yankee, liberal, conservative)? Well, guess what? *They do.* Because that's what people do. But when you go about provin' 'em wrong or fighting their judgments—or the redneck favorite of trying super hard to prove to 'em ya don't care—you're not really doing anything but hurting yourself. Let go of these chips, y'all.

My momma told me a lot growin' up, and almost none of it stuck, shamefully. But here are two lessons she told me that won't get out of my head or heart: "Be kind. And for God's sake, Drew, don't ever be boring."

Lord, people who follow that philosophy make for the best rednecks. *And* the best Yankees. And the best foreigners and, hell, even the best conservatives (though they struggle with the boring part).

Be kind, y'all. And don't be boring.

DM

We love all of you. Love each other as much as ya can. Thanks so much for stoppin' by. Come back and see us sometime. We will prolly be turnt all the way up, singin' "Simple Man." You can join in or just sit there and cry. See yuns soon.

Skew,

Trae, Corey, and Drew

PS: Also, fellers, look: we absolutely 100 percent *promise you* that no one is coming to take your guns. Okay? Swear.

The Ten Commandments
of the New South

1. **Thou shalt not put your God above everyone else's life and rights.**

   Praise God however you want, but keep it to yourself and out of the government. When someone tells you of a tragedy, and you say you will pray, that sounds loving. When someone tells you they're Muslim or atheist or thinking about becoming vegetarian, and you smugly tell 'em you will pray for them, you're being a dick.

2. **Thou shalt not make bad music and call it "country," "Southern," "blues," "dirty south," or "hick hop."**

   If you wanna make shitty pop rock with an accent and sing every single song about a truck you've never worked out of, go ahead. But don't call it country. Don't call "rap" music with no originality or skill "hick hop." Don't call bad music anything related to the South. Call it shit. That's what it is.

3. **Thou shalt remember all of the past in order to allow for a better future.**

   Slavery happened. That flag stands for segregation. We have

monuments to Civil War generals and slave owners, as well as preserved plantations. But we have only *one* slavery museum, and that was built by a private citizen. We have *no national or federal slavery museum*. There is no government-funded slavery museum. A proposal to put one in Virginia came through in 2001 and went unfunded and failed. Another one in Richmond reached a similar fate. This is *absolutely shameful*.

4. **Thou shalt not live off the government if thou canst help it.**
   This goes for all people, but, more importantly, big companies like Walmart (which is based in Arkansas). Most of its employees receive benefits from the government because the retail giant keeps salaries so low. Yes, that's right, we're cofunding Walmart's payroll with our taxes. Get off the draw, Walmart. Same for everyone else, if you can. Welfare is fine, but it can't be your plan. We shall *all* overcome.

5. **Thou shalt not ruin thy family by puttin' pills up thy nose.**
   Seriously, cannot stress enough that while pills feel good, thy ruin lives. Hillbilly heroin got that nickname because our region has been decimated. Stop.

6. **Thou shalt fry it.**[1]
   Fry the chicken. Catfish should be breaded and dipped in the bubbling grease. Baked fries ain't fries. Some foods are just better that way. We all know it. We aren't saying have a fried Oreo after every single meal, but in our quests to be healthy and modern, let's not forget who we are and what makes our food great. Fry some shit every once in a while—at least on Sundays. But seriously, also eat a vegetable.

---

1. **But also eat a damn vegetable.**

7. **Thou shalt honor thy red-ass mother, father, and ancestors.**
   In all your ventures and every aspect of your life, never, ever forget who you are and what you come from. We're some of the toughest, smartest, and also most fun-loving people on the planet. We *must* be embarrassed by being last in education and near the top in obesity, and by having so many people beneath the poverty line. But by the same token, *never* be ashamed of your sleeveless uncle telling dirty jokes at Christmas, don't let anyone believe you're stupid because you talk openly about going to Dollywood, and *never, ever, ever* change your accent.

8. **Thou shalt not drink shitty booze.**
   Unless you're on the lake and you need super-light beer to stay hydrated. Hey, we get it, you're "redneck." We can allow one go-to brand of light beer, but when you live in the land of so much good whiskey, bourbon, craft beer, and even wine, there's no excuse for drinking gross libations. Especially when our bartenders and mixologists have so many amazing local ingredients to work with.

9. **Thou shalt be a responsible gun owner.**
   Keep your gun in a safe. Handle it only when you're sober. (Yes, we have all broken this rule, but let's try harder.) Train your whole family to respect and fear the guns you have and make sure your angry-ass kids do not know how to get access to them without you.

10. **Go see thy mamaw.**
   Now. The chicken's almost ready, and she has pie.

Thank-Yous

All of us: Amy Hughes for believing in us. Leslie Meredith, Judith Curr, Peter Borland, Paul Olsewski, David Brown, Melanie Iglesias Pérez, Albert Tang, Dana Sloan, and Benjamin Holmes at Atria for busting ass to get this done. Bessie Gantt for helping us make a book.

Corey: My mom, dad, and sister for believing in me. My two favorite teachers, Lori Vann and Irene Staub, who always encouraged me to write. Comedian Tim Wilson (RIP) for inspiring me to speak my mind and for sparking my interest in comedy at an early age. The Robertsons (Kris, Robbie, Lexis, Jessica, and Bubba Chase) for being as close to brothers and sisters as you can get when I was growing up. The Tuttons for sharing holiday dinners and making me feel like family. Michael Alfano, who gave me stage time even when I may not have deserved it. DJ Lewis for riding to every open mic with me for so many years and forcing me to get as good as I possibly could. Waylon for all your contributions to the book. Nat Goldberg for taking a risk on me. Amber Roberts for sticking with me through $20 bar shows and sacrificing her Saturday nights to watch me write this book in a living room. And to all my friends who let me run bits by them against their will for most of our lives.

Drew: Mom, because you were everything. Dad, because you showed me true strength and willpower. Jim and Angela for treating me like your own. Karen Starr, because you put me in the gifted class instead of detention. Bryan, because you never treated me differently. Dustin for being a good brother. Daniel J. Lewis for being the funniest and realest human I know, especially when I need it. My boys for making NYC feel like home (y'all know who). Rick for your contributions to the book. Nat for seeing what I sometimes didn't see myself. Anyone who ever came to a show when it was four people in the crowd. And finally, mostly, and humbly, Andi: thank you for being as hopeful and weird and loving and supportive as you are. I love yuns.

Trae: My boys, Bishop and Benton, for being my primary motivation, my steady ground, my life, my heart, my world—from your first day until my last. Their momma and my wife, Katie, without whom literally none of this would be possible, for standing by her man, who has not made that particularly easy on her at times. My dad for daring to encourage his son's heathen notions from Day One (and for so much else). Mama, Mema, Uncle Tim, and Paige for always genuinely believing in me and supporting literally every decision I've ever made. The Celina Boys (Thompson, Nunk, the Brothers Bane, Shine, Duck, Key Daddy, Ol' Porno, Jeremy, Colby, Big James, and honorary member Cholly Pop) and Seth, Jarrod, and Bryce, y'all made a lot of shitty times a lot less shitty and made me laugh harder than anyone else ever has, onstage or off. Everybody at my old DOE job for being way cooler about my dream-chasin' than you ever had to be. Doug for your contributions to the book. Nat Goldberg for taking a flyer on a credit-less father-of-two comedian from the middle of nowhere when so many others did not. And to every single one of you beautiful MFers who shared that first video and are reading this now: you changed my life, and I'm eternally grateful. I love y'all, I do.